5,000 km
per second

Manuele Fior

5,000 km per second

Fantagraphics
Books

Criss-crossing railways,
sitting in abandoned wagons
I watched the present furrow the past
stopping at the glass.
And your face is the color
of a phantom summer
that you let slip slowly away
like a dress.

– Diaframma, "Elena" (1984)

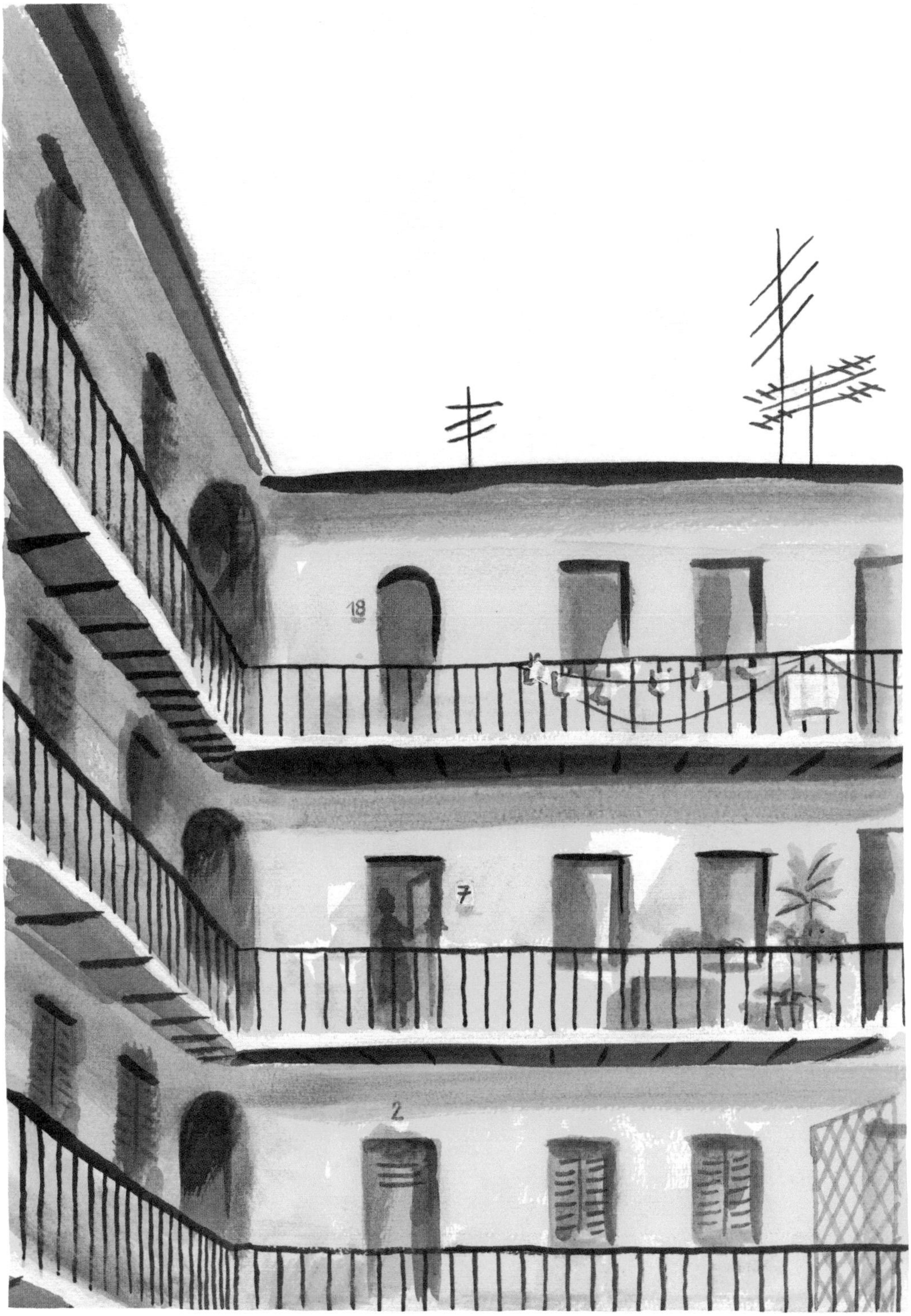
18
7
2

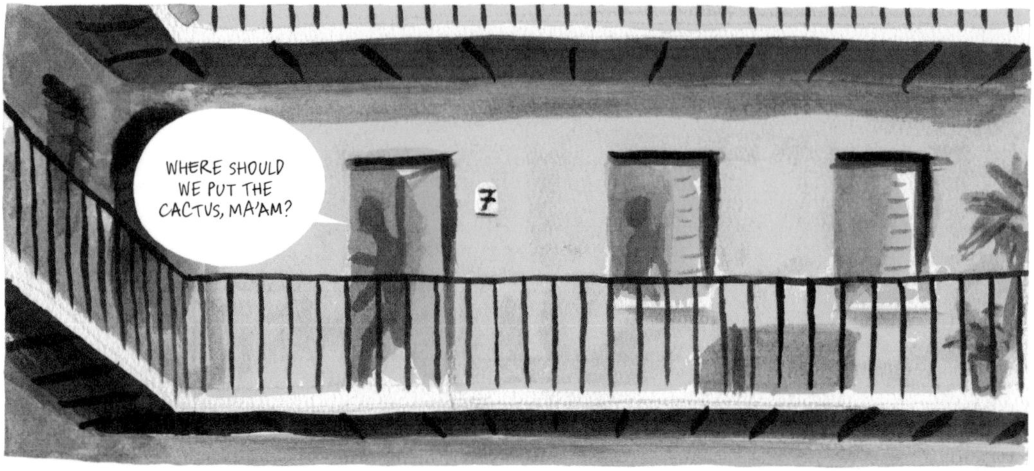
WHERE SHOULD WE PUT THE CACTUS, MA'AM?
7

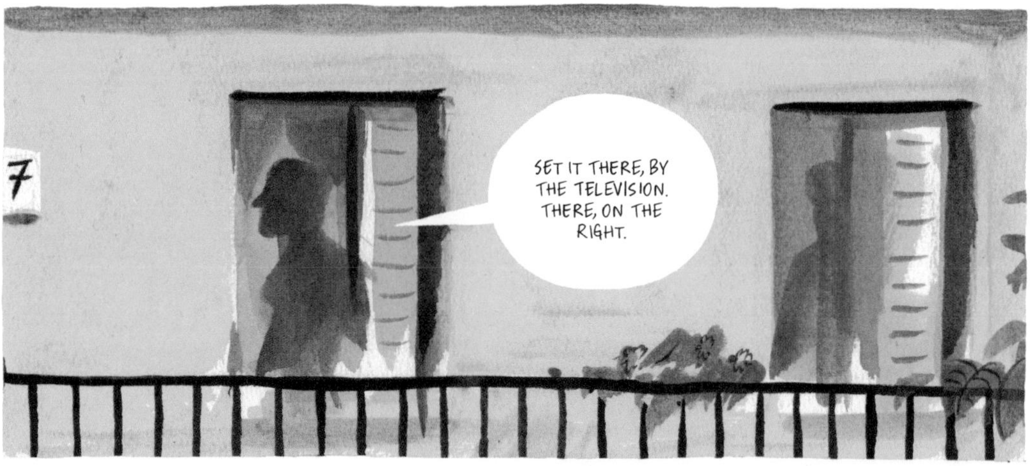
7
SET IT THERE, BY THE TELEVISION. THERE, ON THE RIGHT.

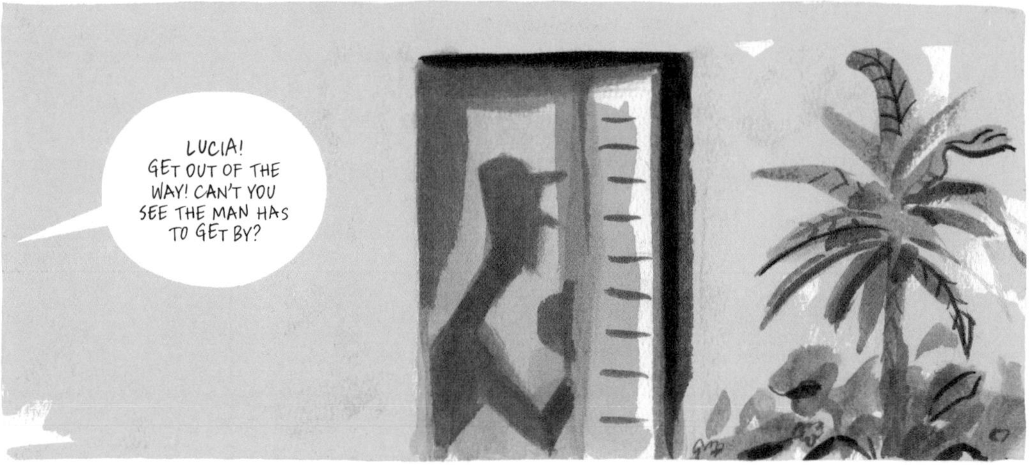
LUCIA! GET OUT OF THE WAY! CAN'T YOU SEE THE MAN HAS TO GET BY?

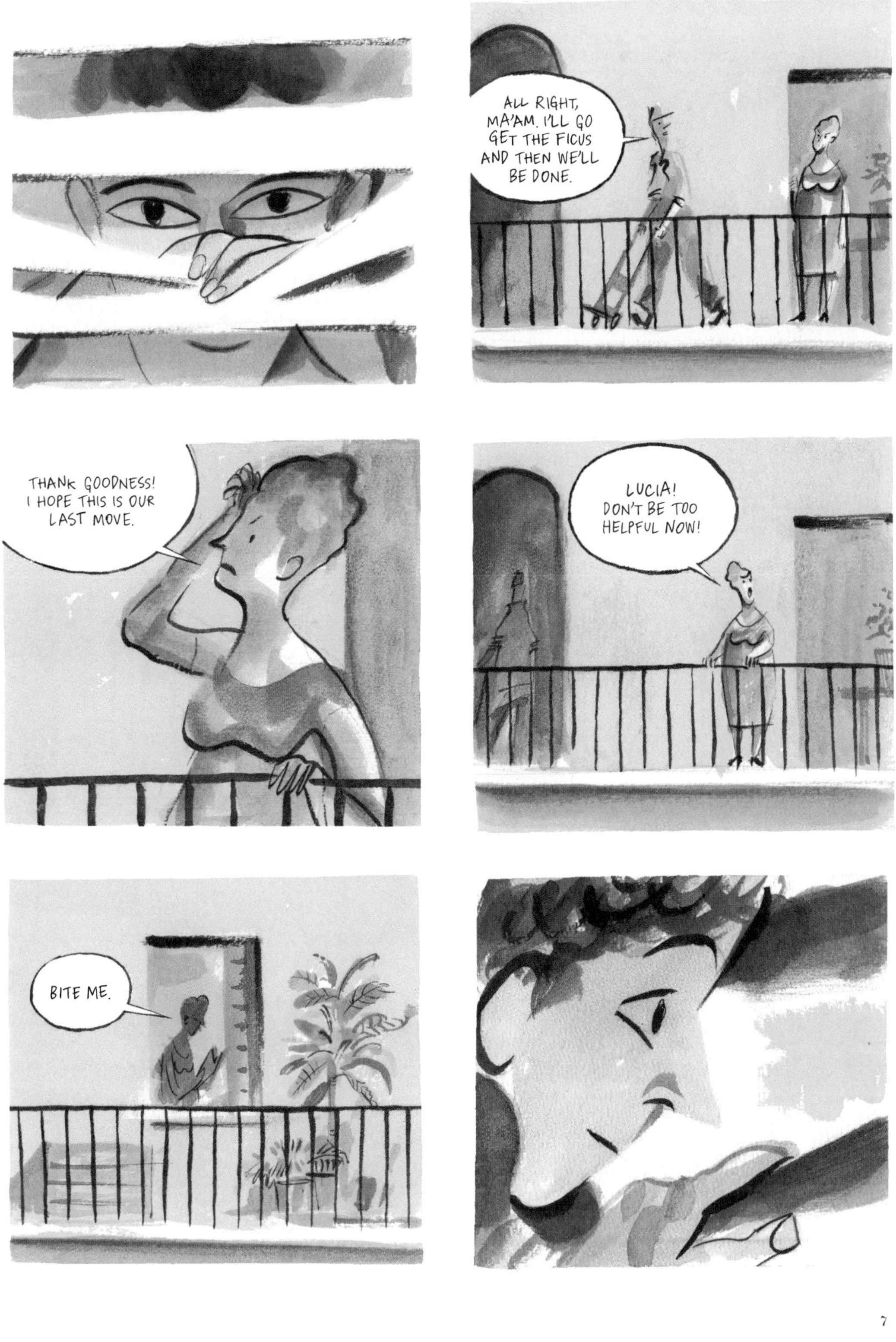
ALL RIGHT, MA'AM. I'LL GO GET THE FICUS AND THEN WE'LL BE DONE.
THANK GOODNESS! I HOPE THIS IS OUR LAST MOVE.
LUCIA! DON'T BE TOO HELPFUL NOW!
BITE ME.

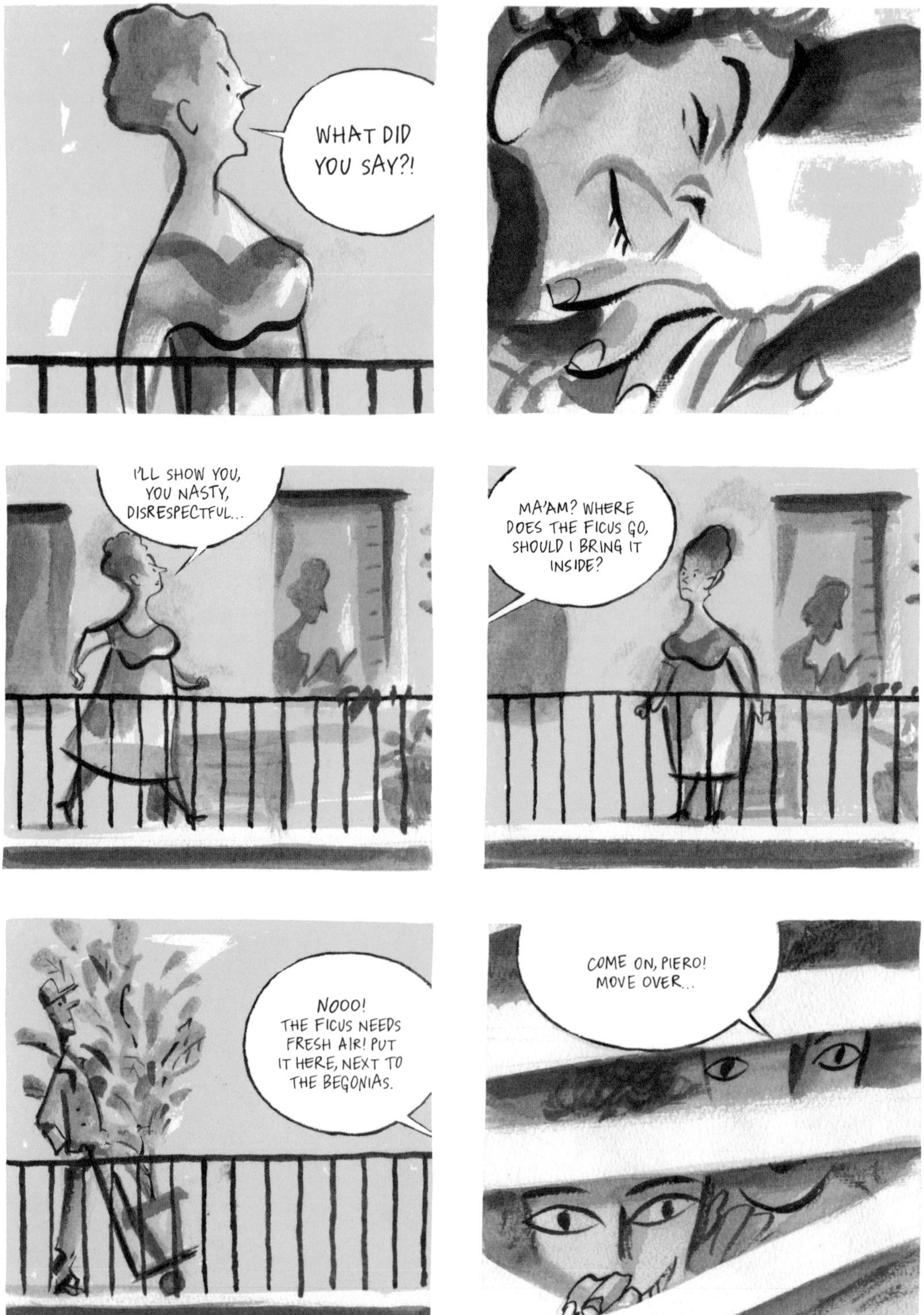
WHAT DID YOU SAY?!
I'LL SHOW YOU, YOU NASTY, DISRESPECTFUL...
MA'AM? WHERE DOES THE FICUS GO, SHOULD I BRING IT INSIDE?
NOOO! THE FICUS NEEDS FRESH AIR! PUT IT HERE, NEXT TO THE BEGONIAS.
COME ON, PIERO! MOVE OVER...

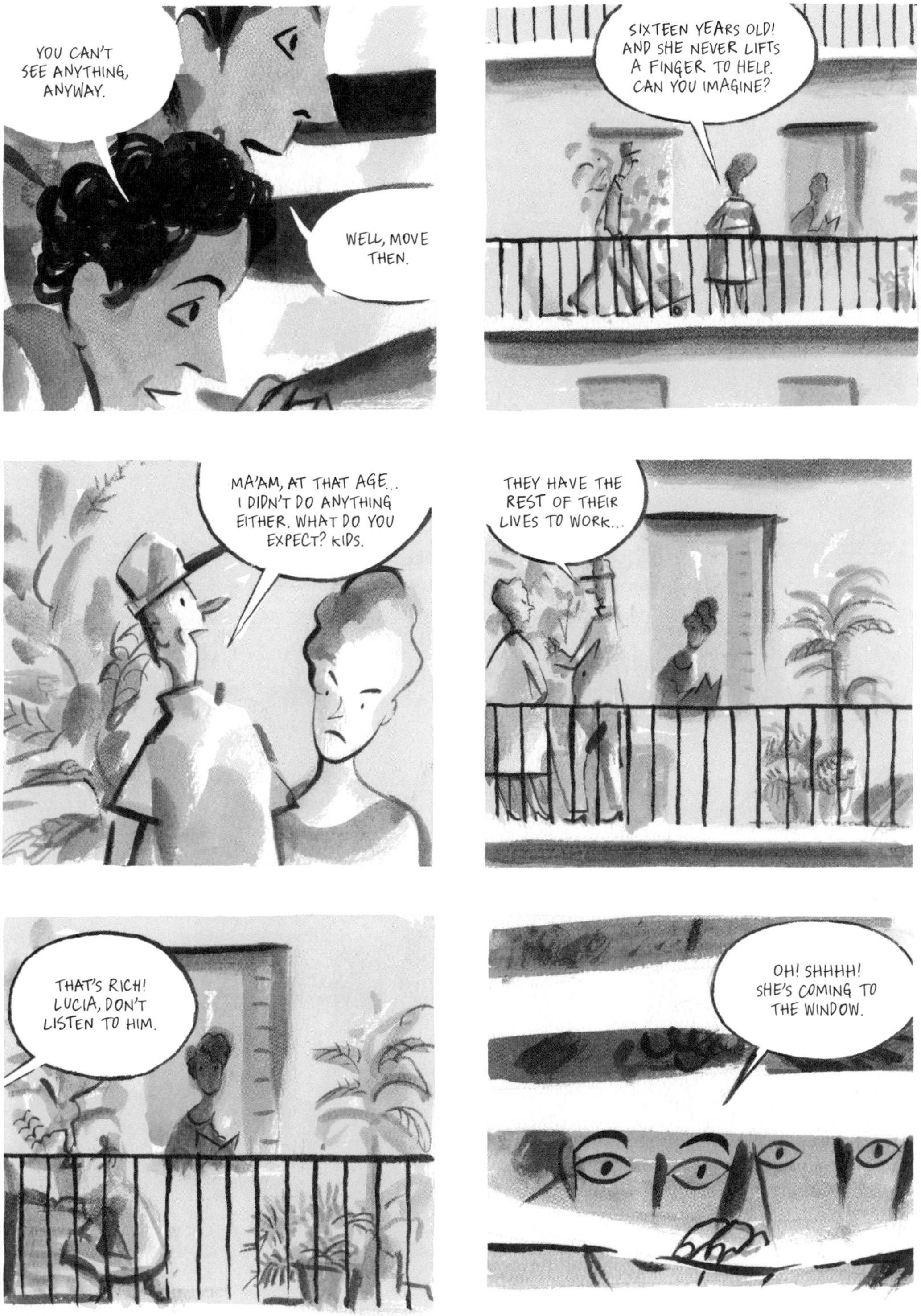
YOU CAN'T SEE ANYTHING, ANYWAY.
WELL, MOVE THEN.
SIXTEEN YEARS OLD! AND SHE NEVER LIFTS A FINGER TO HELP. CAN YOU IMAGINE?
MA'AM, AT THAT AGE... I DIDN'T DO ANYTHING EITHER. WHAT DO YOU EXPECT? KIDS.
THEY HAVE THE REST OF THEIR LIVES TO WORK...
THAT'S RICH! LUCIA, DON'T LISTEN TO HIM.
OH! SHHHH! SHE'S COMING TO THE WINDOW.

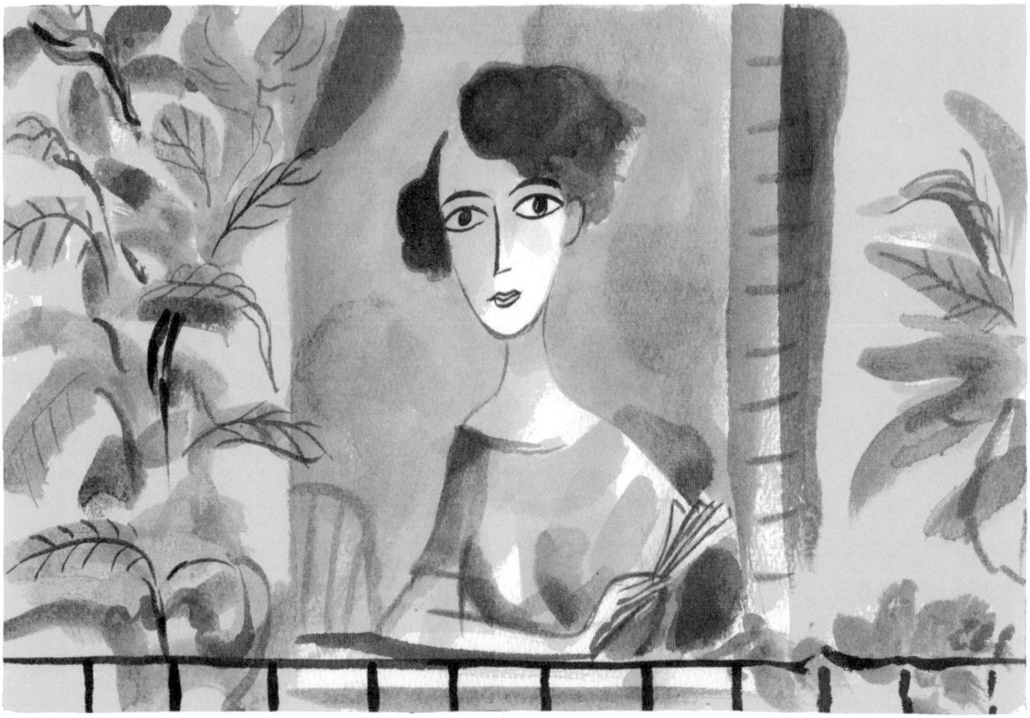

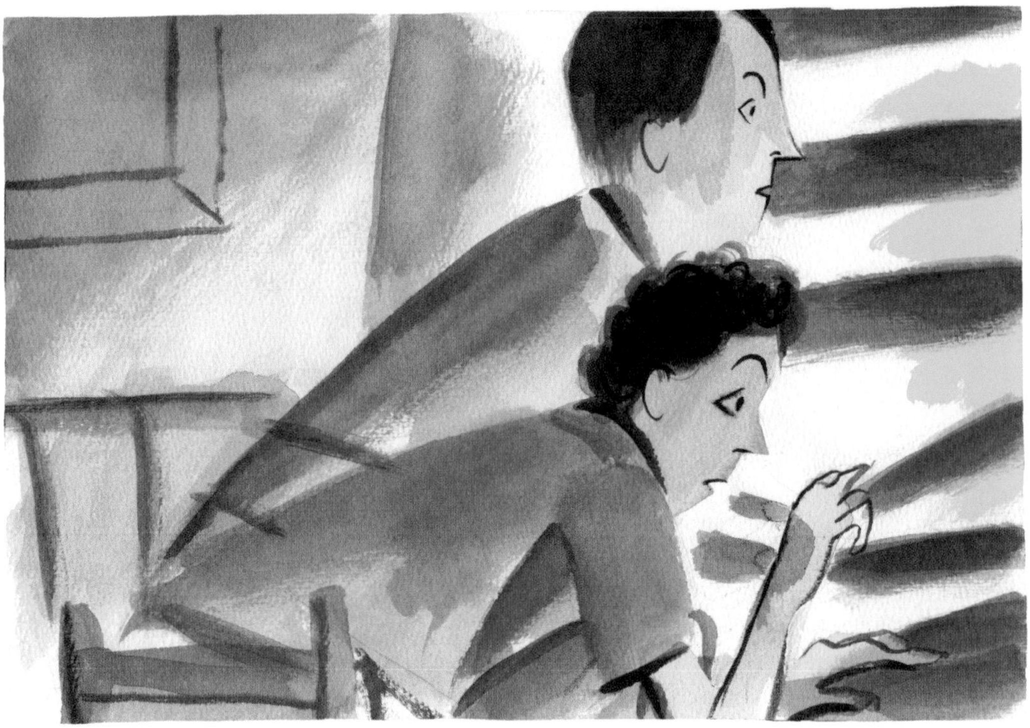

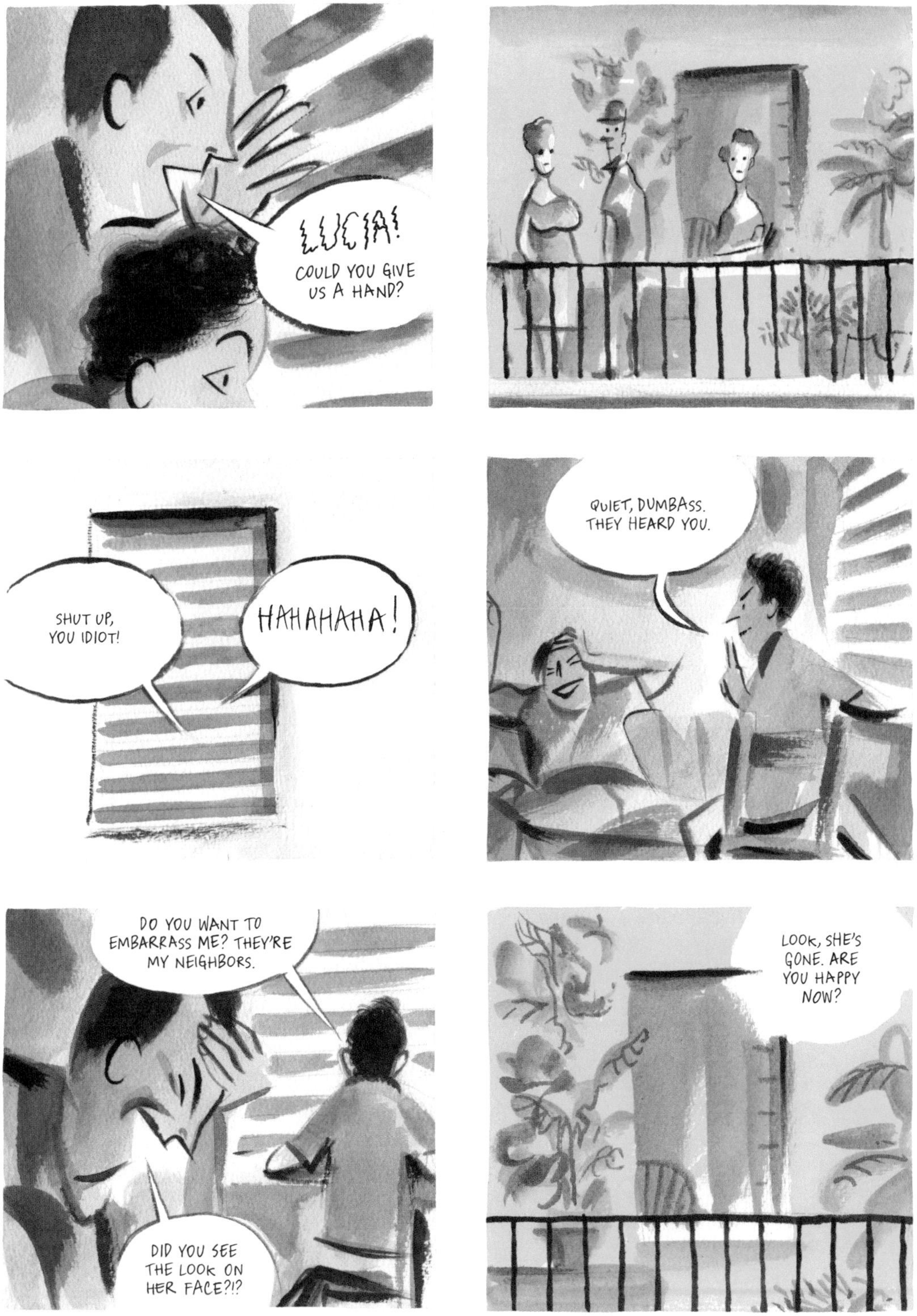
LUCIA!
COULD YOU GIVE US A HAND?
SHUT UP, YOU IDIOT!
HAHAHAHA!
QUIET, DUMBASS. THEY HEARD YOU.
DO YOU WANT TO EMBARRASS ME? THEY'RE MY NEIGHBORS.
DID YOU SEE THE LOOK ON HER FACE?!?
LOOK, SHE'S GONE. ARE YOU HAPPY NOW?

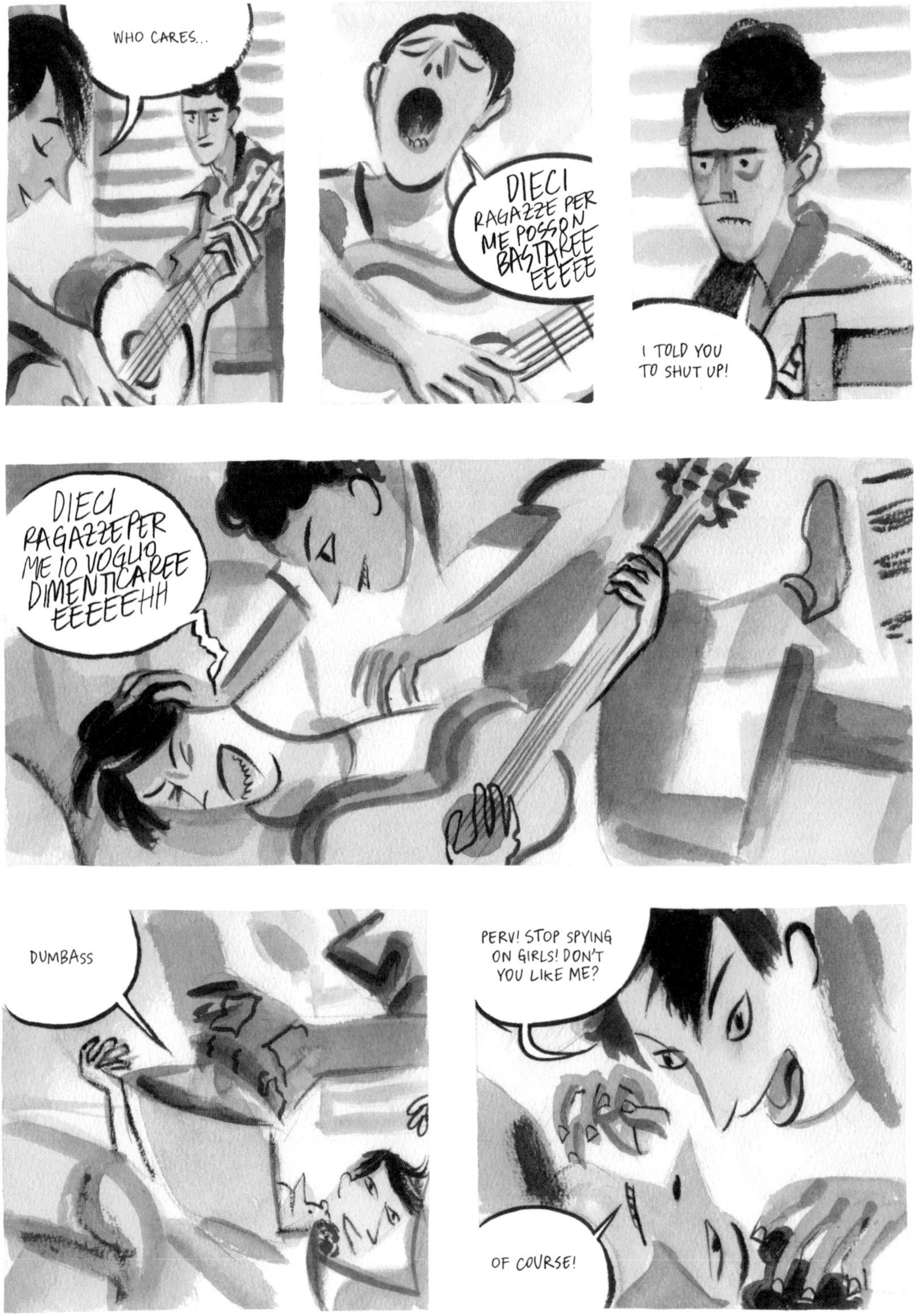
WHO CARES...
DIECI RAGAZZE PER ME POSSON BASTAREE EEEEE
I TOLD YOU TO SHUT UP!
DIECI RAGAZZE PER ME IO VOGLIO DIMENTICAREE EEEEEHH
DUMBASS
PERV! STOP SPYING ON GIRLS! DON'T YOU LIKE ME?
OF COURSE!

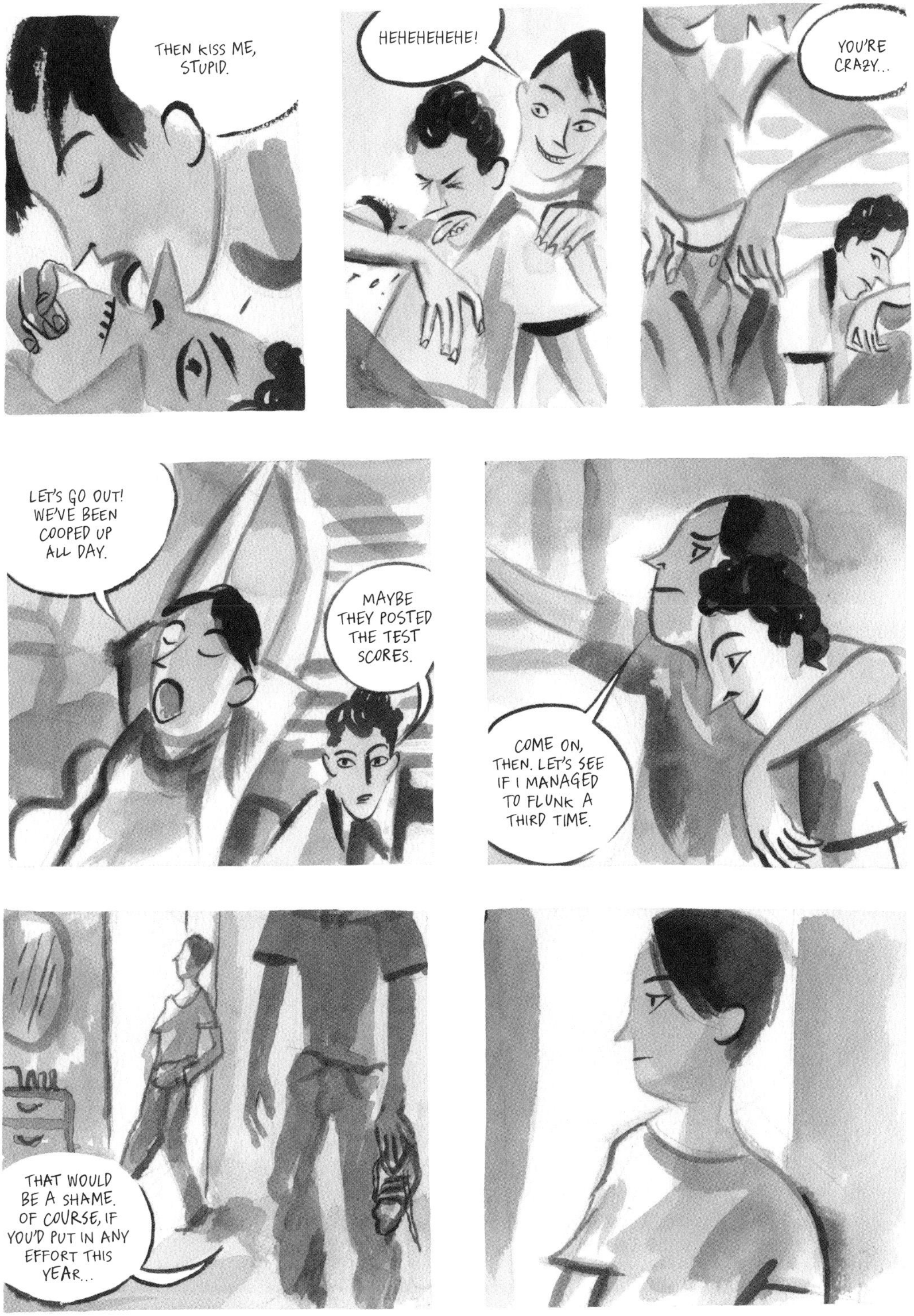
THEN KISS ME, STUPID.
HEHEHEHEHE!
YOU'RE CRAZY...
LET'S GO OUT! WE'VE BEEN COOPED UP ALL DAY.
MAYBE THEY POSTED THE TEST SCORES.
COME ON, THEN. LET'S SEE IF I MANAGED TO FLUNK A THIRD TIME.
THAT WOULD BE A SHAME. OF COURSE, IF YOU'D PUT IN ANY EFFORT THIS YEAR...

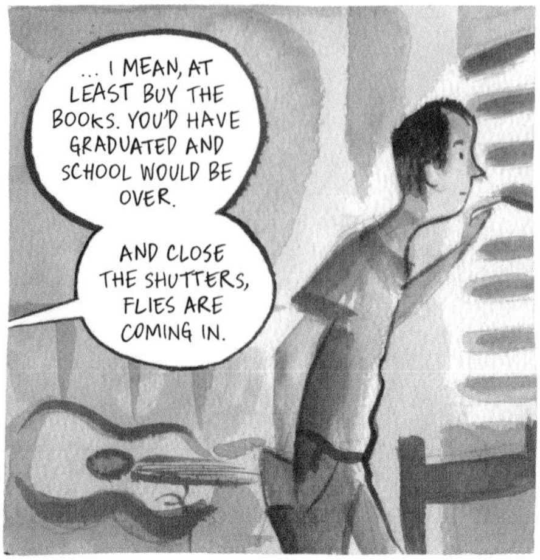
... I MEAN, AT LEAST BUY THE BOOKS. YOU'D HAVE GRADUATED AND SCHOOL WOULD BE OVER.
AND CLOSE THE SHUTTERS, FLIES ARE COMING IN.

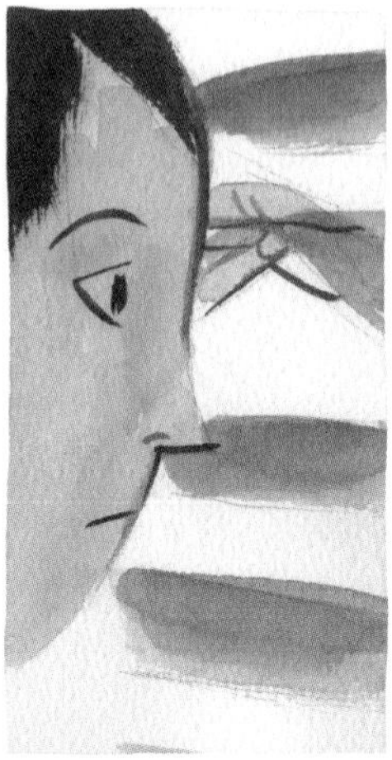

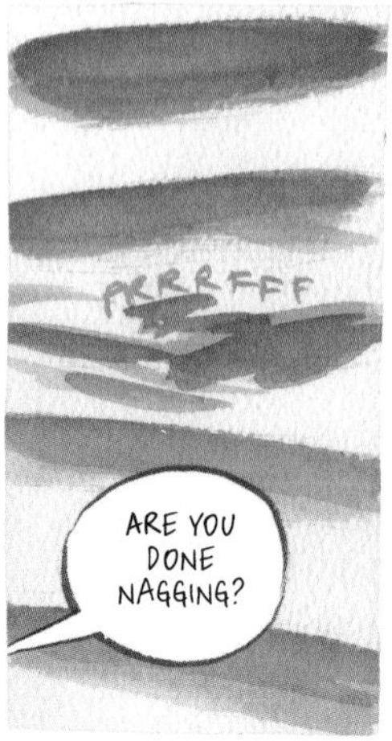
PRRRFFF
ARE YOU DONE NAGGING?

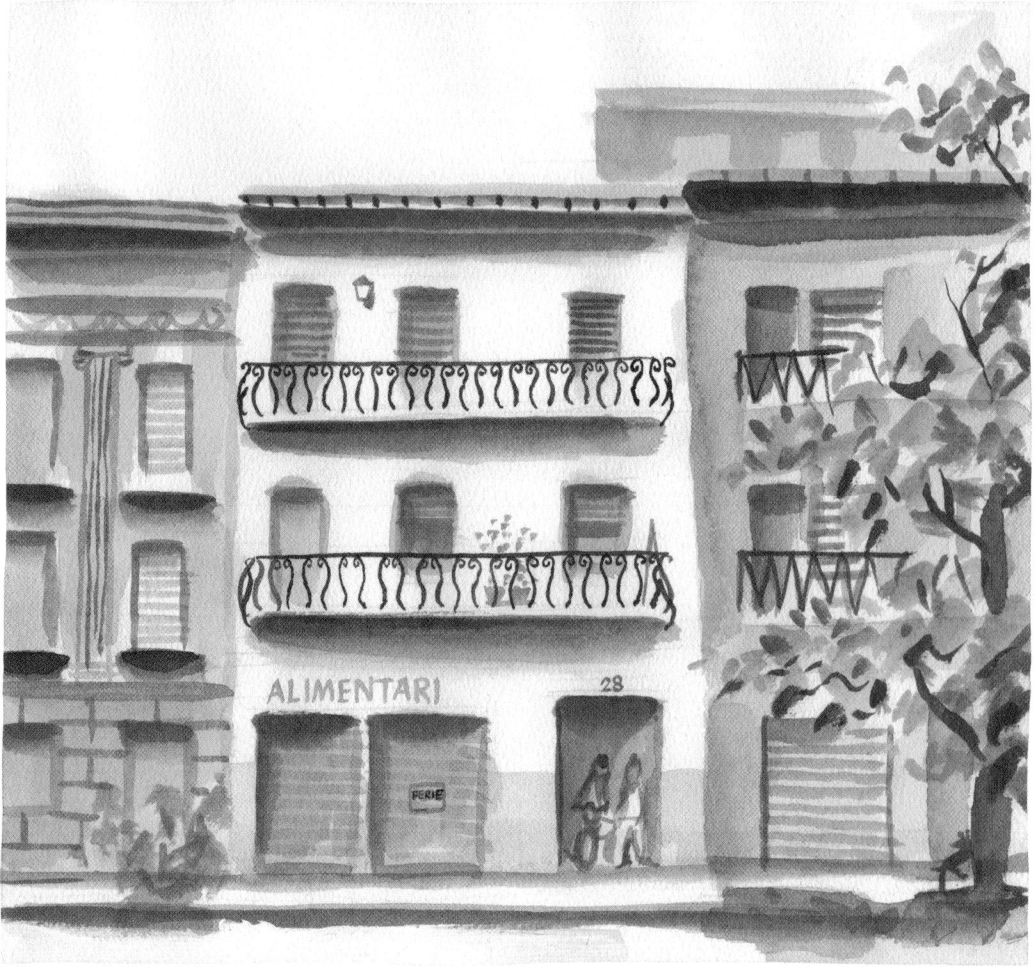
ALIMENTARI
28
FERIE

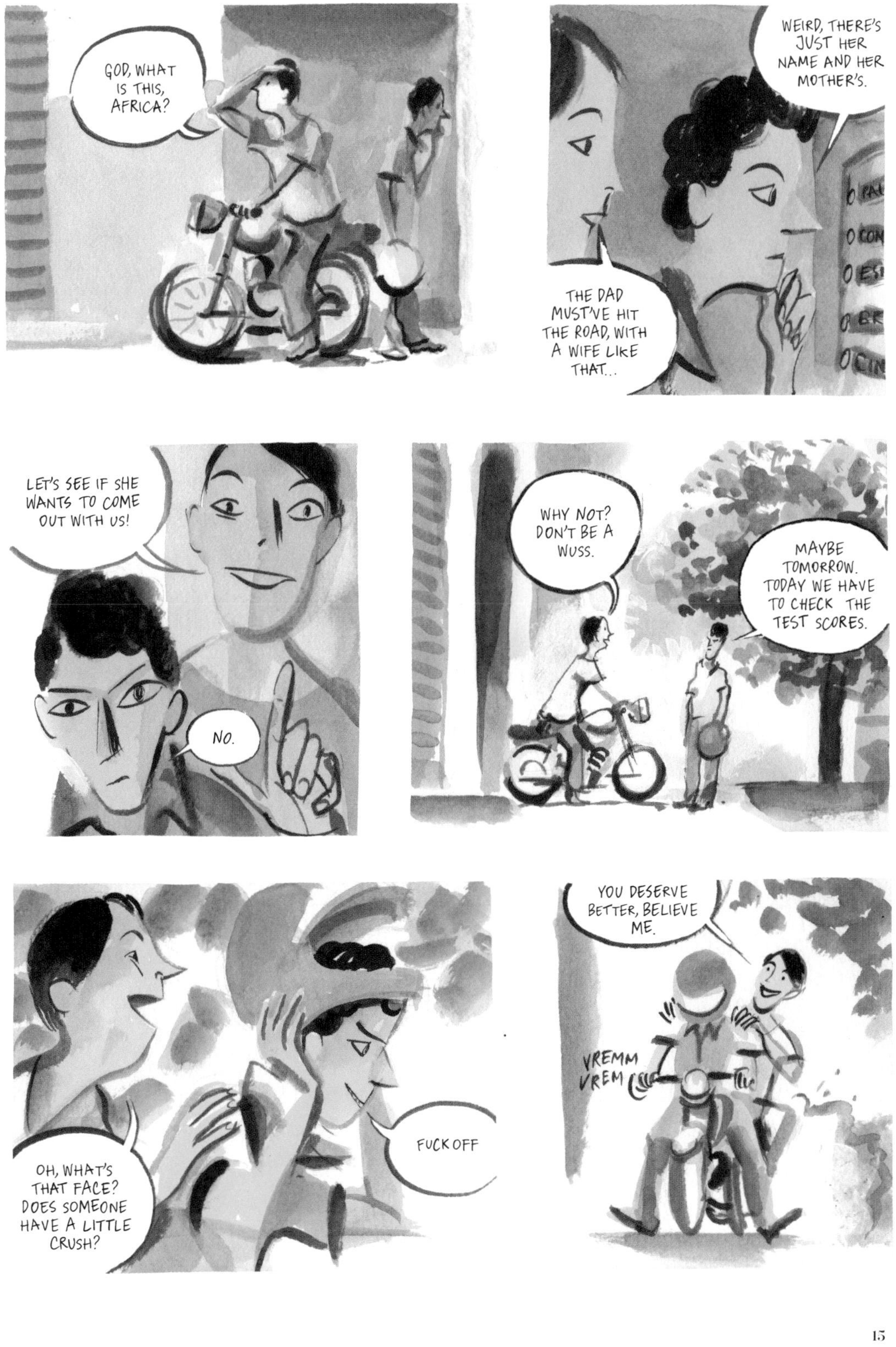
GOD, WHAT IS THIS, AFRICA?
WEIRD, THERE'S JUST HER NAME AND HER MOTHER'S.
THE DAD MUST'VE HIT THE ROAD, WITH A WIFE LIKE THAT...
LET'S SEE IF SHE WANTS TO COME OUT WITH US!
NO.
WHY NOT? DON'T BE A WUSS.
MAYBE TOMORROW. TODAY WE HAVE TO CHECK THE TEST SCORES.
OH, WHAT'S THAT FACE? DOES SOMEONE HAVE A LITTLE CRUSH?
FUCK OFF
YOU DESERVE BETTER, BELIEVE ME.
VREMM VREM

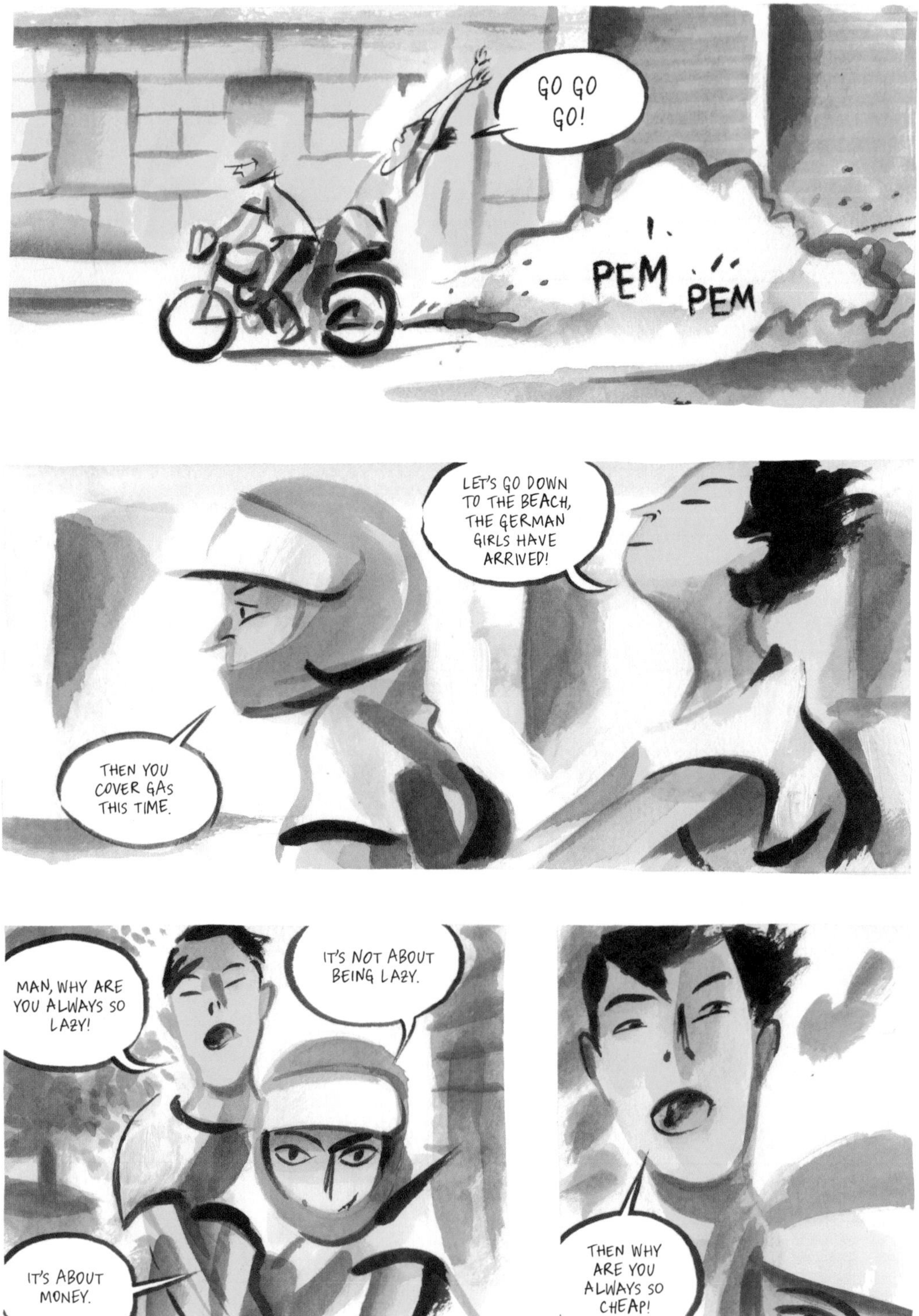
GO GO GO!
PEM PEM
LET'S GO DOWN TO THE BEACH, THE GERMAN GIRLS HAVE ARRIVED!
THEN YOU COVER GAS THIS TIME.
MAN, WHY ARE YOU ALWAYS SO LAZY!
IT'S NOT ABOUT BEING LAZY.
IT'S ABOUT MONEY.
THEN WHY ARE YOU ALWAYS SO CHEAP!

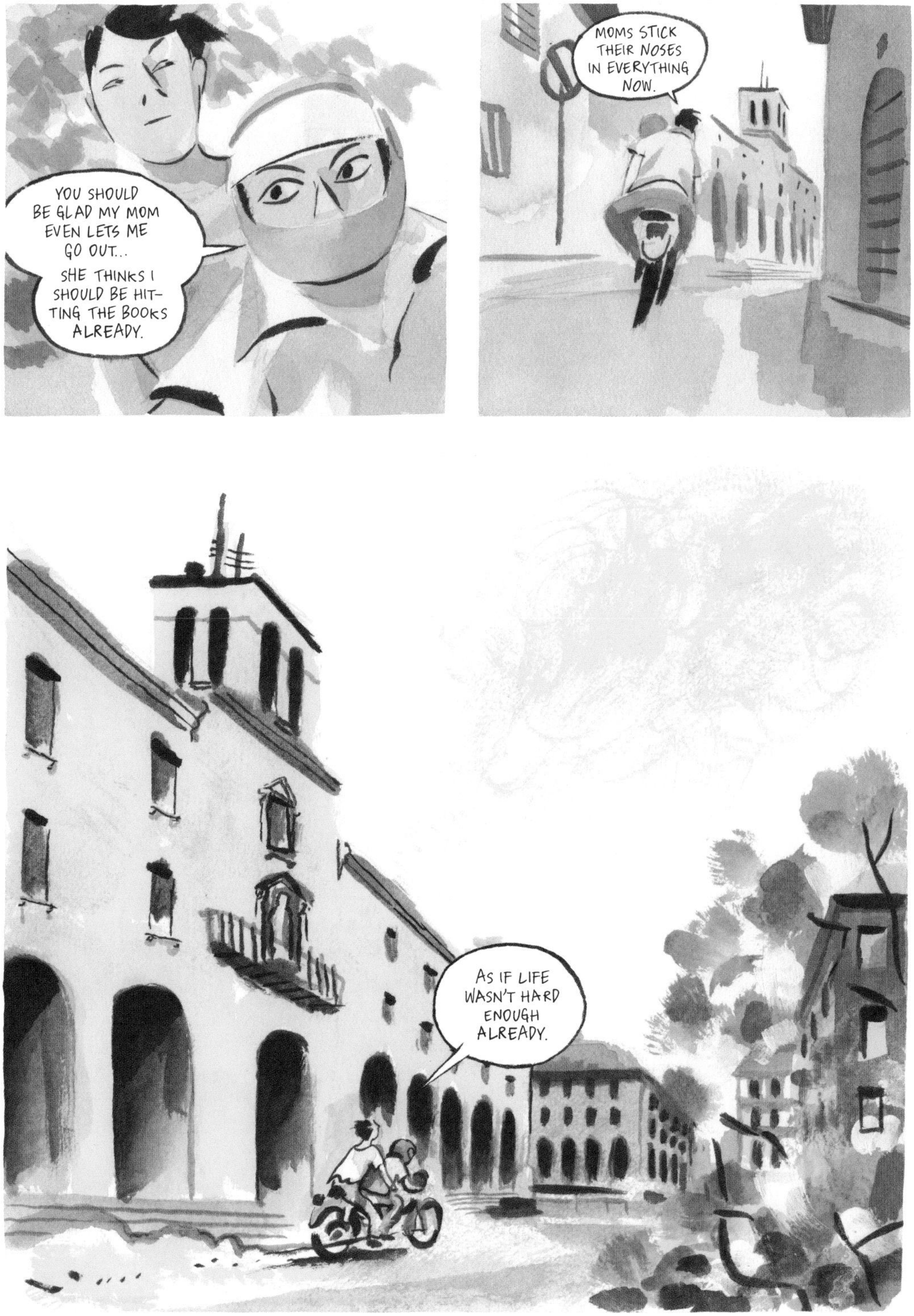
YOU SHOULD BE GLAD MY MOM EVEN LETS ME GO OUT...
SHE THINKS I SHOULD BE HIT-TING THE BOOKS ALREADY.
MOMS STICK THEIR NOSES IN EVERYTHING NOW.
AS IF LIFE WASN'T HARD ENOUGH ALREADY.

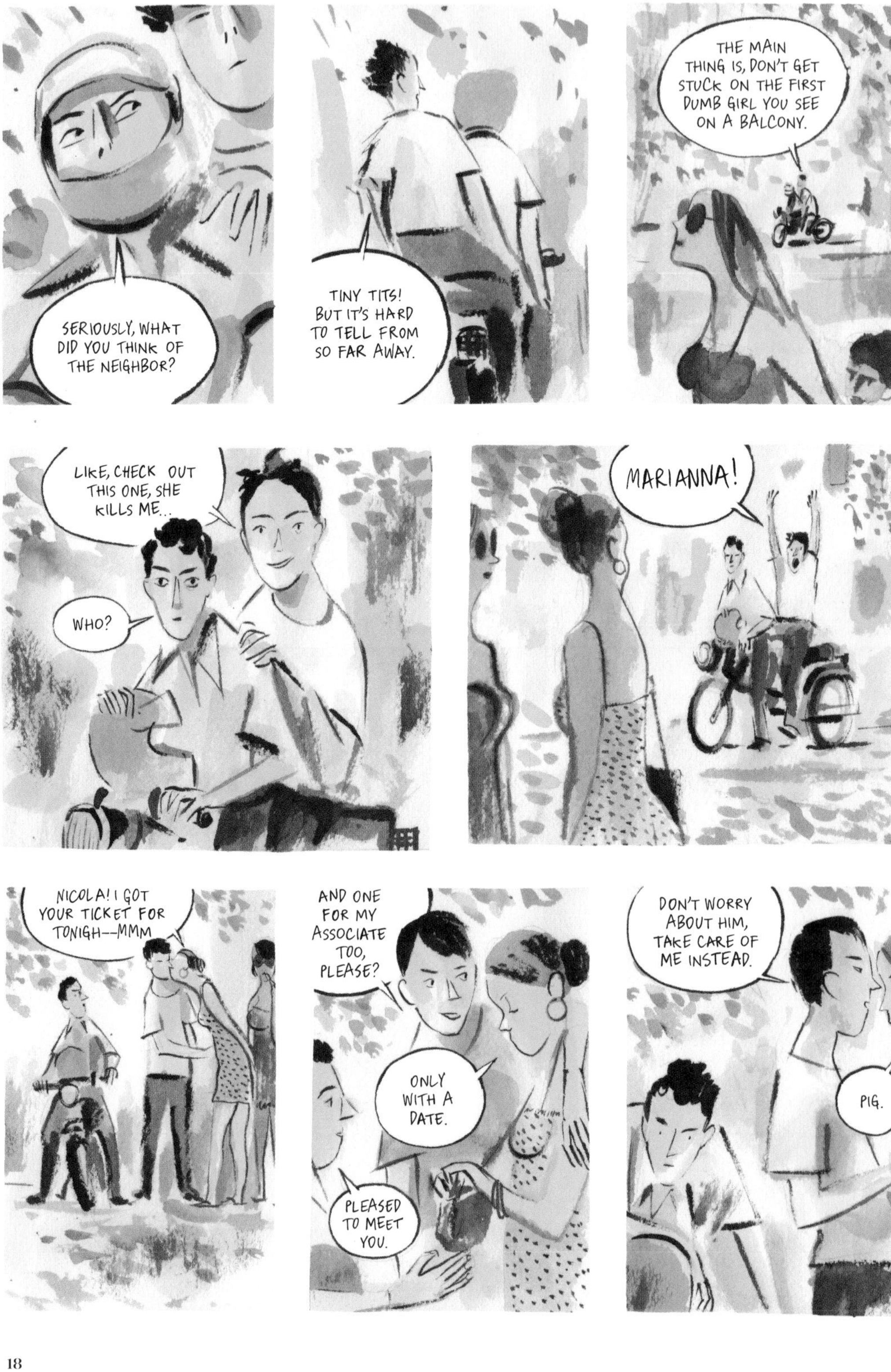
SERIOUSLY, WHAT DID YOU THINK OF THE NEIGHBOR?
TINY TITS! BUT IT'S HARD TO TELL FROM SO FAR AWAY.
THE MAIN THING IS, DON'T GET STUCK ON THE FIRST DUMB GIRL YOU SEE ON A BALCONY.
LIKE, CHECK OUT THIS ONE, SHE KILLS ME...
WHO?
MARIANNA!
NICOLA! I GOT YOUR TICKET FOR TONIGH--MMM
AND ONE FOR MY ASSOCIATE TOO, PLEASE?
ONLY WITH A DATE.
PLEASED TO MEET YOU.
DON'T WORRY ABOUT HIM, TAKE CARE OF ME INSTEAD.
PIG.

Pleased to meet you. WHAT ARE YOU, FROM MEDIEVAL TIMES? WHY ARE YOU SO EMBARRASSING?

PAF!

OUCH!

ANYWAY, TONIGHT YOU SHOULD INVITE YOUR NEIGHBOR IF YOU WANT TO GET INTO THE CLUB.

JUST RELAX, SAY HI, GET HER ATTENTION VALENTINA!

THE FIRST IMPRESSION IS ESSENTIAL, YOU KNOW? IF YOU MESS IT UP YOU HAVE TO START ALL OVER AGAIN. PHYSICAL CONTACT, FOR EXAMPLE, IS IMPORTANT...

WOMEN LIKE TO BE TOUCHED, YOU TAKE HER HAND, GIVE IT A LITTLE SQUEEZE, THEN COME OUT WITH A LINE LIKE...

"YOU'RE SO BEAUTIFUL...

FOR EXAMPLE.

AND THEN YOU END UP IN BED.

THEN YOU GET MARRIED AND HAVE KIDS AND GROW OLD TOGETHER.

WHAT WAS THE FIRST STEP, THEN?

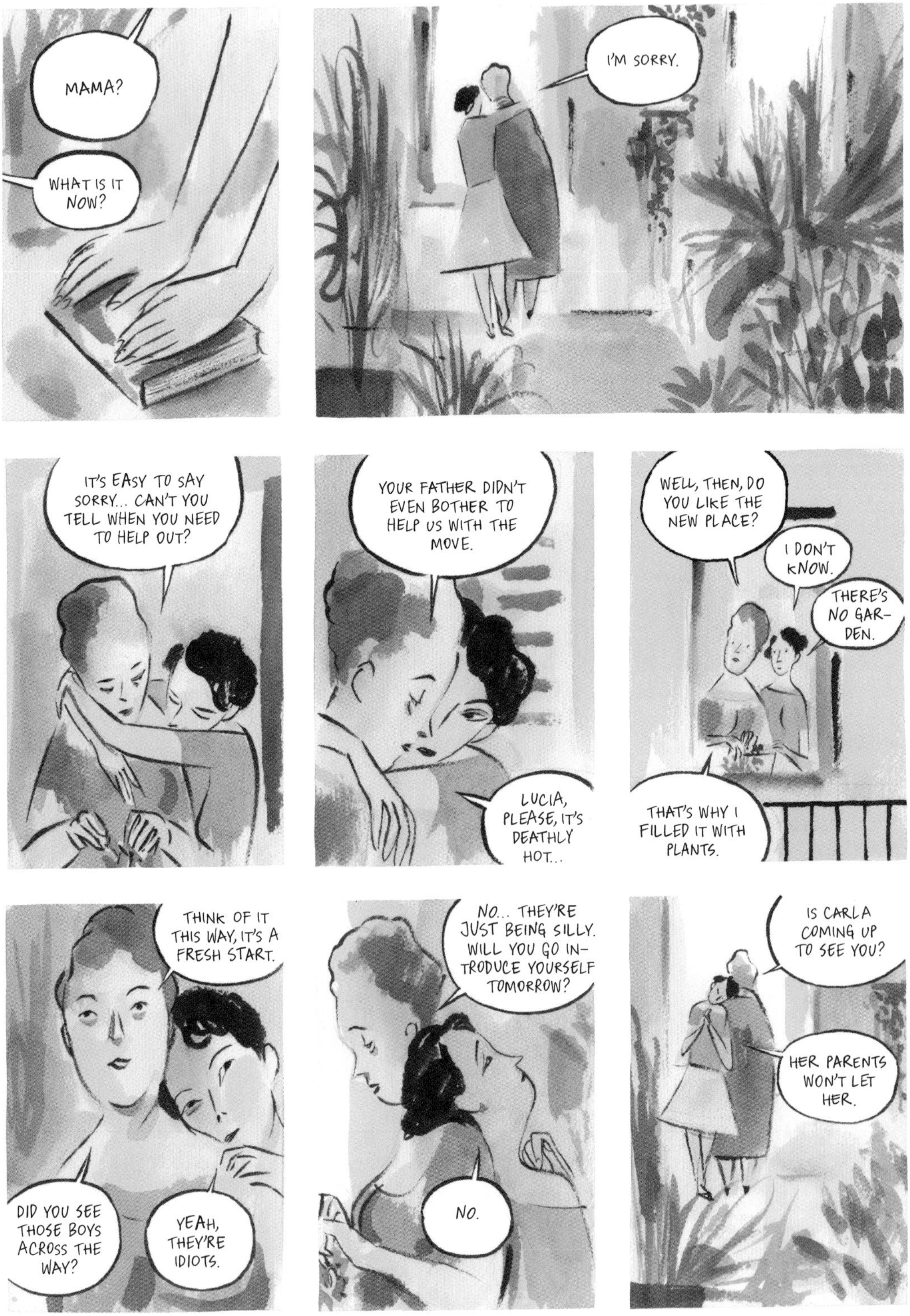
MAMA?
WHAT IS IT NOW?
I'M SORRY.
IT'S EASY TO SAY SORRY... CAN'T YOU TELL WHEN YOU NEED TO HELP OUT?
YOUR FATHER DIDN'T EVEN BOTHER TO HELP US WITH THE MOVE.
LUCIA, PLEASE, IT'S DEATHLY HOT...
WELL, THEN, DO YOU LIKE THE NEW PLACE?
I DON'T KNOW.
THERE'S NO GAR-DEN.
THAT'S WHY I FILLED IT WITH PLANTS.
THINK OF IT THIS WAY, IT'S A FRESH START.
DID YOU SEE THOSE BOYS ACROSS THE WAY?
YEAH, THEY'RE IDIOTS.
NO... THEY'RE JUST BEING SILLY. WILL YOU GO IN-TRODUCE YOURSELF TOMORROW?
NO.
IS CARLA COMING UP TO SEE YOU?
HER PARENTS WON'T LET HER.

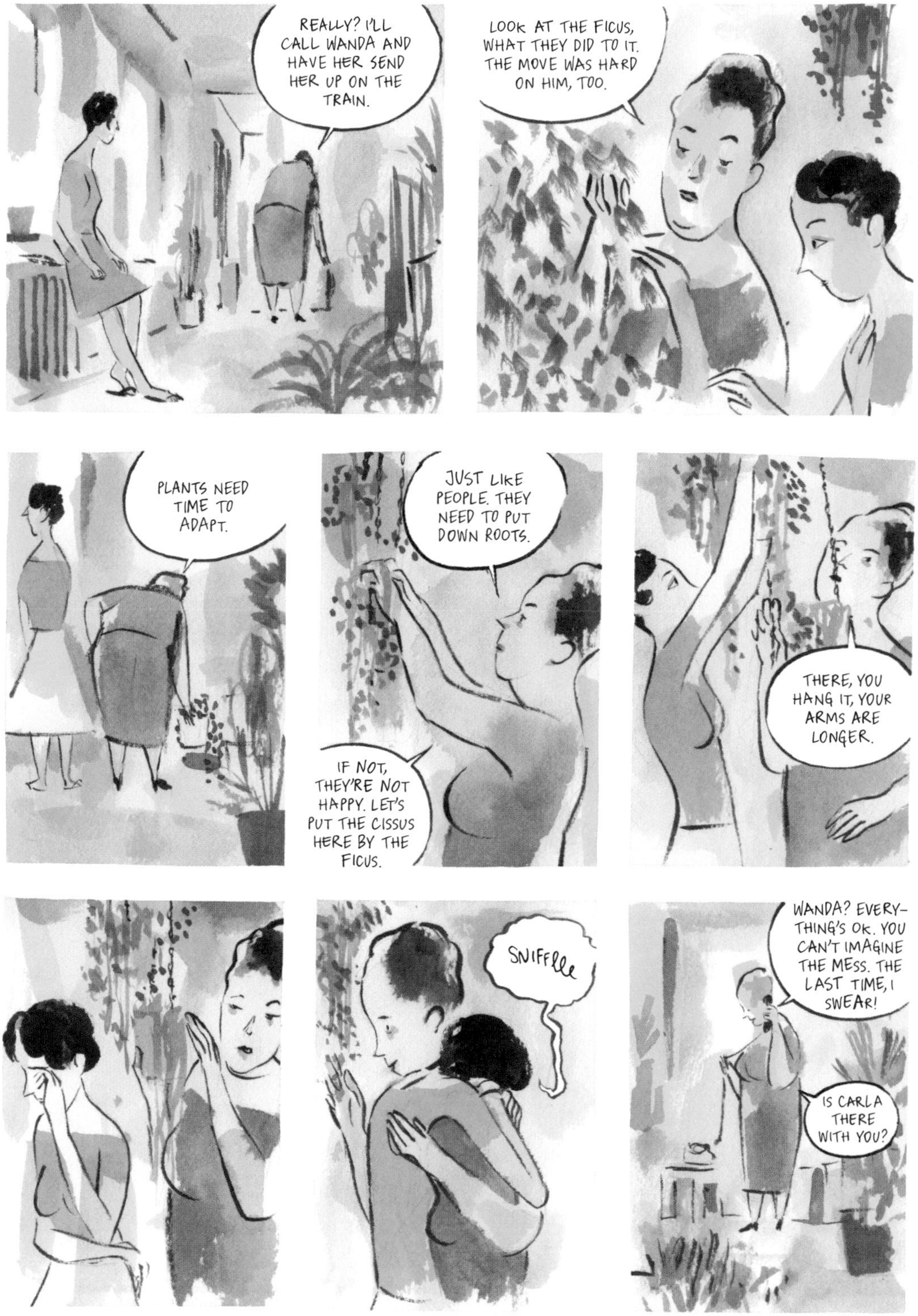
REALLY? I'LL CALL WANDA AND HAVE HER SEND HER UP ON THE TRAIN.
LOOK AT THE FICUS, WHAT THEY DID TO IT. THE MOVE WAS HARD ON HIM, TOO.
PLANTS NEED TIME TO ADAPT.
JUST LIKE PEOPLE. THEY NEED TO PUT DOWN ROOTS.
IF NOT, THEY'RE NOT HAPPY. LET'S PUT THE CISSUS HERE BY THE FICUS.
THERE, YOU HANG IT, YOUR ARMS ARE LONGER.
SNIFFLLE
WANDA? EVERY-THING'S OK. YOU CAN'T IMAGINE THE MESS. THE LAST TIME, I SWEAR!
IS CARLA THERE WITH YOU?

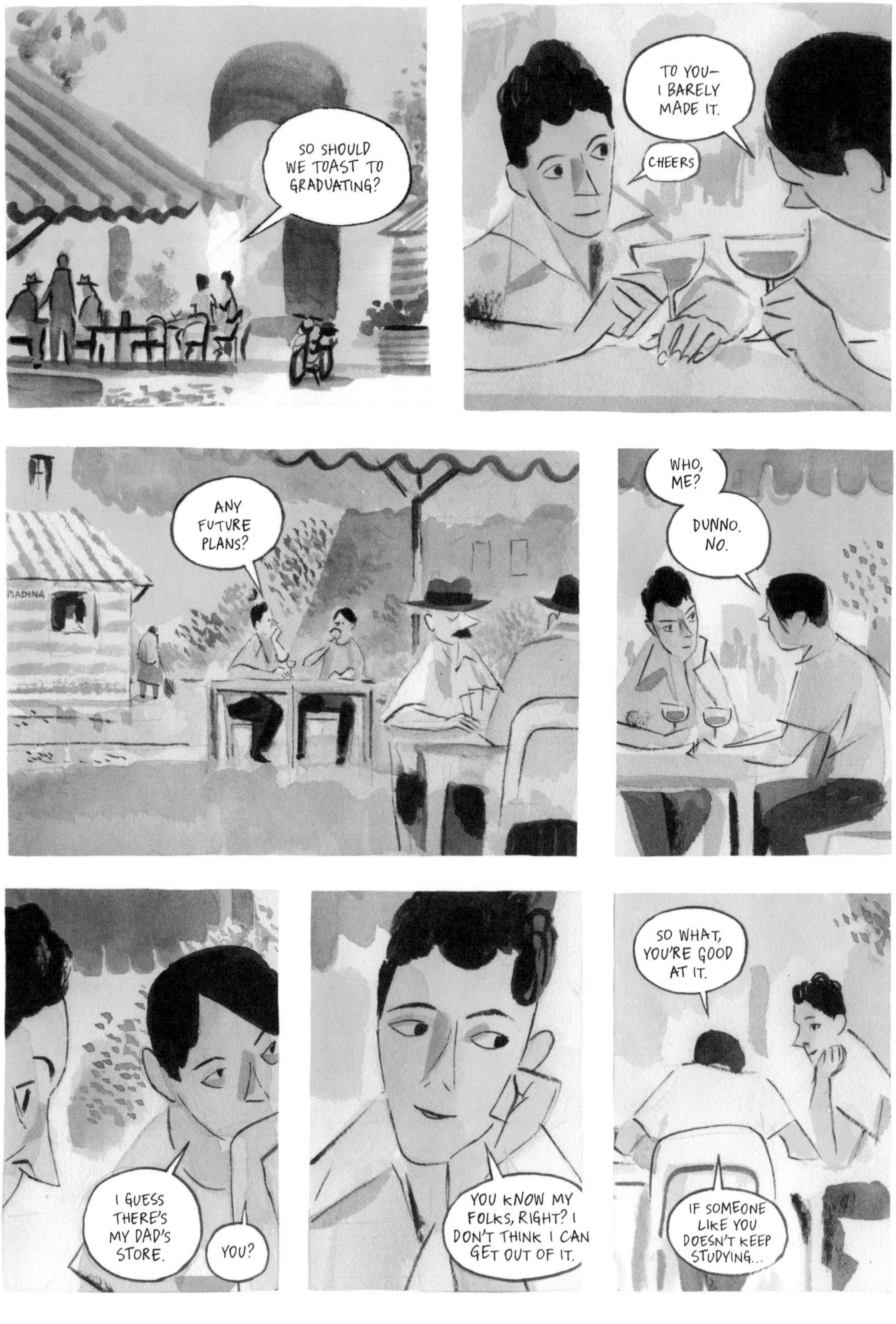
SO SHOULD WE TOAST TO GRADUATING?
TO YOU— I BARELY MADE IT.
CHEERS
ANY FUTURE PLANS?
WHO, ME?
DUNNO. NO.
I GUESS THERE'S MY DAD'S STORE.
YOU?
YOU KNOW MY FOLKS, RIGHT? I DON'T THINK I CAN GET OUT OF IT.
SO WHAT, YOU'RE GOOD AT IT.
IF SOMEONE LIKE YOU DOESN'T KEEP STUDYING...

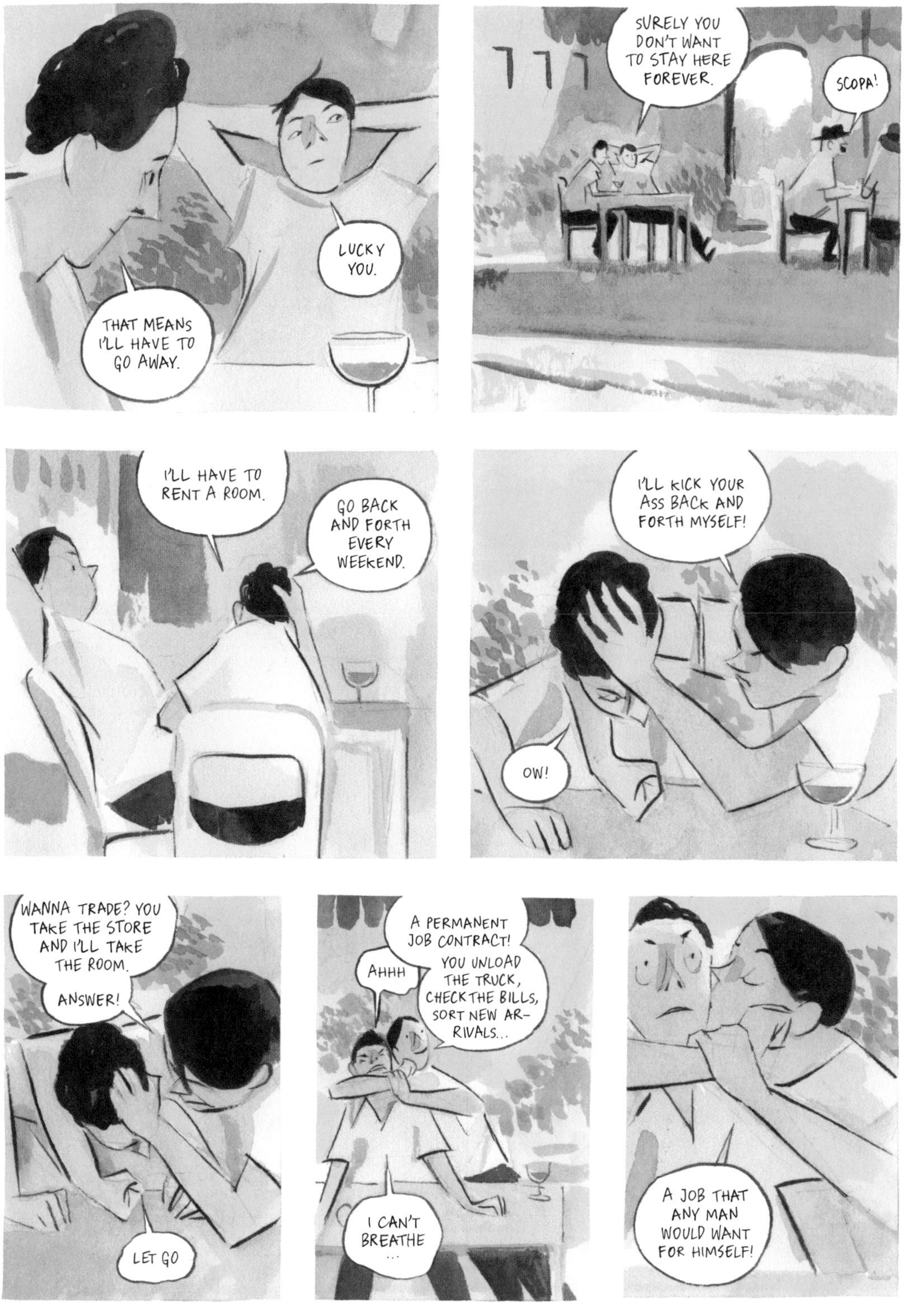
THAT MEANS I'LL HAVE TO GO AWAY.
LUCKY YOU.
SURELY YOU DON'T WANT TO STAY HERE FOREVER.
SCOPA!
I'LL HAVE TO RENT A ROOM.
GO BACK AND FORTH EVERY WEEKEND.
I'LL KICK YOUR ASS BACK AND FORTH MYSELF!
OW!
WANNA TRADE? YOU TAKE THE STORE AND I'LL TAKE THE ROOM.
ANSWER!
LET GO
A PERMANENT JOB CONTRACT!
AHHH
YOU UNLOAD THE TRUCK, CHECK THE BILLS, SORT NEW AR-RIVALS...
I CAN'T BREATHE ...
A JOB THAT ANY MAN WOULD WANT FOR HIMSELF!

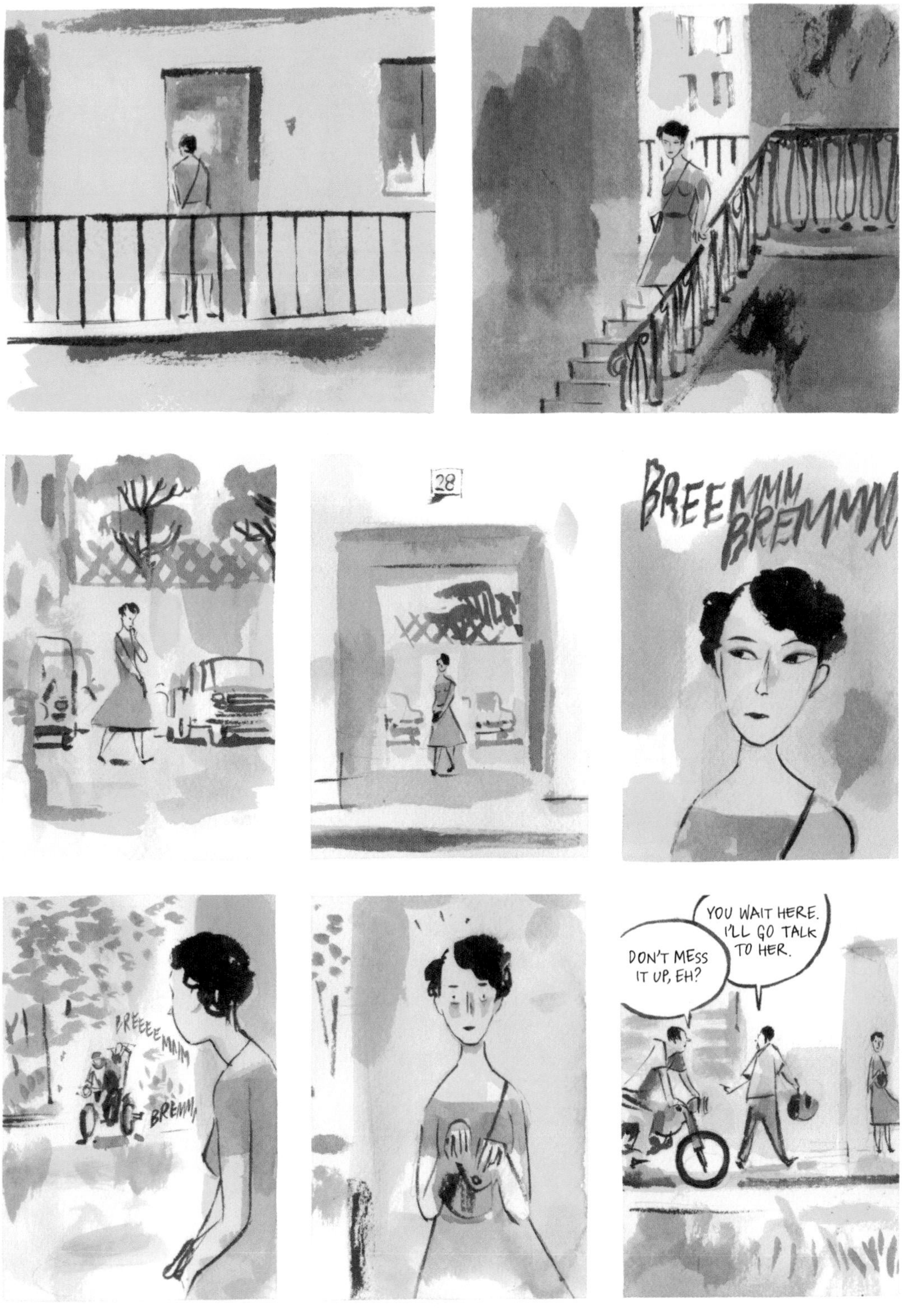
28
YOU WAIT HERE. I'LL GO TALK TO HER.
DON'T MESS IT UP, EH?

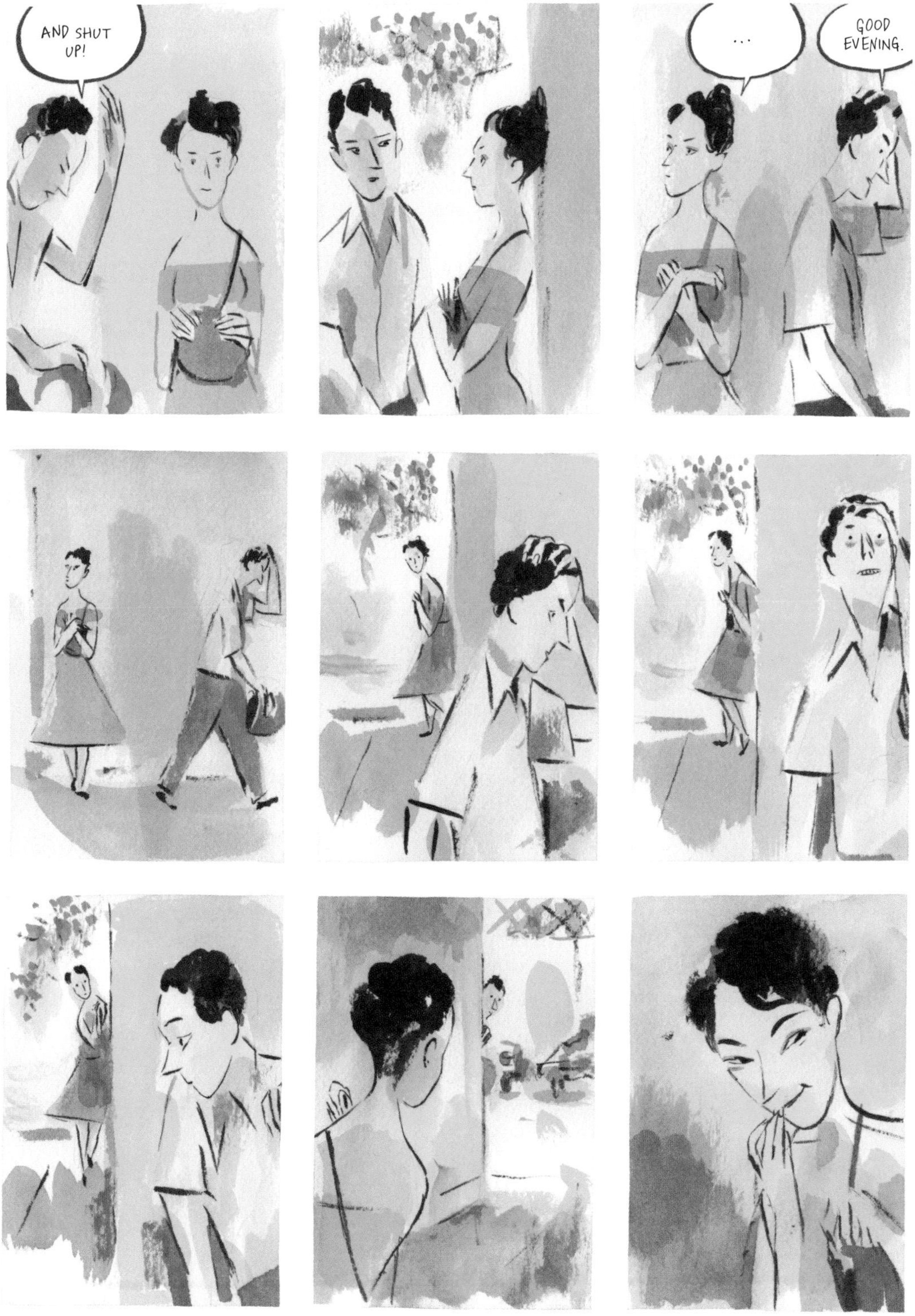
AND SHUT UP!
...
GOOD EVENING.

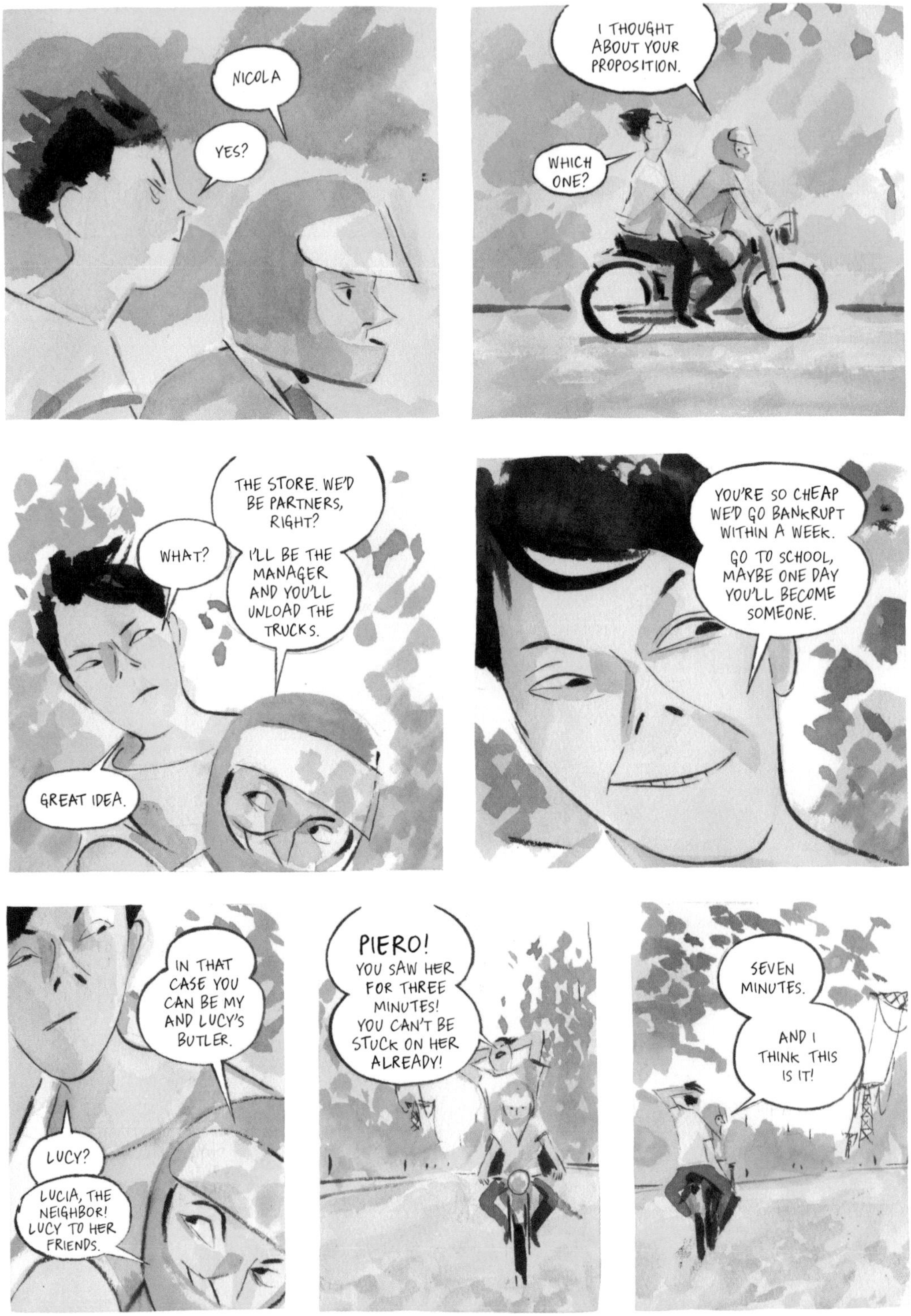
NICOLA
YES?
I THOUGHT ABOUT YOUR PROPOSITION.
WHICH ONE?
THE STORE. WE'D BE PARTNERS, RIGHT?
WHAT?
I'LL BE THE MANAGER AND YOU'LL UNLOAD THE TRUCKS.
GREAT IDEA.
YOU'RE SO CHEAP WE'D GO BANKRUPT WITHIN A WEEK.
GO TO SCHOOL, MAYBE ONE DAY YOU'LL BECOME SOMEONE.
IN THAT CASE YOU CAN BE MY AND LUCY'S BUTLER.
LUCY?
LUCIA, THE NEIGHBOR! LUCY TO HER FRIENDS.
PIERO! YOU SAW HER FOR THREE MINUTES! YOU CAN'T BE STUCK ON HER ALREADY!
SEVEN MINUTES.
AND I THINK THIS IS IT!

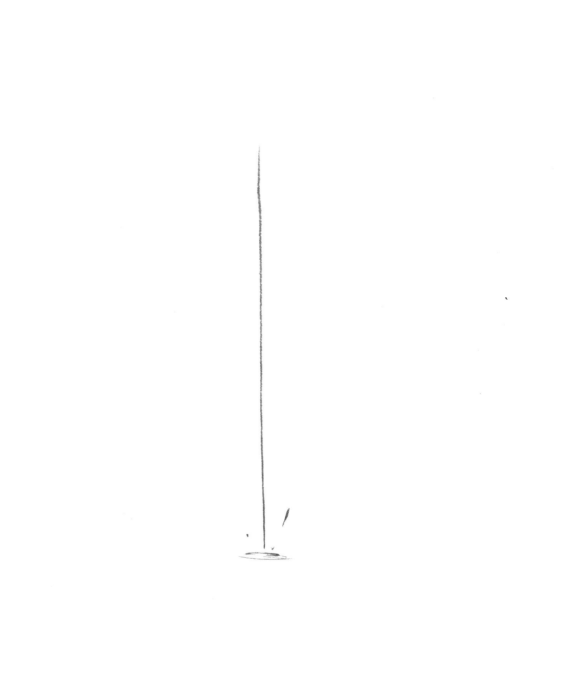

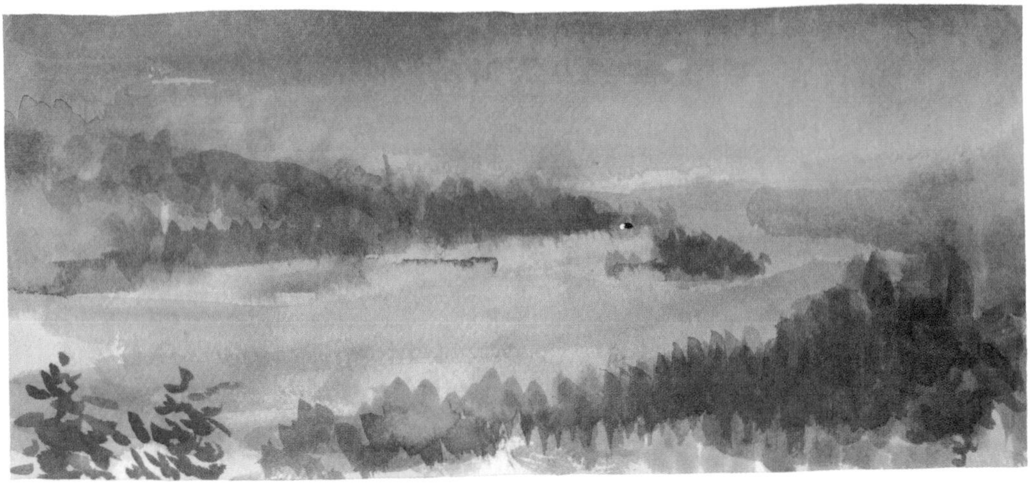

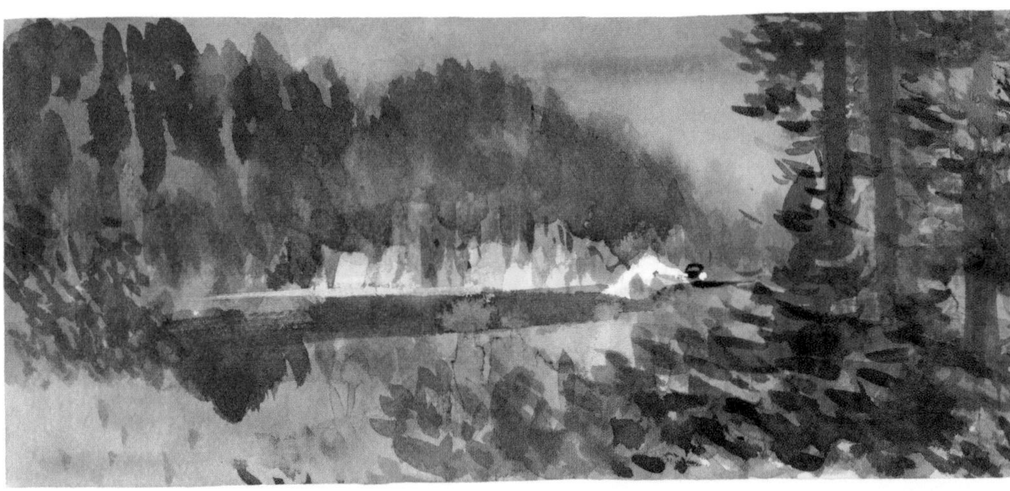

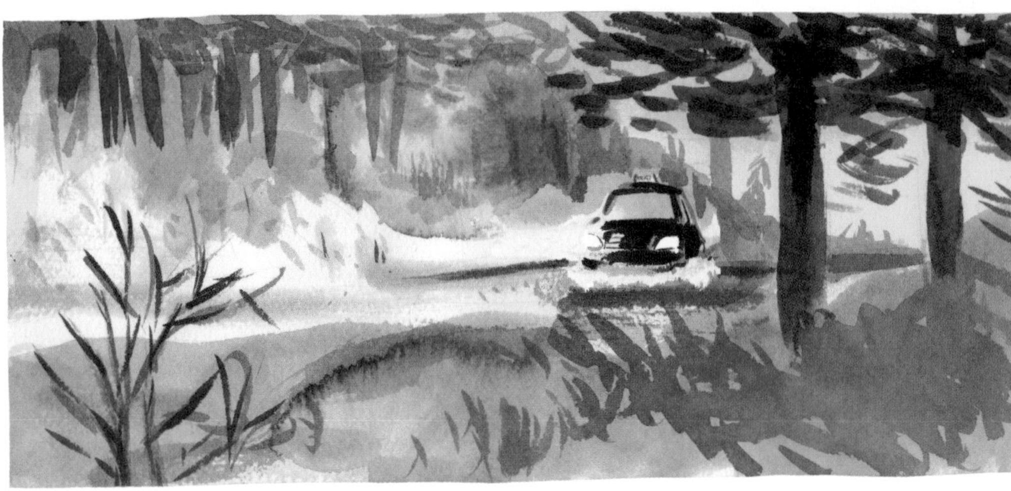

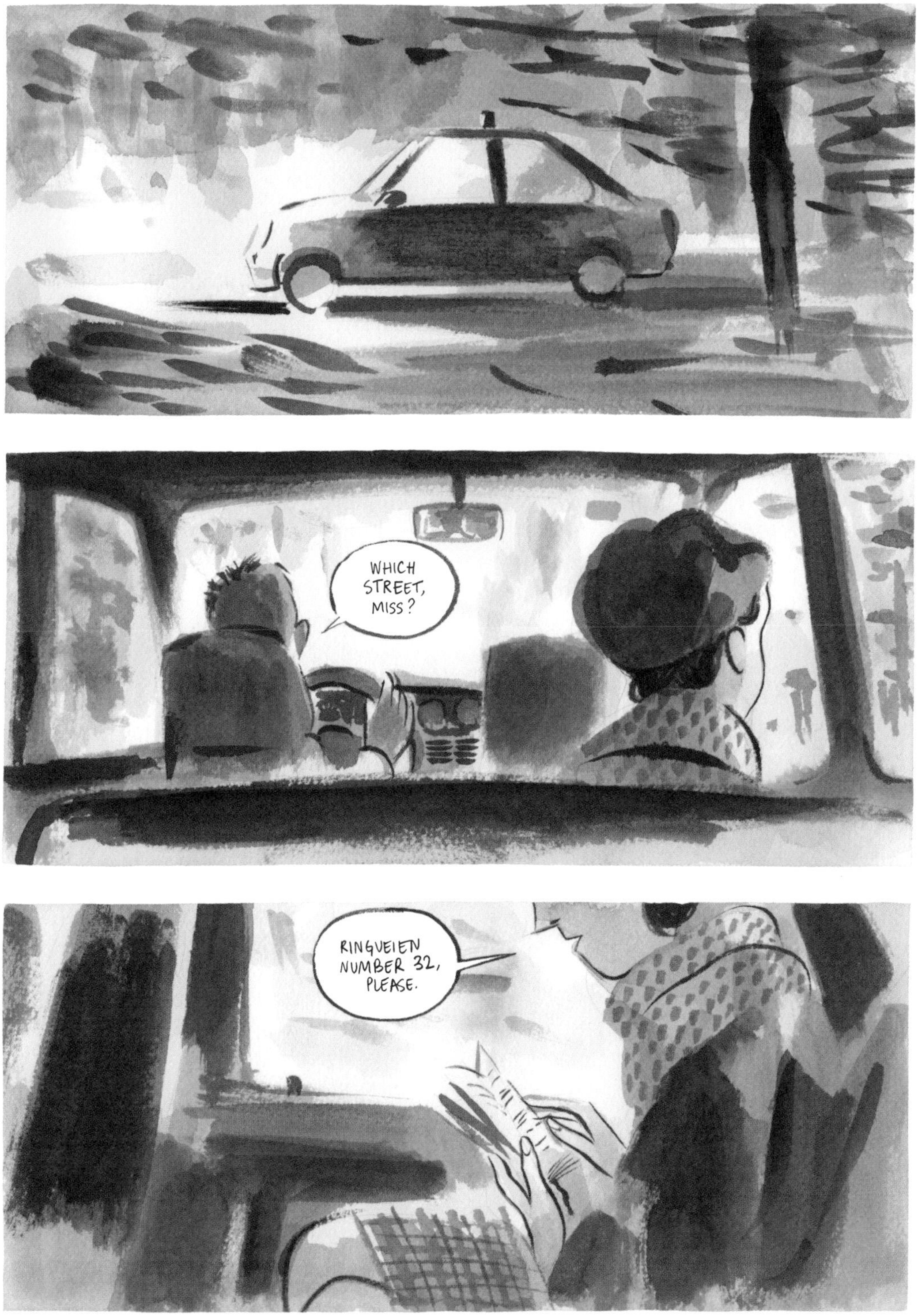
WHICH STREET, MISS?
RINGVEIEN NUMBER 32, PLEASE.

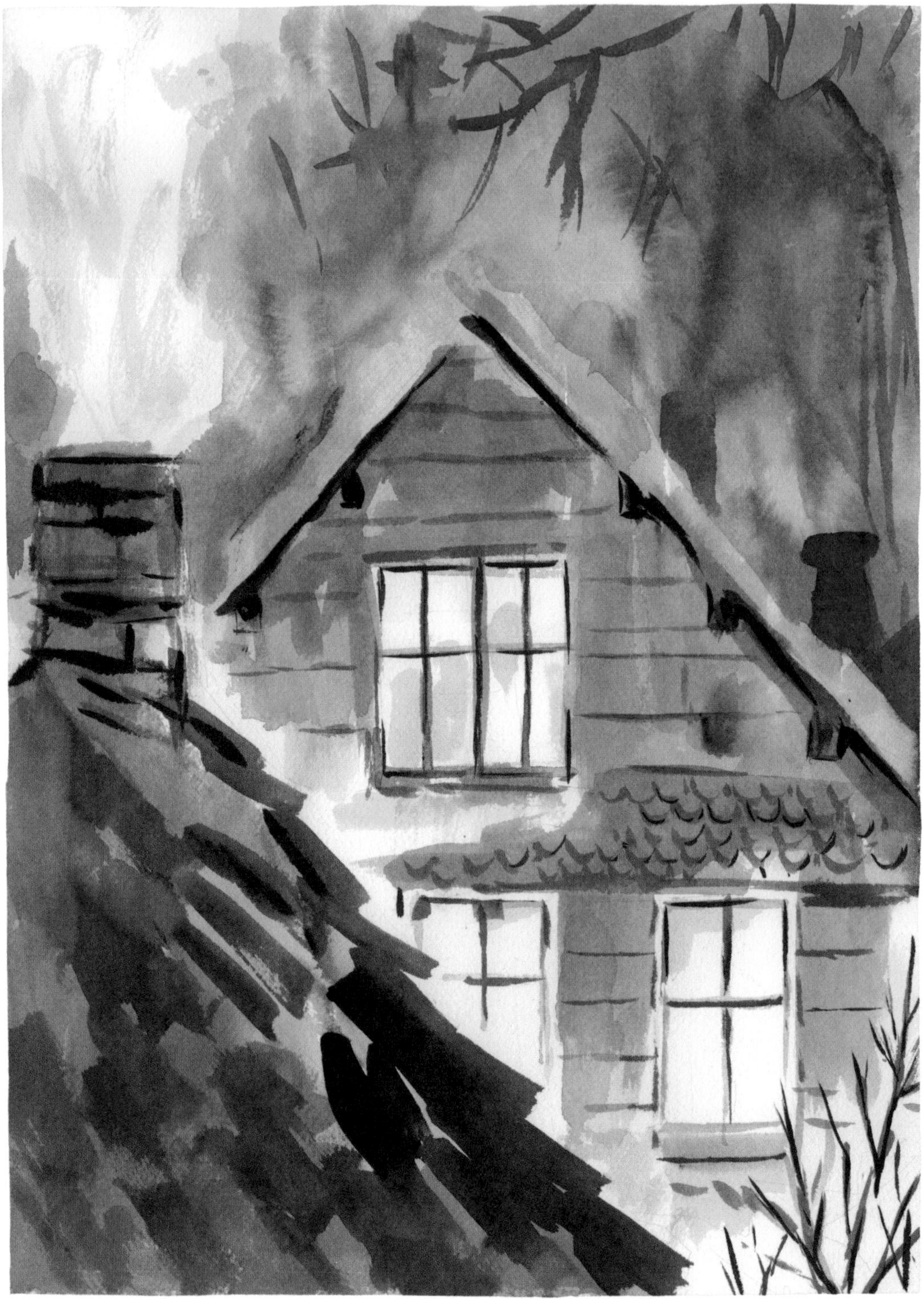

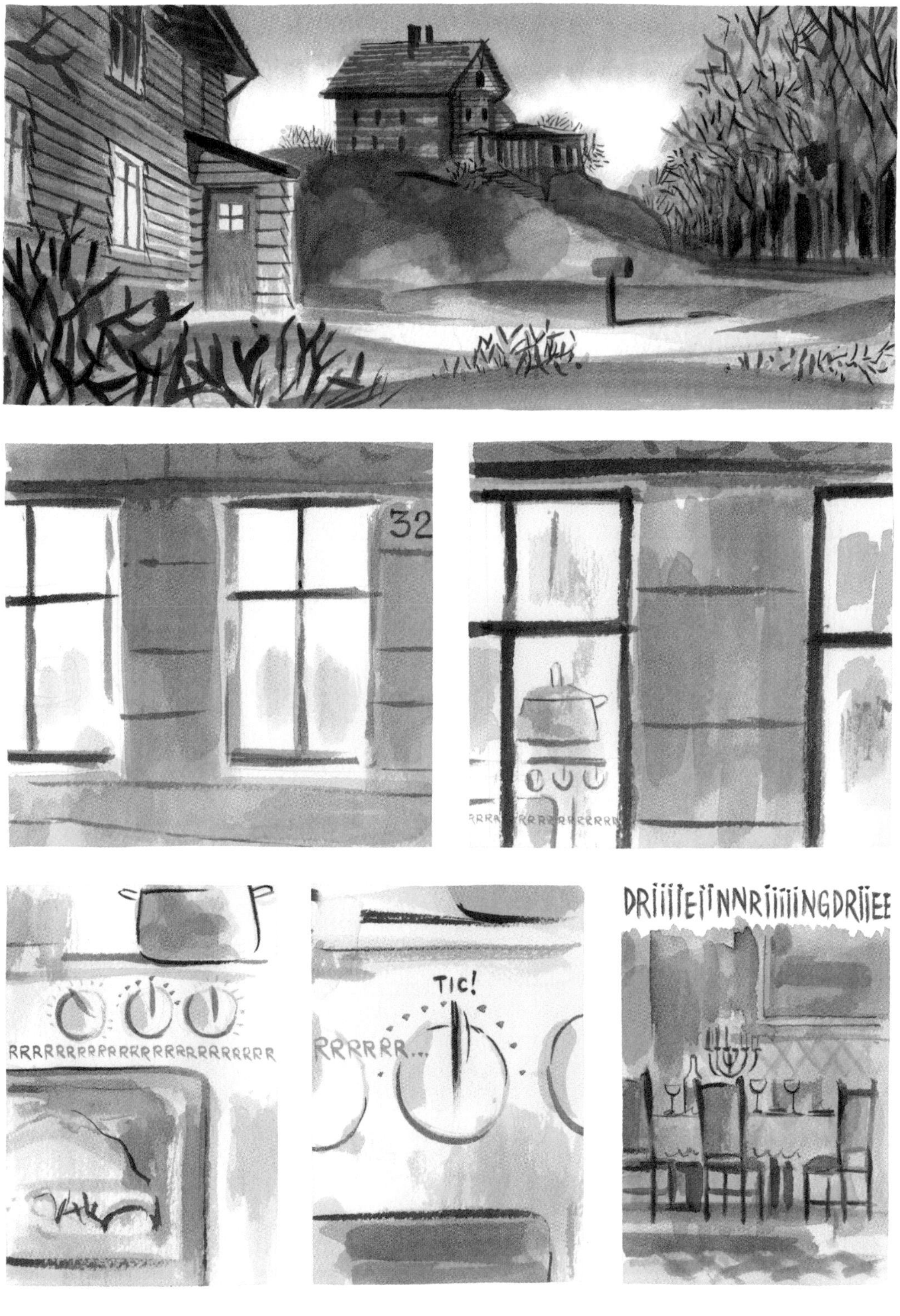
32
RRRRRRRRRRRRRRRR
RRRRRRRRRRRRRRRRRRRRRR
RRRRRR...
TIC!
DRiiiiEiiNNRiiiiiNGDRiiEE

Rͮiͥͥͥiͥe͡iͥͥͥͥͥiͥNNNiͥͥiͥNGGRRRR

iͥͥͥͥͥNNNGGRiͥͥͥͥͥiͥEEͥiͥͥNNRR

RRRPDRRRRRRiͥͥͥͥͥiͥEENNRDRiͥͥͥ

HERREGUD, JEG GLEMTE DET STEKE!

RRDRiͥͥͥͥͥiͥiͥNNNG!

DRiͥͥͥiͥEͥiͥNNRiͥͥͥͥNGDRiͥEE

Oh no, I forgot the roast!

RRRPDRRRRRRiͥͥͥͥͥiͥEENNRDRiͥͥͥ

SSSSSSP

TI MINUTTER IGJEN...

Ten more minutes...

SVEN! ER DU FERDIG?

SVEN! Are you ready?

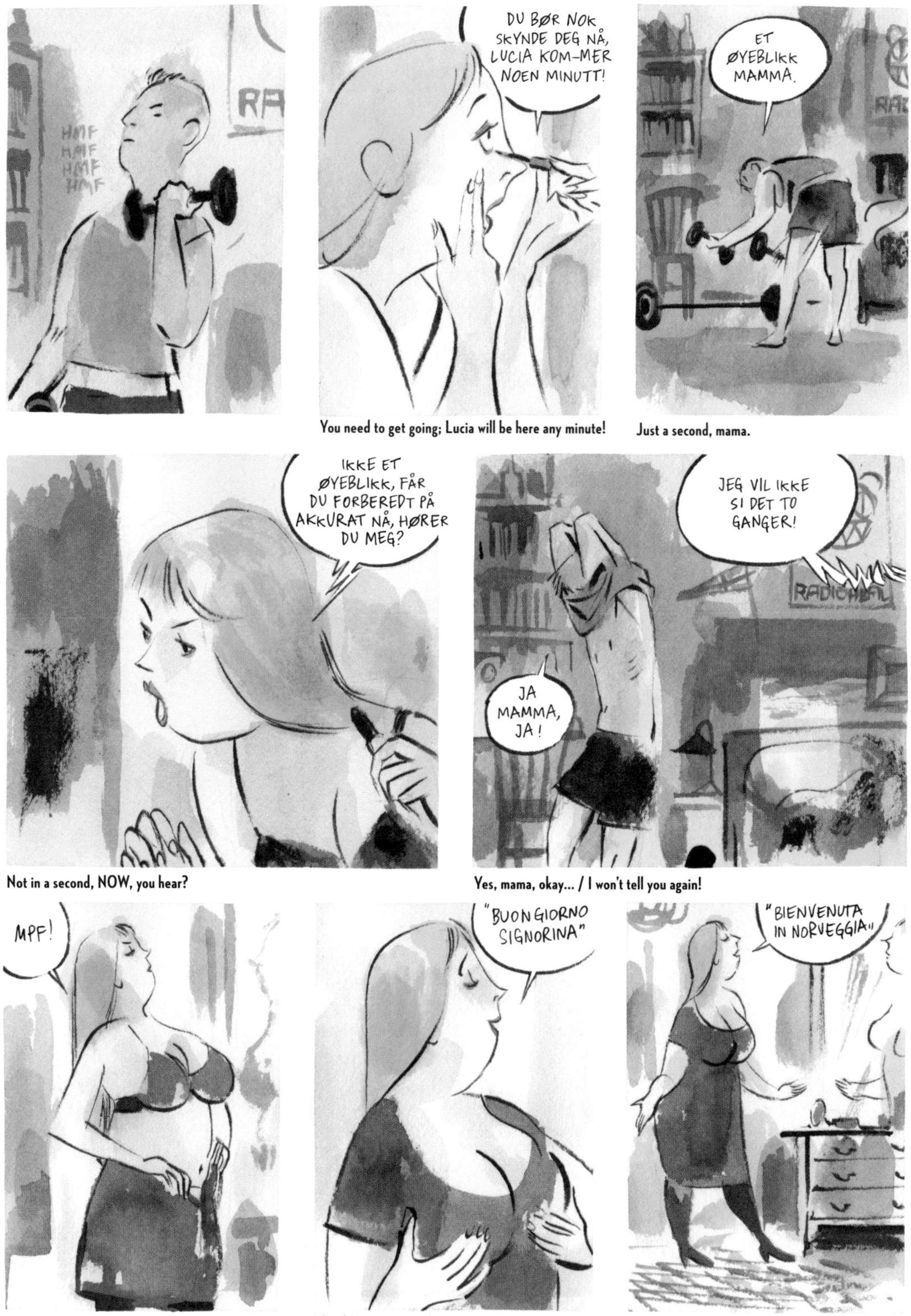
HMF
HMF
HMF
HMF
DU BØR NOK SKYNDE DEG NÅ, LUCIA KOM-MER NOEN MINUTT!
ET ØYEBLIKK MAMMA.
IKKE ET ØYEBLIKK, FÅR DU FORBEREDT PÅ AKKURAT NÅ, HØRER DU MEG?
JEG VIL IKKE SI DET TO GANGER!
JA MAMMA, JA!
MPF!
"BUONGIORNO SIGNORINA"
"BIENVENUTA IN NORVEGGIA"

You need to get going; Lucia will be here any minute!

Just a second, mama.

Not in a second, NOW, you hear?

Yes, mama, okay... / I won't tell you again!

"Good Morning, Miss."

"Welcome in Norway."

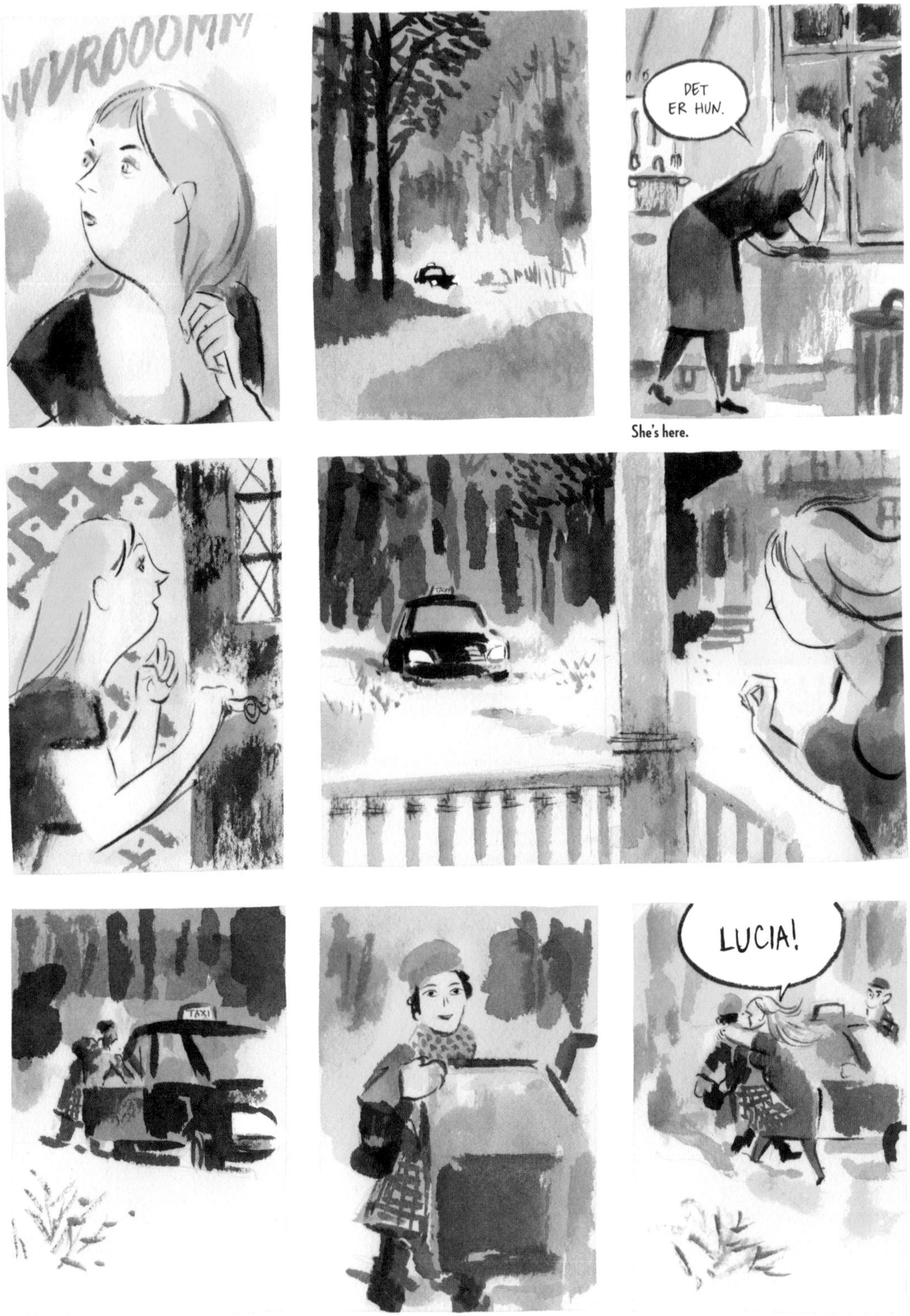
VVVROOOMM
DET ER HUN.
She's here.
LUCIA!

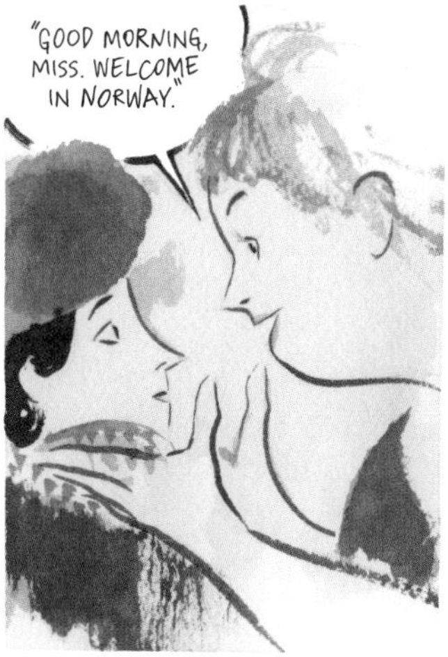
"GOOD MORNING, MISS. WELCOME IN NORWAY."

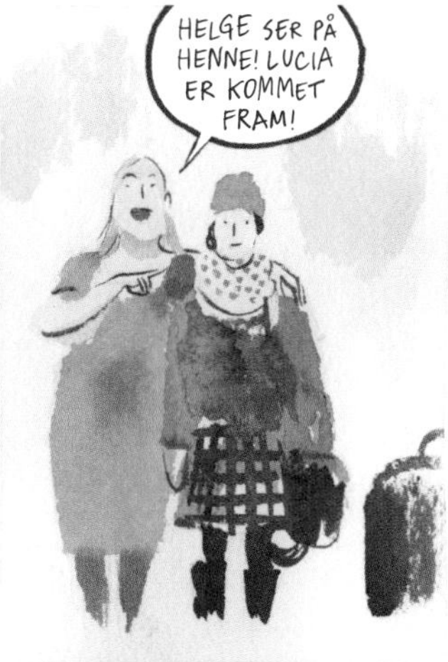
HELGE SER PÅ HENNE! LUCIA ER KOMMET FRAM!

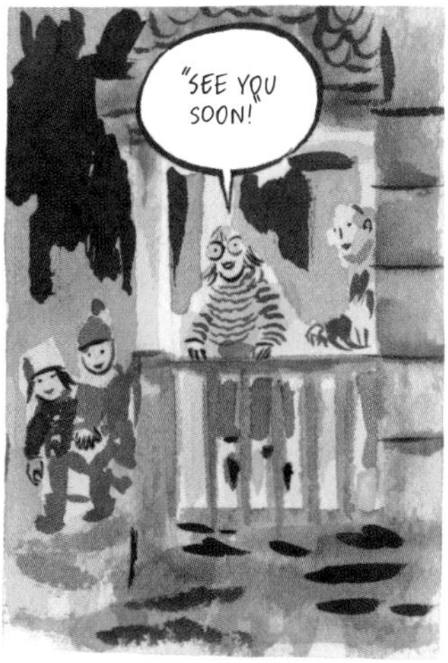
"SEE YOU SOON!"

Helge, look ! Lucia is here!

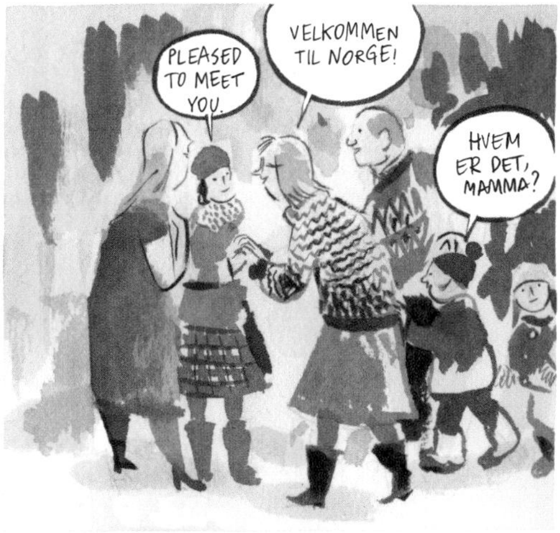
PLEASED TO MEET YOU.
VELKOMMEN TIL NORGE!
HVEM ER DET, MAMMA?

Welcome to Norway! / Who's that, Mama?

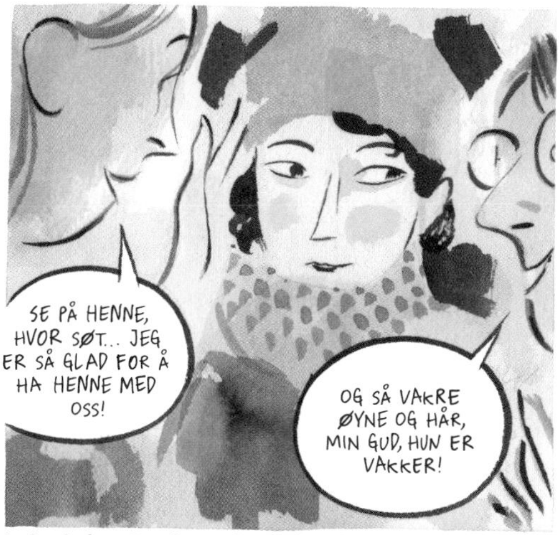
SE PÅ HENNE, HVOR SØT... JEG ER SÅ GLAD FOR Å HA HENNE MED OSS!
OG SÅ VAKRE ØYNE OG HÅR, MIN GUD, HUN ER VAKKER!

Look at this face... I'm so happy to have you here! / And those eyes, what a beauty!

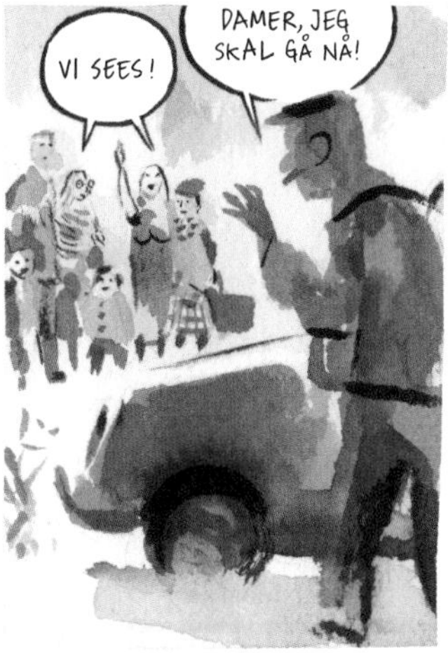
VI SEES!
DAMER, JEG SKAL GÅ NÅ!

Ladies, I'm off! / Goodbye!

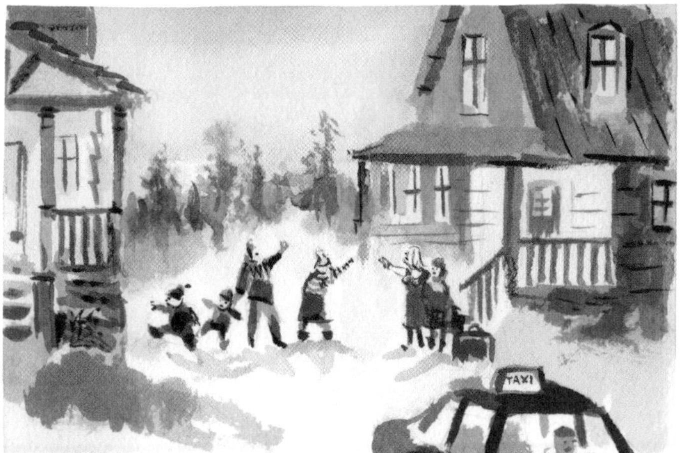
TAXI

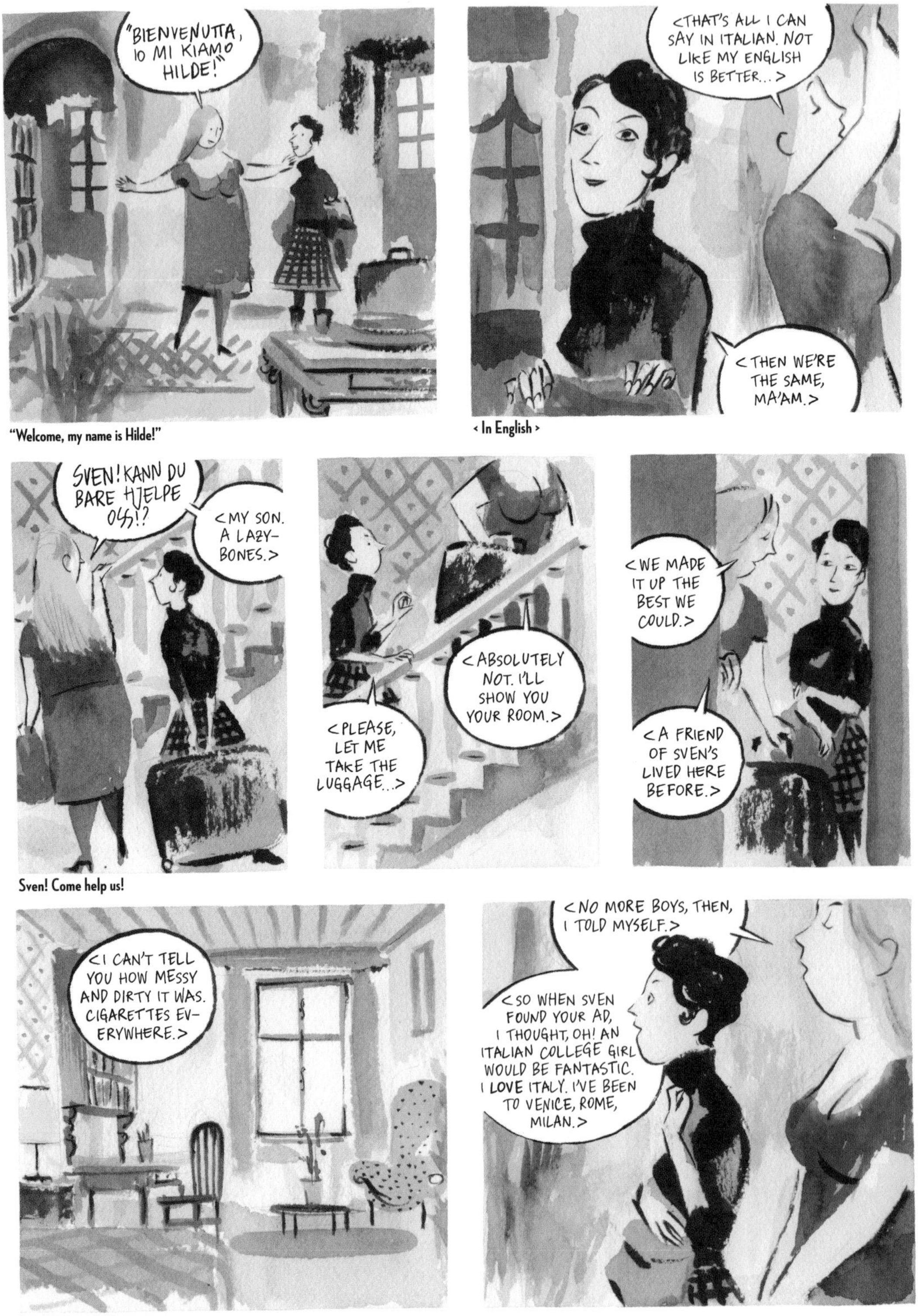
"BIENVENUTTA, IO MI KIAMO HILDE!"
<THAT'S ALL I CAN SAY IN ITALIAN. NOT LIKE MY ENGLISH IS BETTER...>
<THEN WE'RE THE SAME, MA'AM.>
SVEN! KANN DU BARE HJELPE OSS!?
<MY SON. A LAZY-BONES.>
<PLEASE, LET ME TAKE THE LUGGAGE...>
<ABSOLUTELY NOT. I'LL SHOW YOU YOUR ROOM.>
<WE MADE IT UP THE BEST WE COULD.>
<A FRIEND OF SVEN'S LIVED HERE BEFORE.>
<I CAN'T TELL YOU HOW MESSY AND DIRTY IT WAS. CIGARETTES EV-ERYWHERE.>
<NO MORE BOYS, THEN, I TOLD MYSELF.>
<SO WHEN SVEN FOUND YOUR AD, I THOUGHT, OH! AN ITALIAN COLLEGE GIRL WOULD BE FANTASTIC. I **LOVE** ITALY. I'VE BEEN TO VENICE, ROME, MILAN.>

"Welcome, my name is Hilde!"

< In English >

Sven! Come help us!

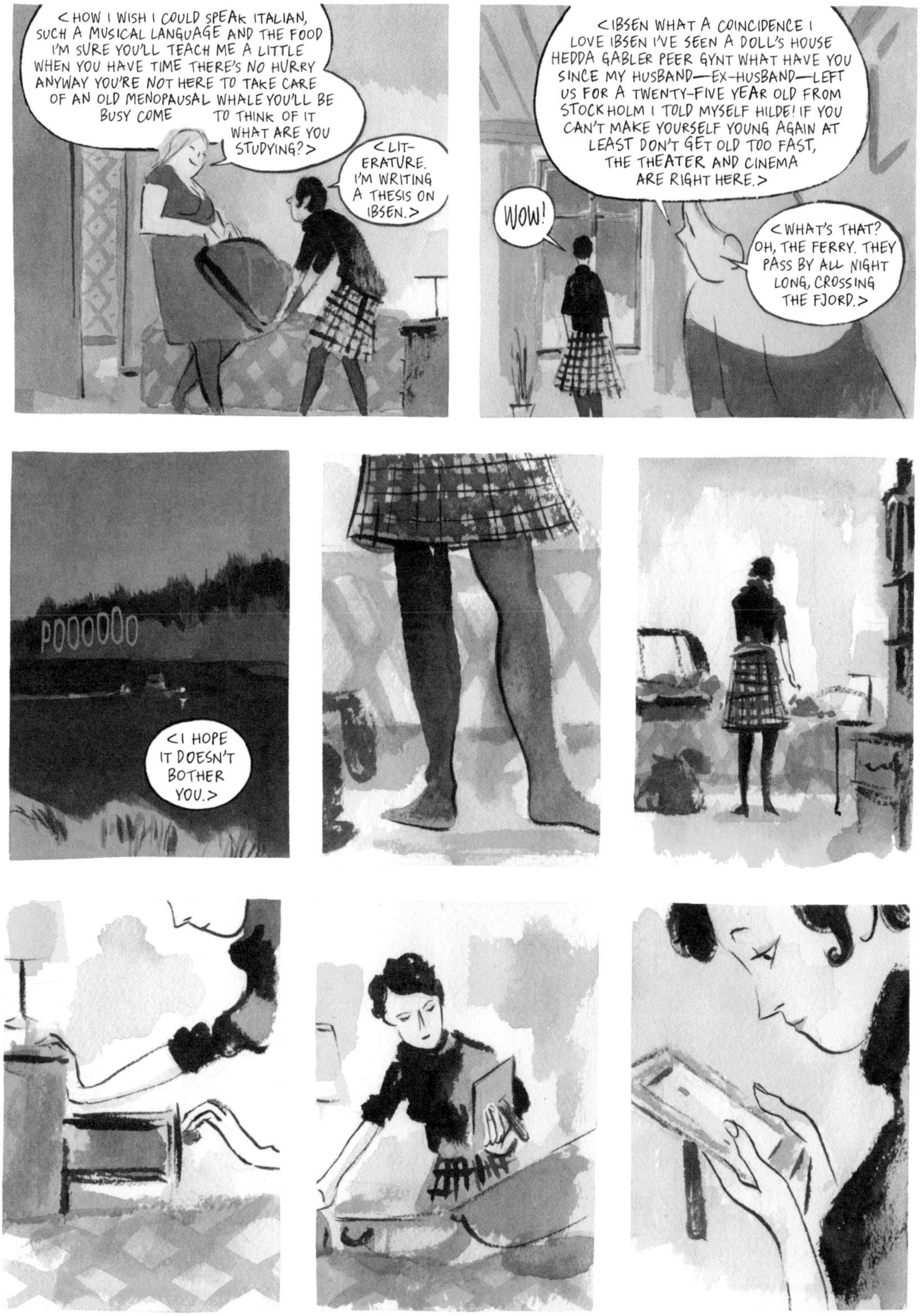
<HOW I WISH I COULD SPEAK ITALIAN, SUCH A MUSICAL LANGUAGE AND THE FOOD I'M SURE YOU'LL TEACH ME A LITTLE WHEN YOU HAVE TIME THERE'S NO HURRY ANYWAY YOU'RE NOT HERE TO TAKE CARE OF AN OLD MENOPAUSAL WHALE YOU'LL BE BUSY COME TO THINK OF IT WHAT ARE YOU STUDYING?>
<LIT-ERATURE. I'M WRITING A THESIS ON IBSEN.>
<IBSEN WHAT A COINCIDENCE I LOVE IBSEN I'VE SEEN A DOLL'S HOUSE HEDDA GABLER PEER GYNT WHAT HAVE YOU SINCE MY HUSBAND—EX-HUSBAND—LEFT US FOR A TWENTY-FIVE YEAR OLD FROM STOCKHOLM I TOLD MYSELF HILDE! IF YOU CAN'T MAKE YOURSELF YOUNG AGAIN AT LEAST DON'T GET OLD TOO FAST, THE THEATER AND CINEMA ARE RIGHT HERE.>
WOW!
<WHAT'S THAT? OH, THE FERRY. THEY PASS BY ALL NIGHT LONG, CROSSING THE FJORD.>
POOOOOO
<I HOPE IT DOESN'T BOTHER YOU.>

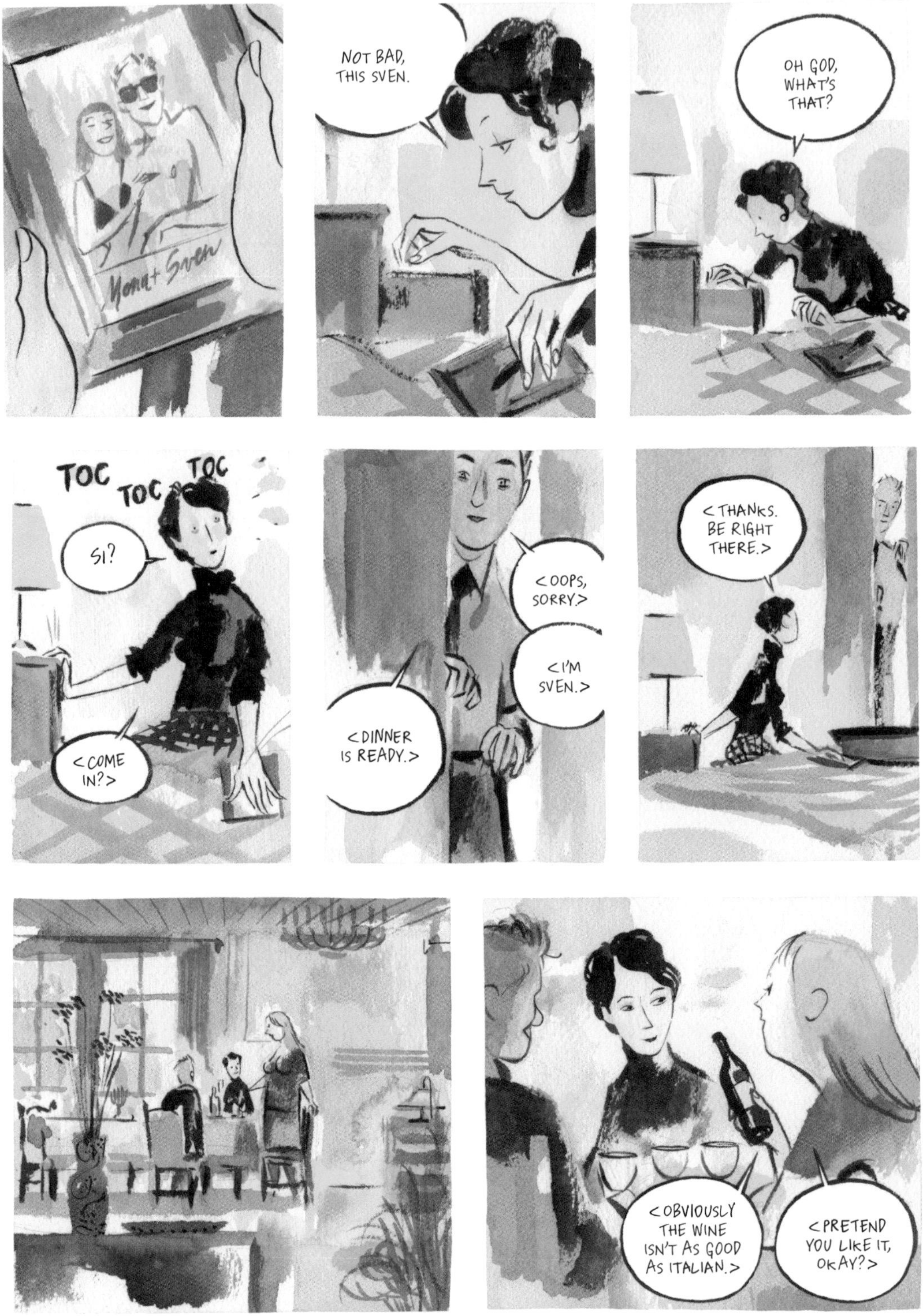
NOT BAD, THIS SVEN.
OH GOD, WHAT'S THAT?
TOC TOC TOC
SI?
<COME IN?>
<OOPS, SORRY.>
<I'M SVEN.>
<DINNER IS READY.>
<THANKS. BE RIGHT THERE.>
<OBVIOUSLY THE WINE ISN'T AS GOOD AS ITALIAN.>
<PRETEND YOU LIKE IT, OKAY?>

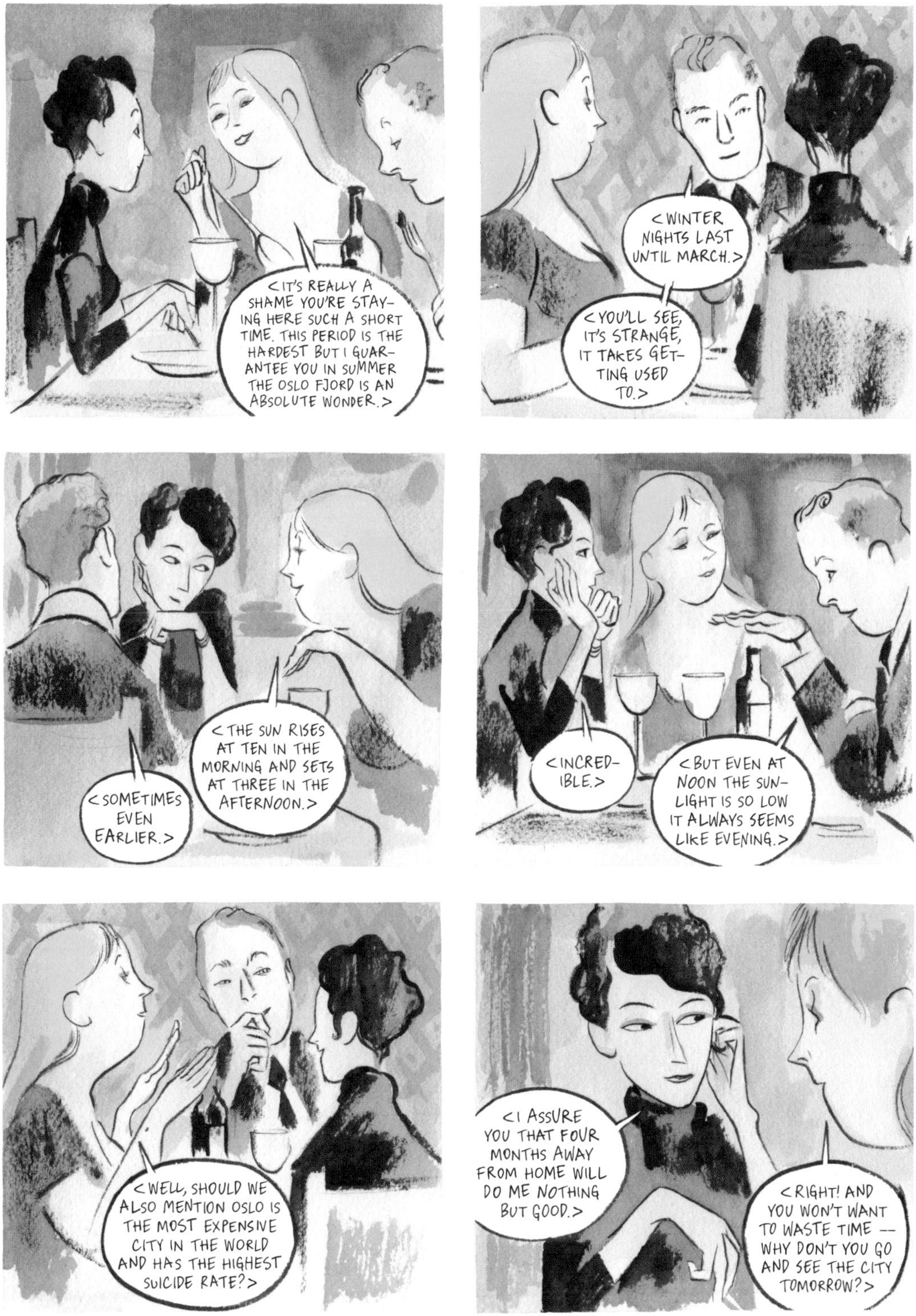
<IT'S REALLY A SHAME YOU'RE STAYING HERE SUCH A SHORT TIME. THIS PERIOD IS THE HARDEST BUT I GUARANTEE YOU IN SUMMER THE OSLO FJORD IS AN ABSOLUTE WONDER.>
<WINTER NIGHTS LAST UNTIL MARCH.>
<YOU'LL SEE, IT'S STRANGE, IT TAKES GETTING USED TO.>
<THE SUN RISES AT TEN IN THE MORNING AND SETS AT THREE IN THE AFTERNOON.>
<SOMETIMES EVEN EARLIER.>
<INCREDIBLE.>
<BUT EVEN AT NOON THE SUNLIGHT IS SO LOW IT ALWAYS SEEMS LIKE EVENING.>
<WELL, SHOULD WE ALSO MENTION OSLO IS THE MOST EXPENSIVE CITY IN THE WORLD AND HAS THE HIGHEST SUICIDE RATE?>
<I ASSURE YOU THAT FOUR MONTHS AWAY FROM HOME WILL DO ME NOTHING BUT GOOD.>
<RIGHT! AND YOU WON'T WANT TO WASTE TIME -- WHY DON'T YOU GO AND SEE THE CITY TOMORROW?>

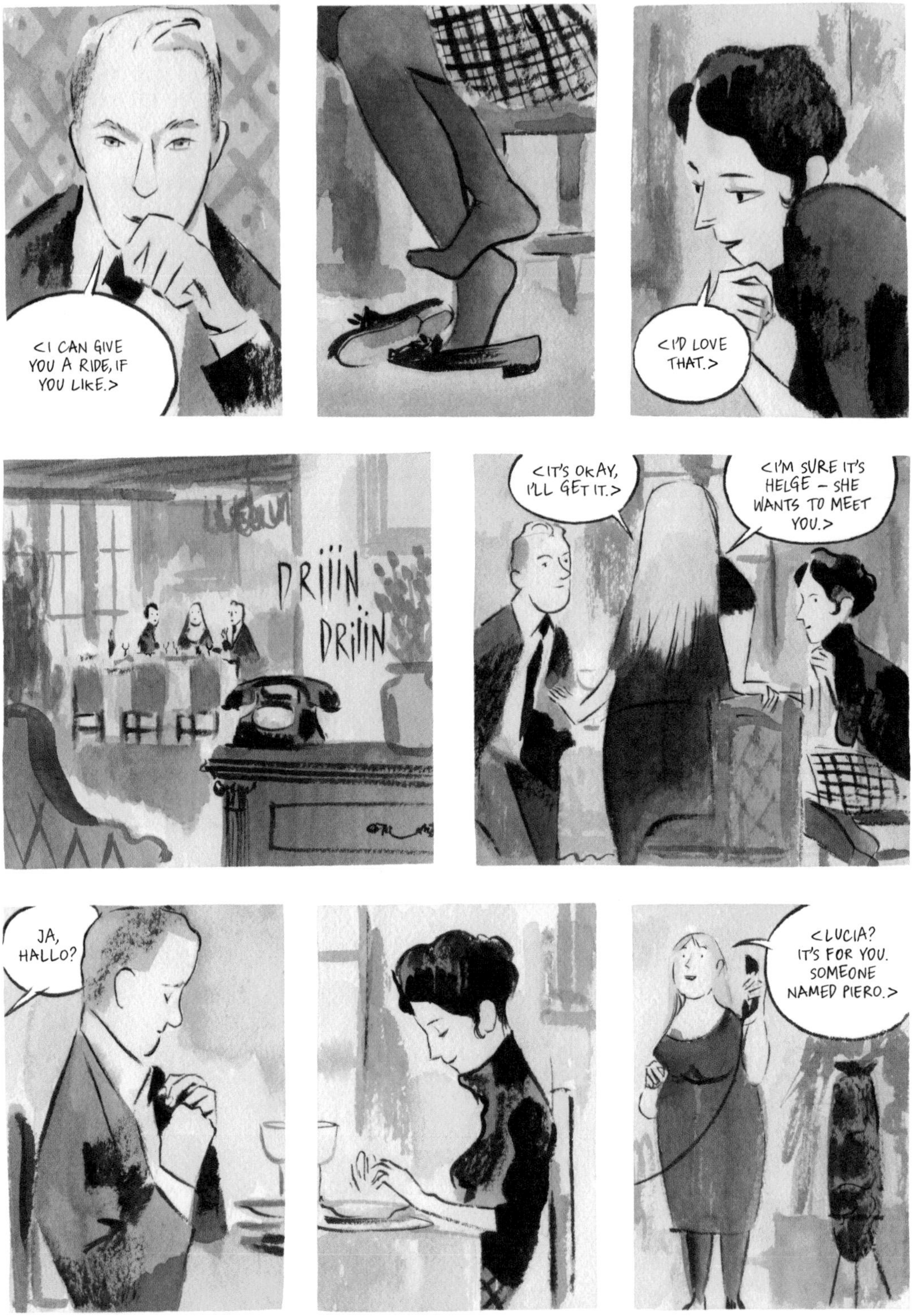

<I CAN GIVE YOU A RIDE, IF YOU LIKE.>
<I'D LOVE THAT.>
DRIIIN DRIIIN
<IT'S OKAY, I'LL GET IT.>
<I'M SURE IT'S HELGE – SHE WANTS TO MEET YOU.>
JA, HALLO?
<LUCIA? IT'S FOR YOU. SOMEONE NAMED PIERO.>

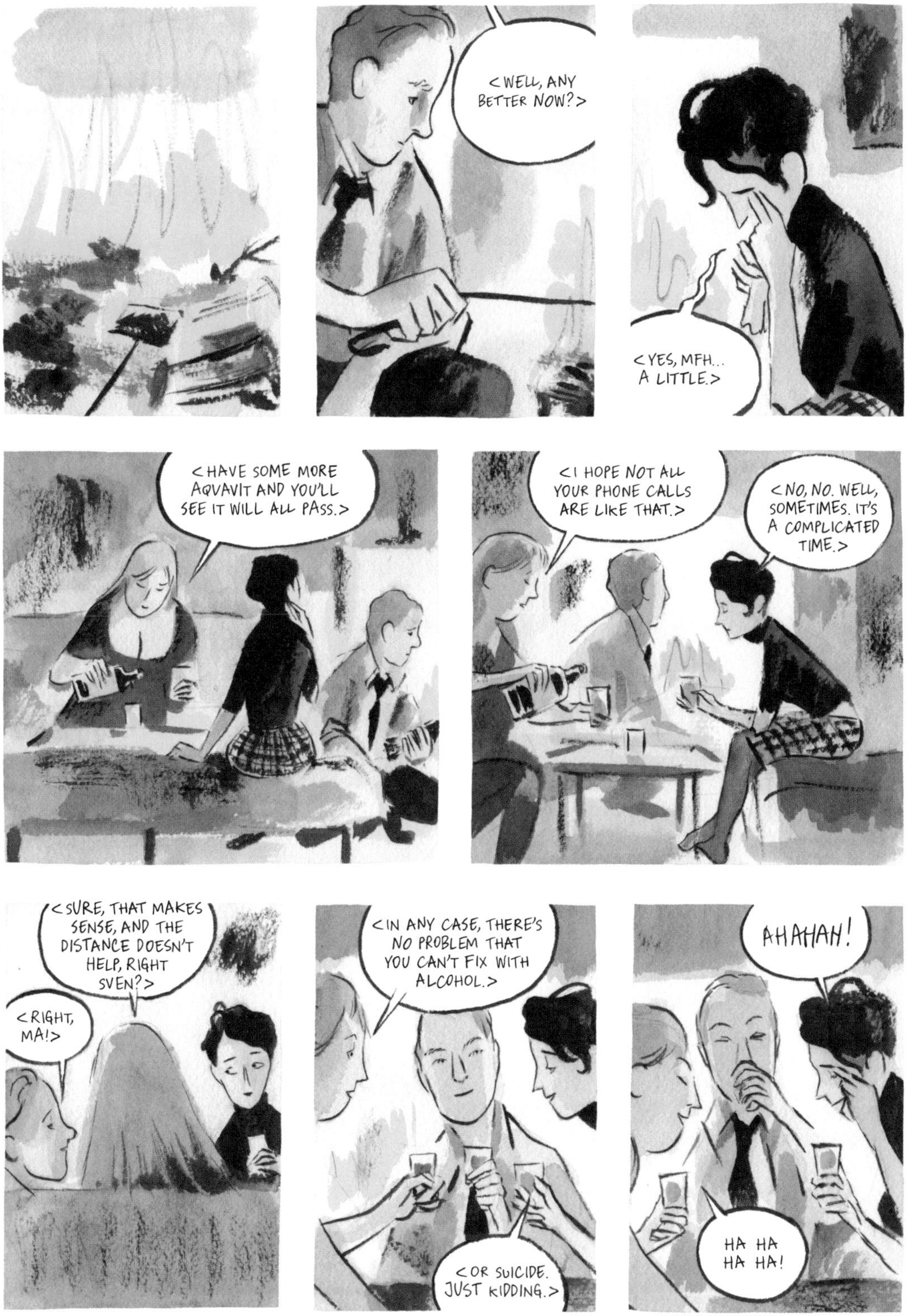
<WELL, ANY BETTER NOW?>
<YES, MFH... A LITTLE.>
<HAVE SOME MORE AQUAVIT AND YOU'LL SEE IT WILL ALL PASS.>
<I HOPE NOT ALL YOUR PHONE CALLS ARE LIKE THAT.>
<NO, NO. WELL, SOMETIMES. IT'S A COMPLICATED TIME.>
<SURE, THAT MAKES SENSE, AND THE DISTANCE DOESN'T HELP, RIGHT SVEN?>
<RIGHT, MA!>
<IN ANY CASE, THERE'S NO PROBLEM THAT YOU CAN'T FIX WITH ALCOHOL.>
<OR SUICIDE. JUST KIDDING.>
AHAHAH!
HA HA HA HA!

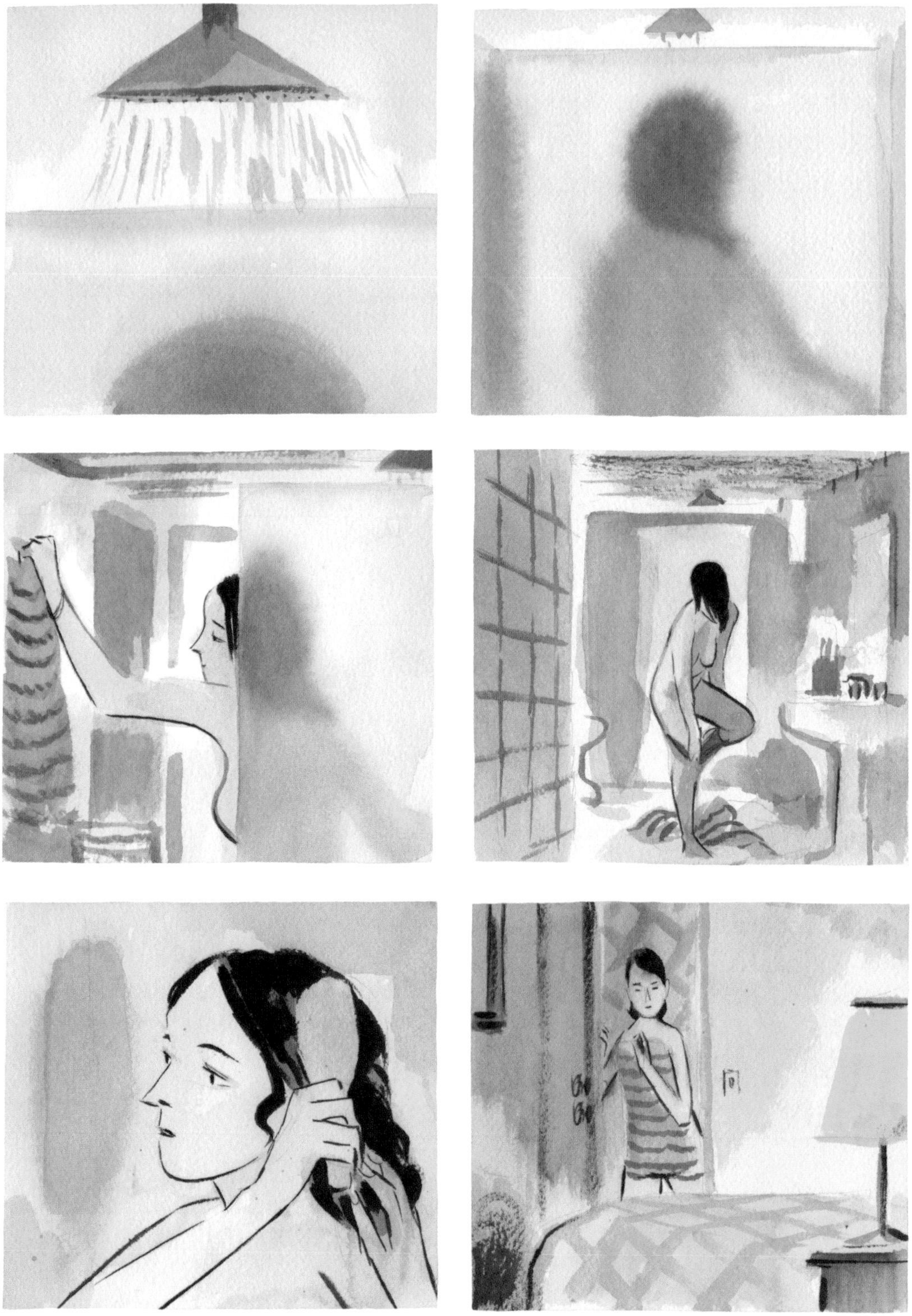

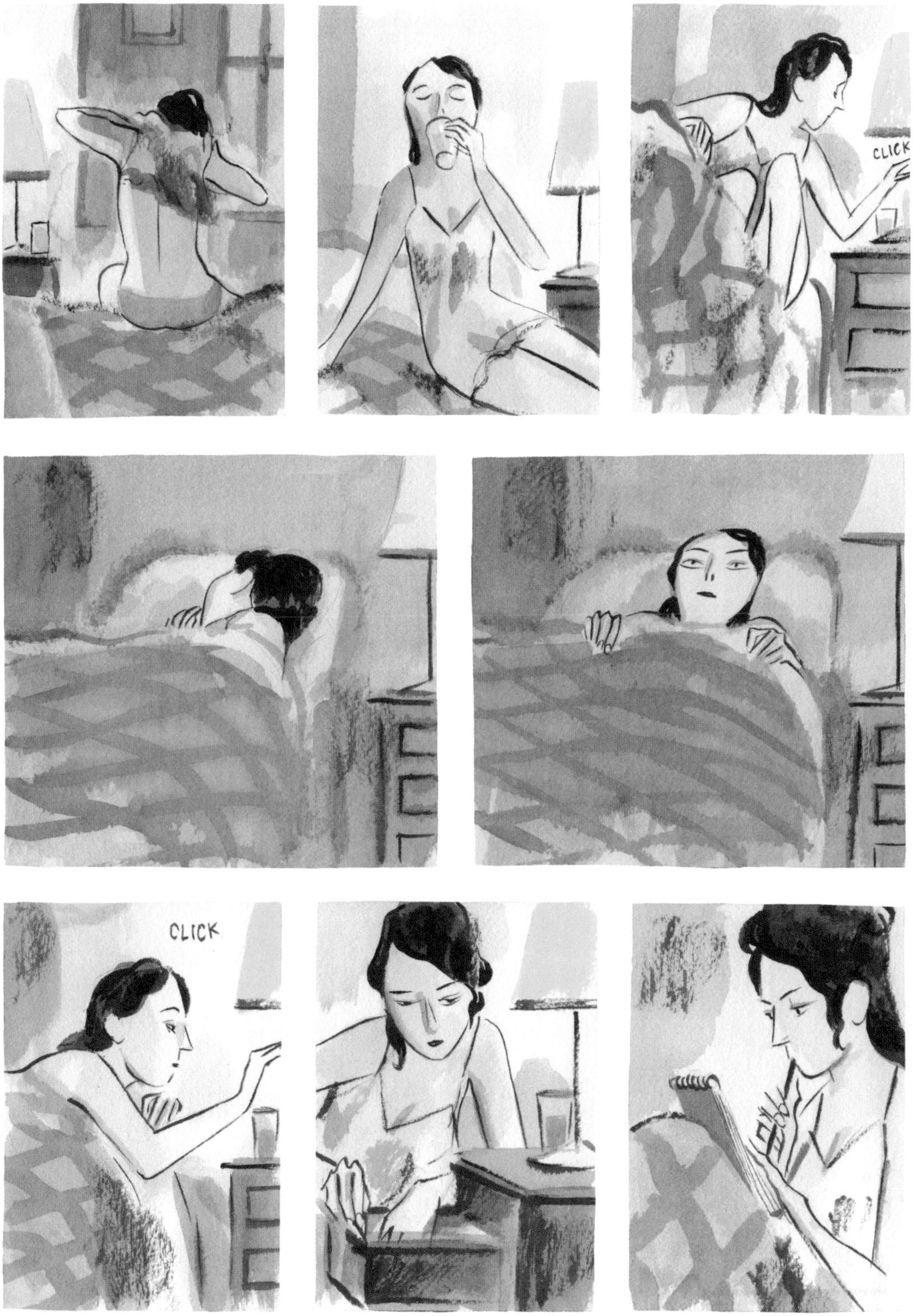
CLICK
CLICK

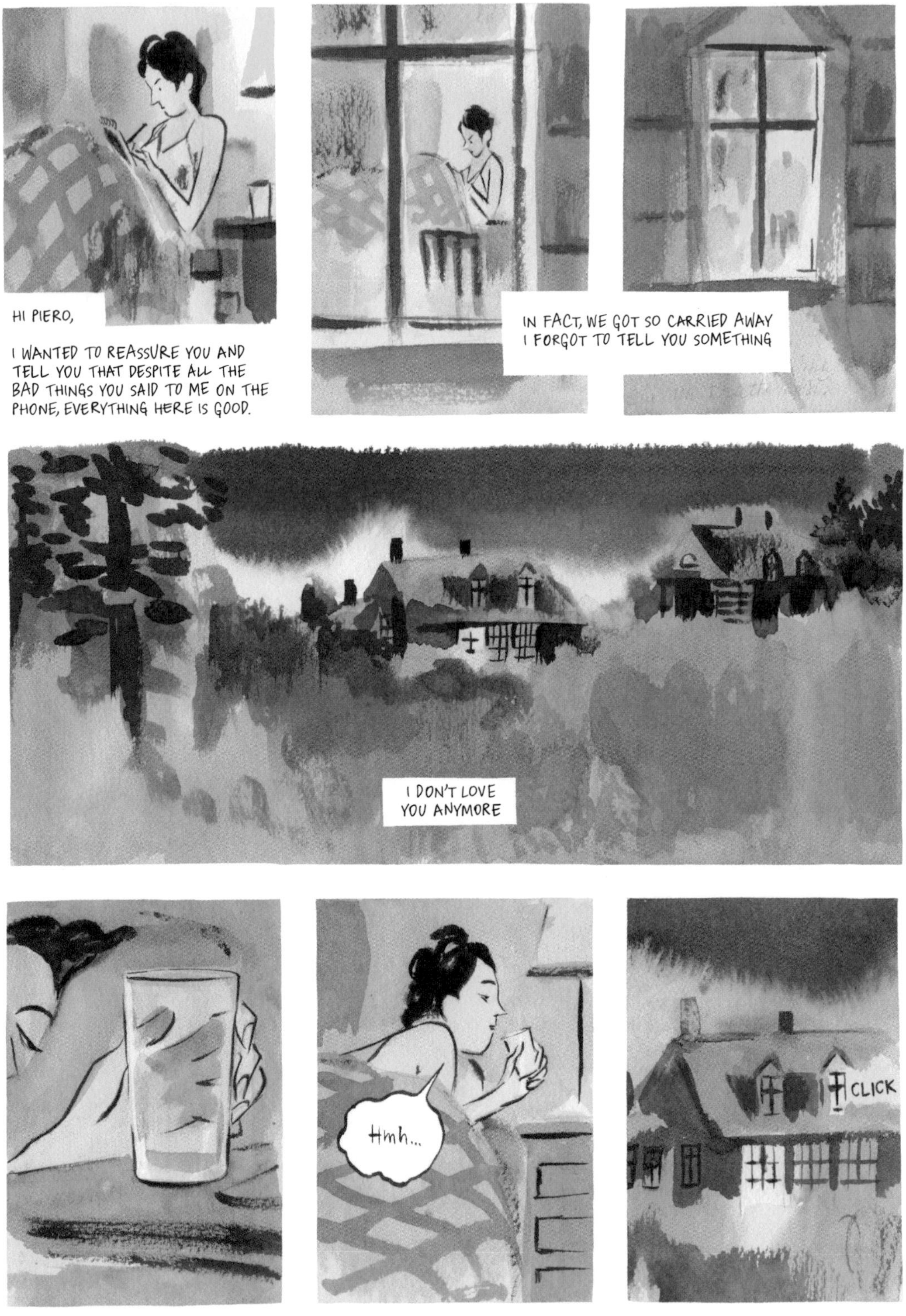
HI PIERO,
I WANTED TO REASSURE YOU AND TELL YOU THAT DESPITE ALL THE BAD THINGS YOU SAID TO ME ON THE PHONE, EVERYTHING HERE IS GOOD.
IN FACT, WE GOT SO CARRIED AWAY I FORGOT TO TELL YOU SOMETHING
I DON'T LOVE YOU ANYMORE
Hmh...
CLICK

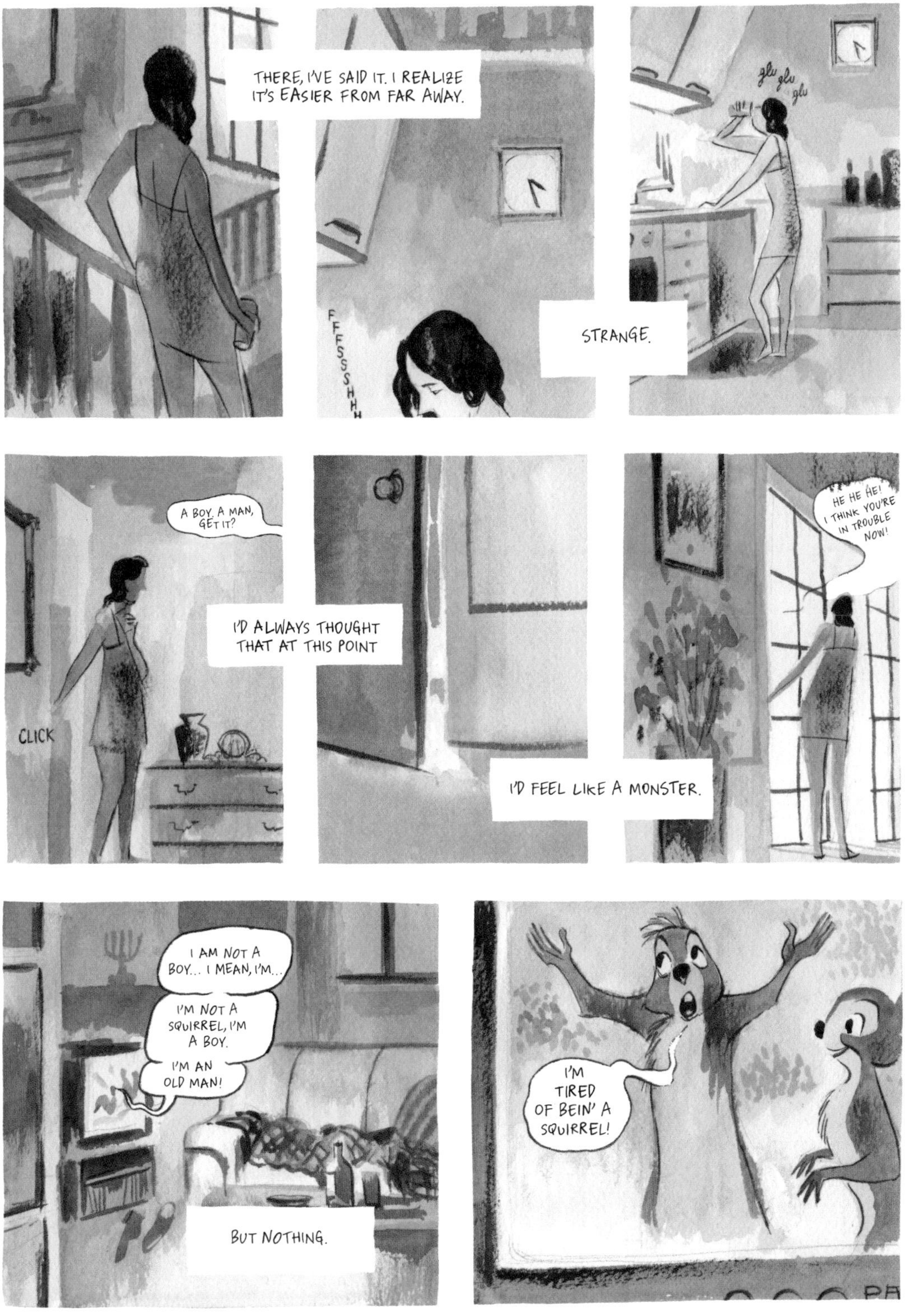
THERE, I'VE SAID IT. I REALIZE IT'S EASIER FROM FAR AWAY.
FFFSSSHHH
glu glu glu
STRANGE.
A BOY. A MAN, GET IT?
CLICK
I'D ALWAYS THOUGHT THAT AT THIS POINT
I'D FEEL LIKE A MONSTER.
HE HE HE! I THINK YOU'RE IN TROUBLE NOW!
I AM NOT A BOY... I MEAN, I'M...
I'M NOT A SQUIRREL, I'M A BOY.
I'M AN OLD MAN!
BUT NOTHING.
I'M TIRED OF BEIN' A SQUIRREL!
PA

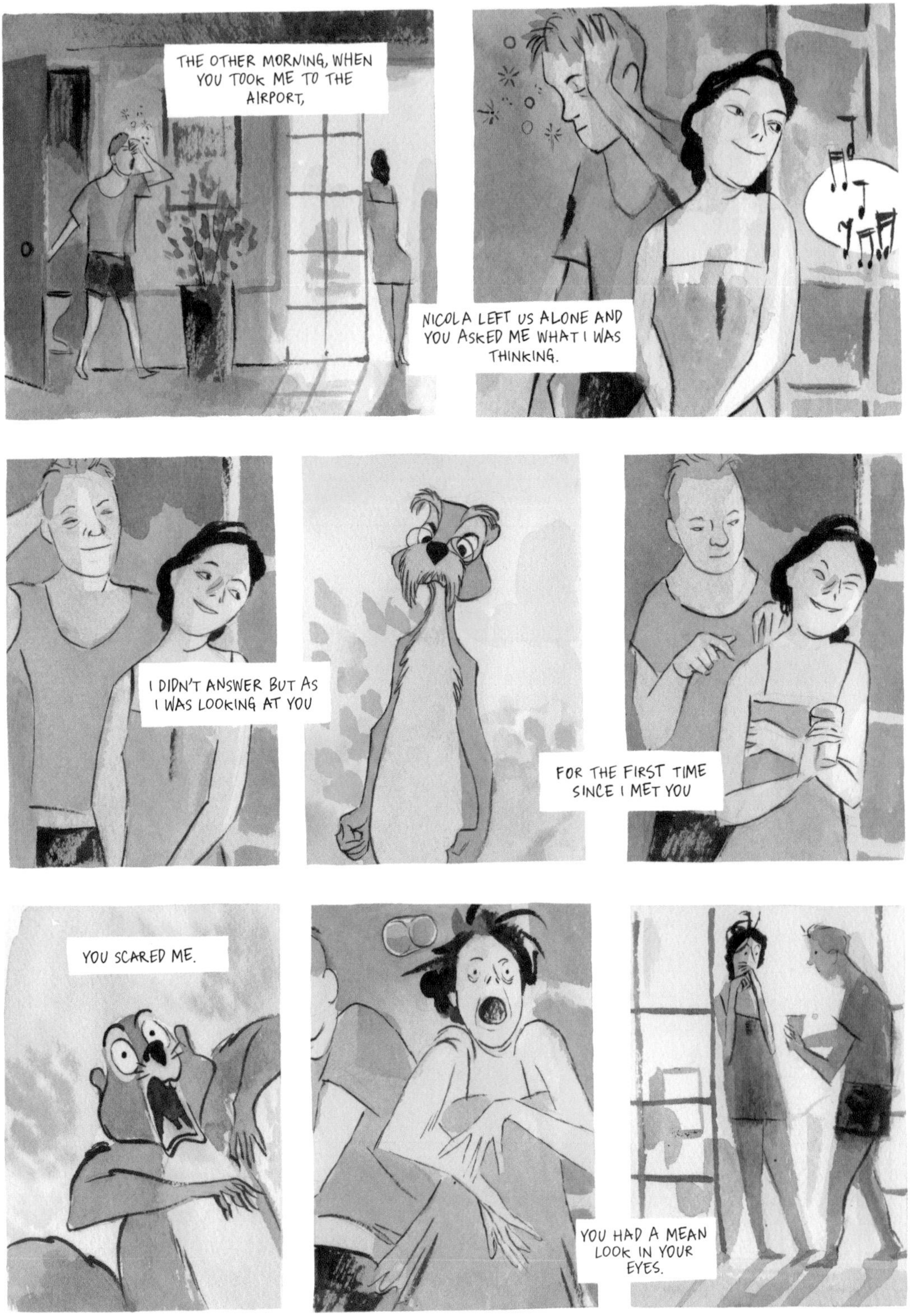
THE OTHER MORNING, WHEN YOU TOOK ME TO THE AIRPORT,
NICOLA LEFT US ALONE AND YOU ASKED ME WHAT I WAS THINKING.
I DIDN'T ANSWER BUT AS I WAS LOOKING AT YOU
FOR THE FIRST TIME SINCE I MET YOU
YOU SCARED ME.
YOU HAD A MEAN LOOK IN YOUR EYES.

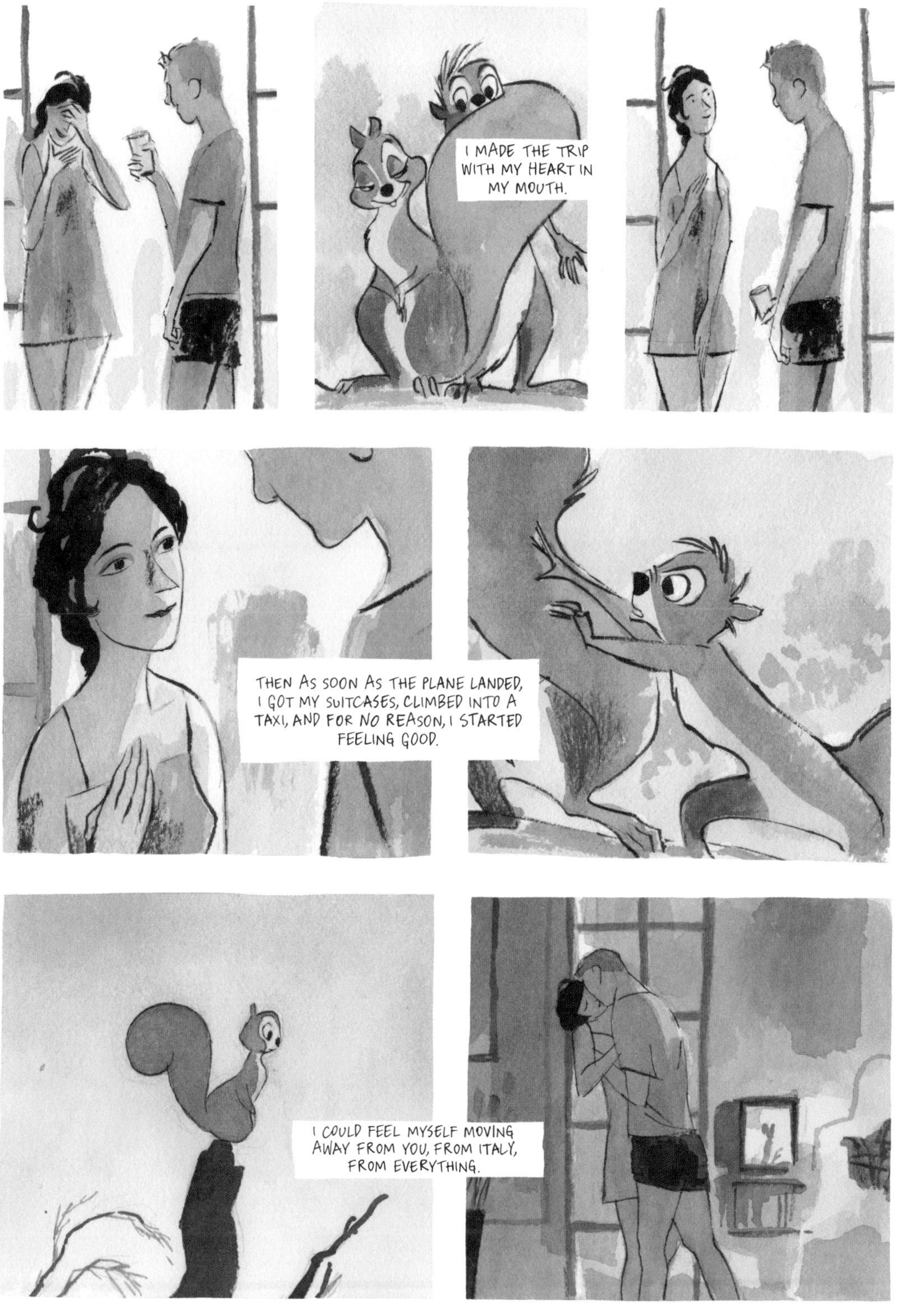
I MADE THE TRIP WITH MY HEART IN MY MOUTH.
THEN AS SOON AS THE PLANE LANDED, I GOT MY SUITCASES, CLIMBED INTO A TAXI, AND FOR NO REASON, I STARTED FEELING GOOD.
I COULD FEEL MYSELF MOVING AWAY FROM YOU, FROM ITALY, FROM EVERYTHING.

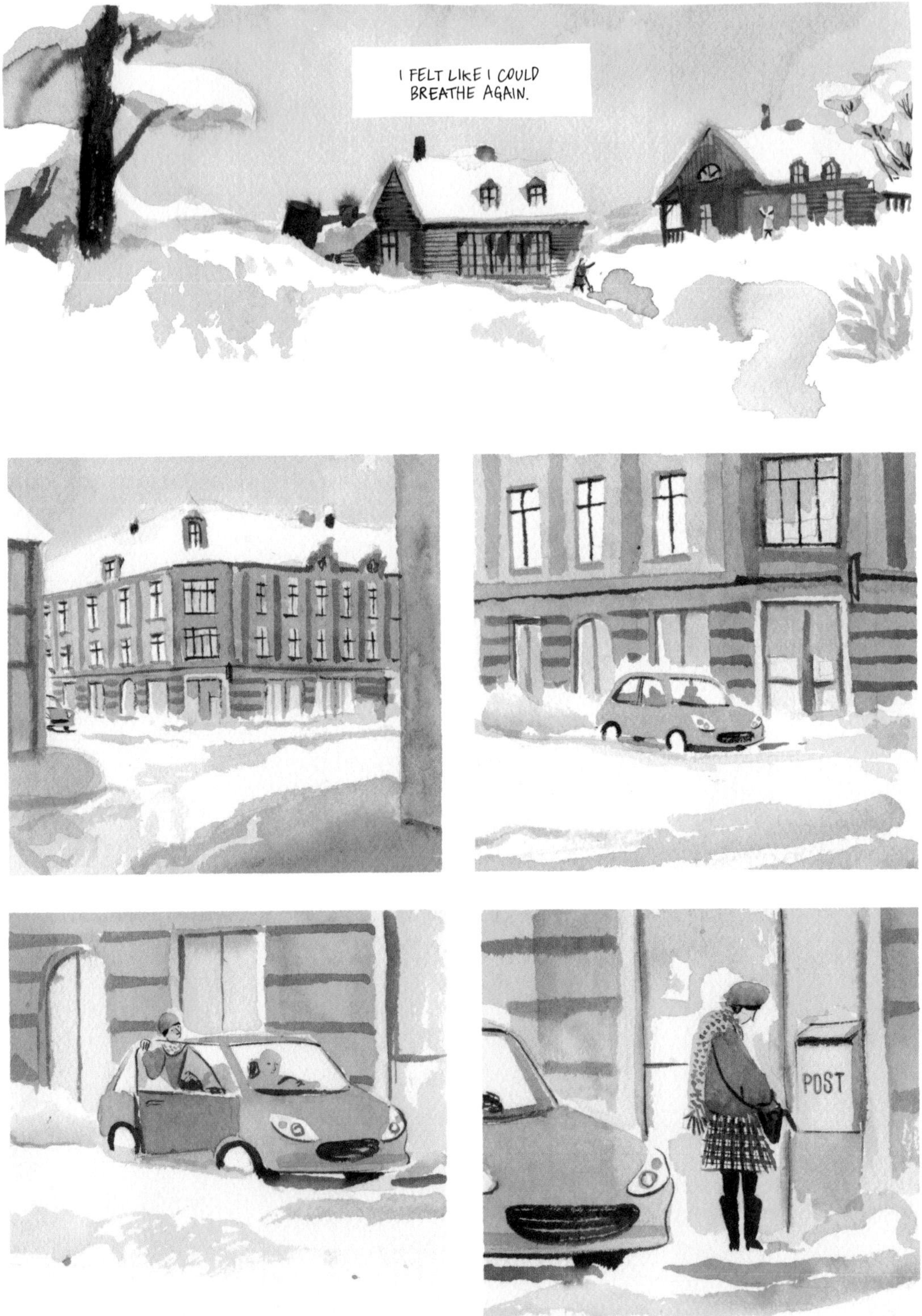
I FELT LIKE I COULD BREATHE AGAIN.
POST

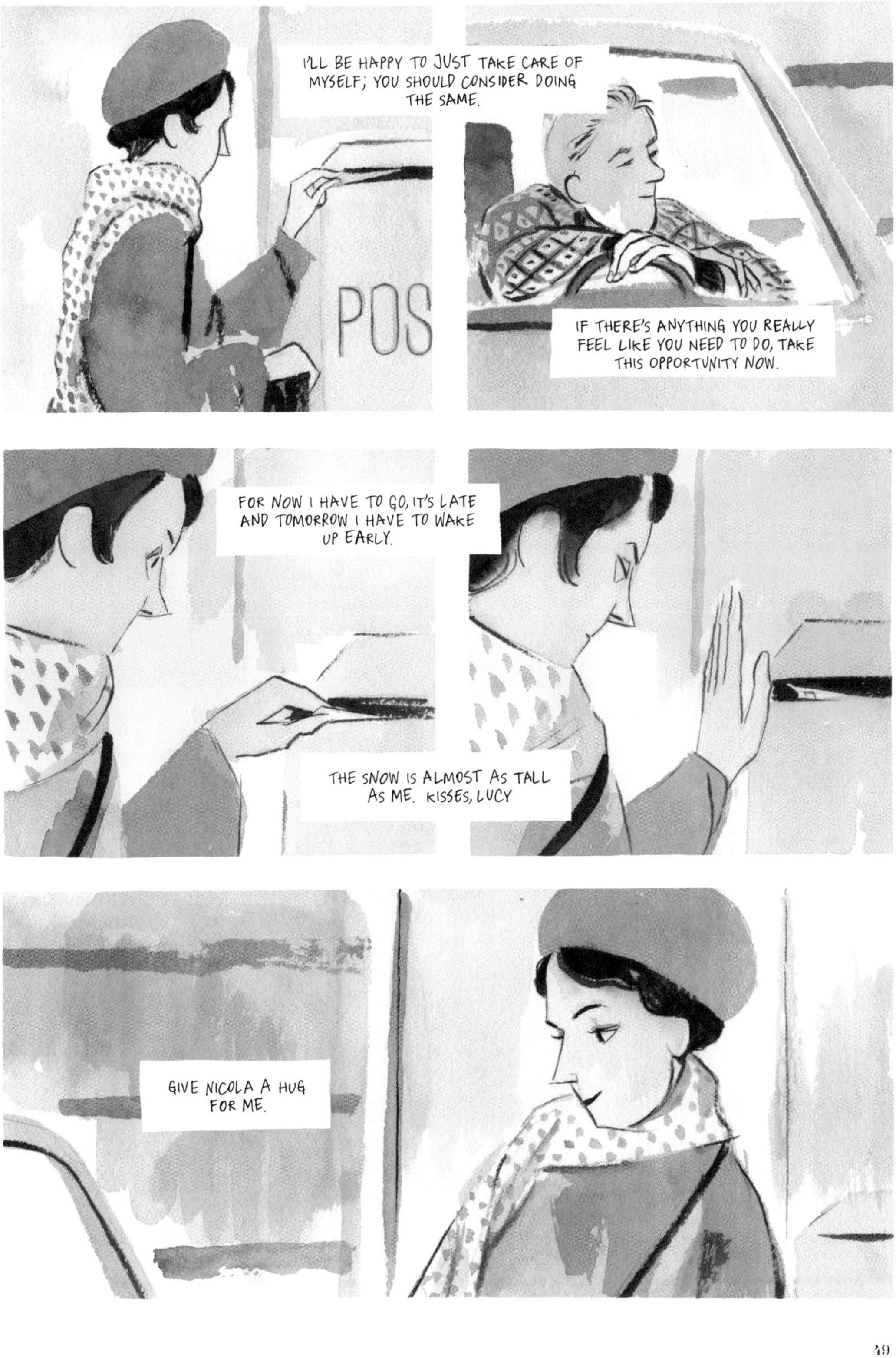
I'LL BE HAPPY TO JUST TAKE CARE OF MYSELF; YOU SHOULD CONSIDER DOING THE SAME.
POS
IF THERE'S ANYTHING YOU REALLY FEEL LIKE YOU NEED TO DO, TAKE THIS OPPORTUNITY NOW.
FOR NOW I HAVE TO GO, IT'S LATE AND TOMORROW I HAVE TO WAKE UP EARLY.
THE SNOW IS ALMOST AS TALL AS ME. KISSES, LUCY
GIVE NICOLA A HUG FOR ME.

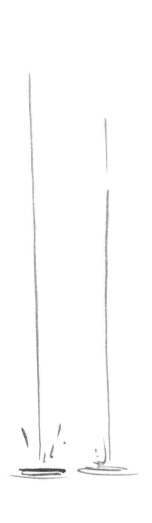

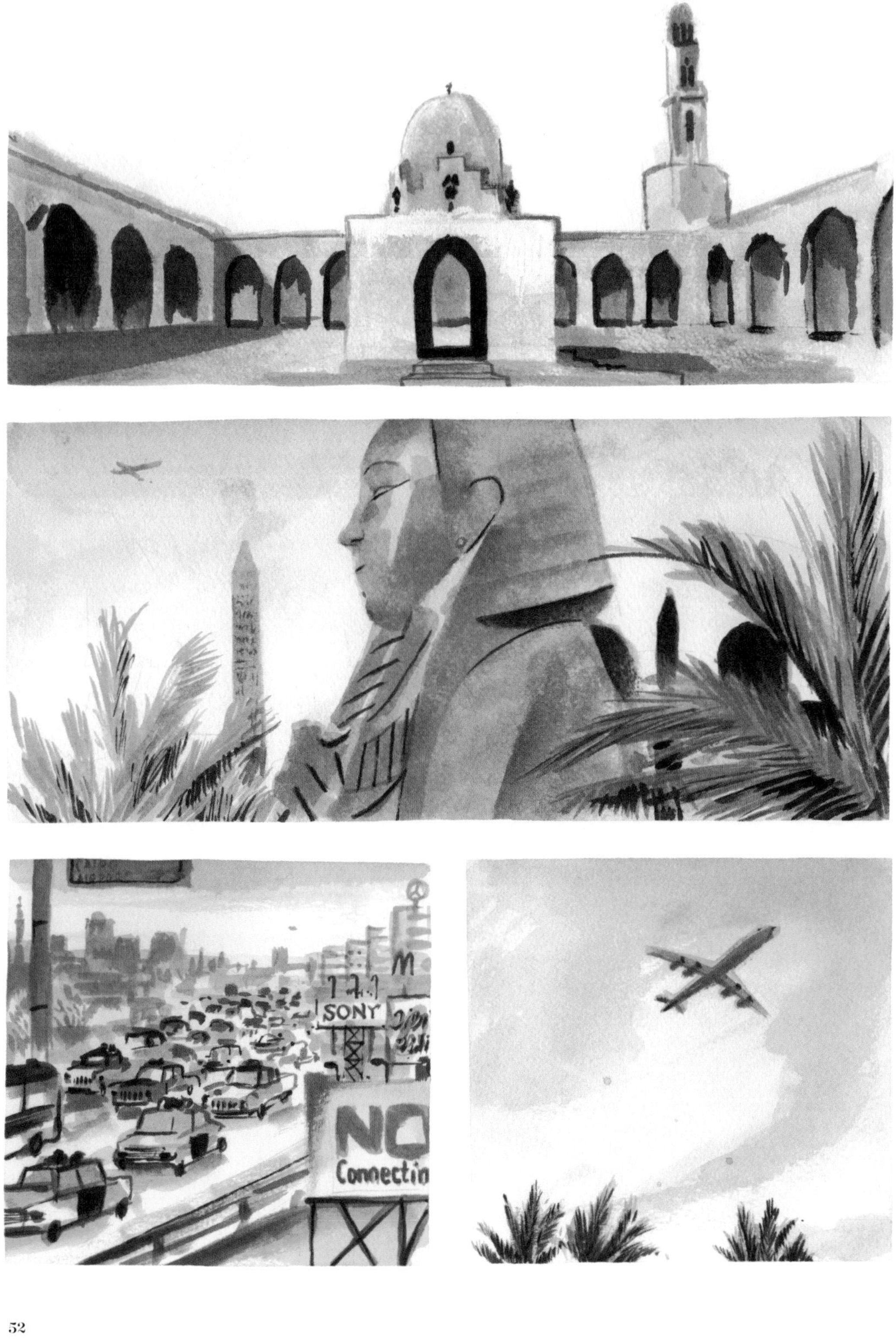
SONY
NO
Connectin

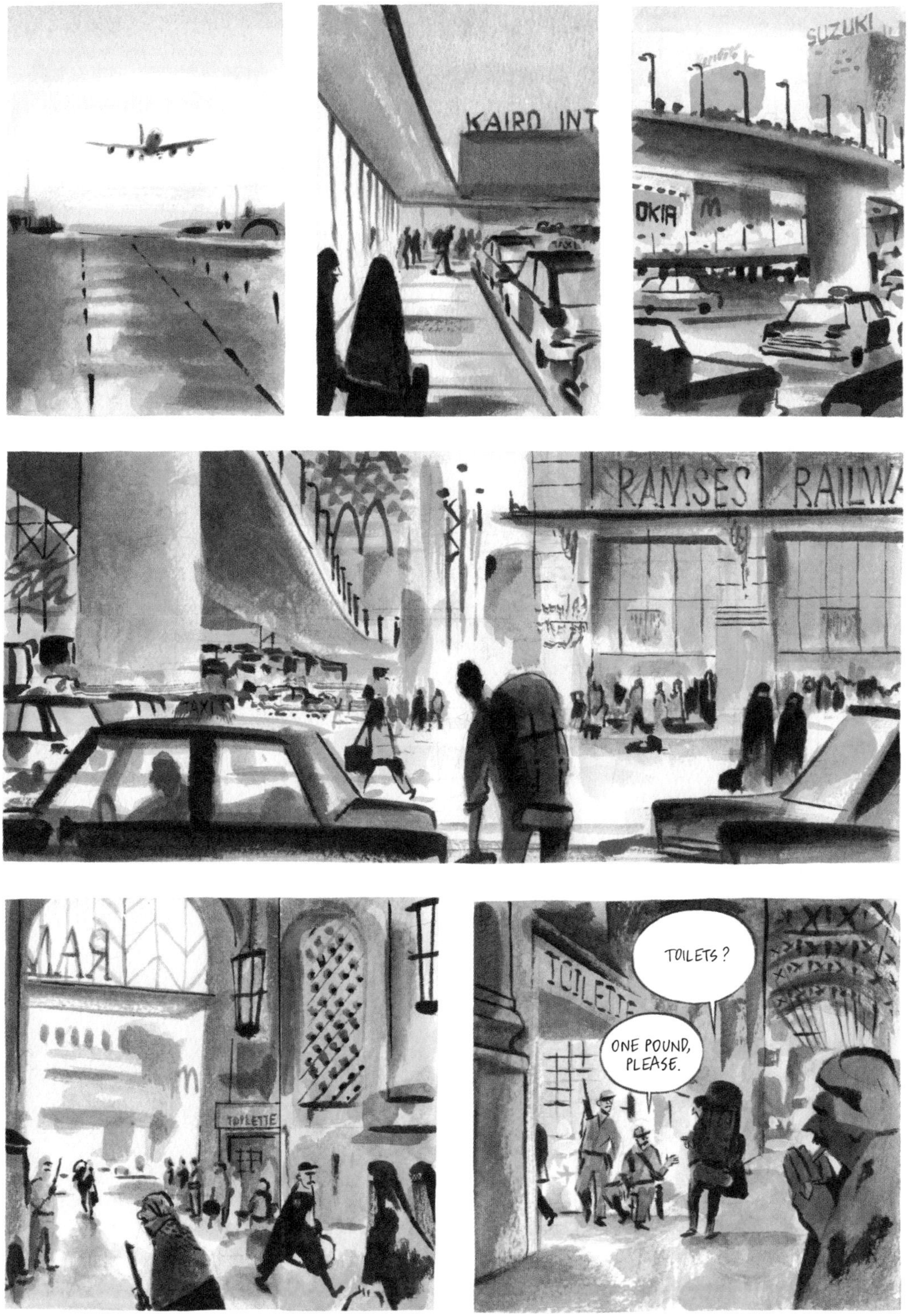
KAIRO INT
SUZUKI
RAMSES RAILWA
TAXI
TOILETTE
TOILETTE
TOILETS ?
ONE POUND, PLEASE.

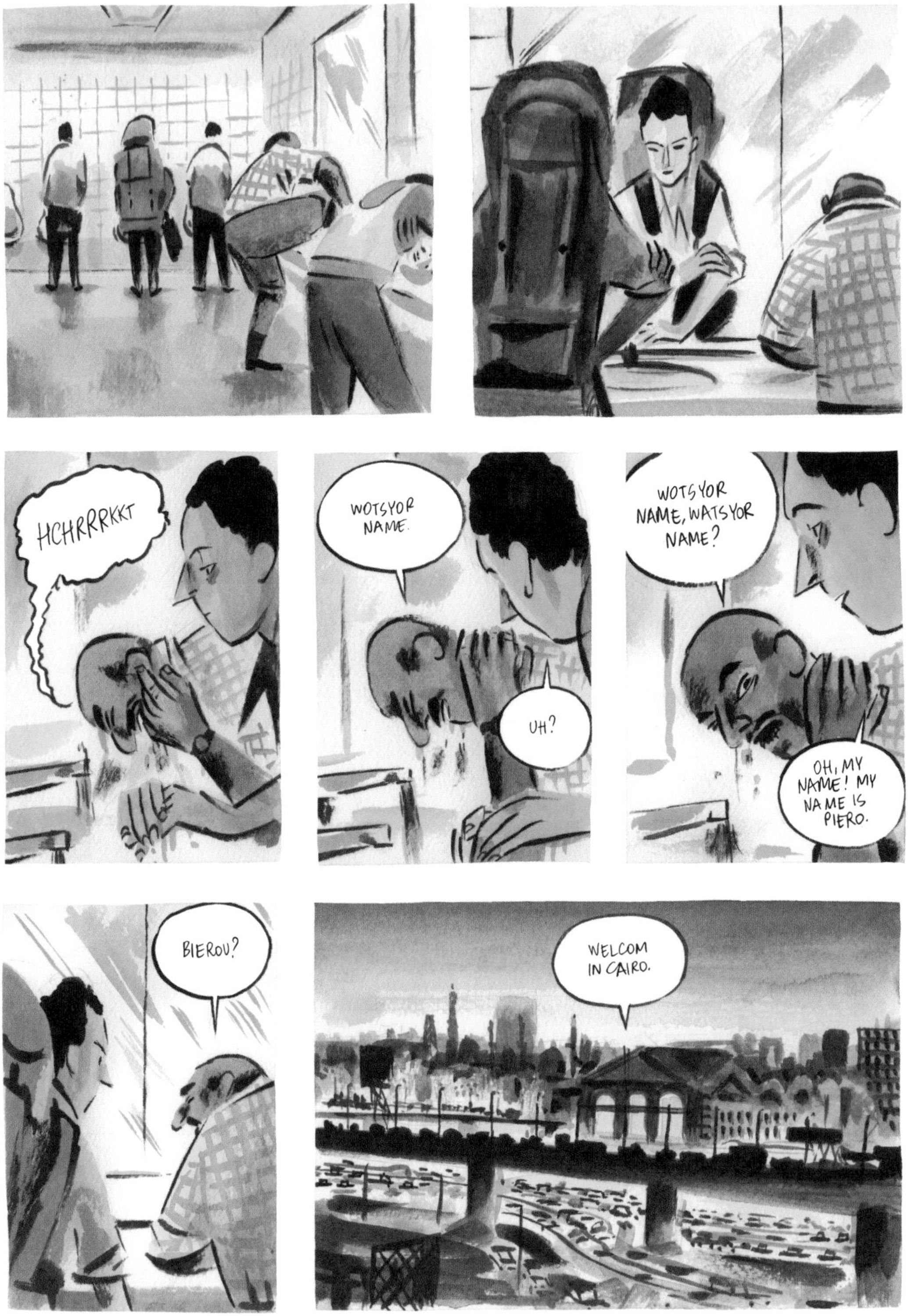
HCHRRRKKT
WOTSYOR NAME.
UH?
WOTSYOR NAME, WATSYOR NAME?
OH, MY NAME! MY NAME IS PIERO.
BIEROU?
WELCOM IN CAIRO.

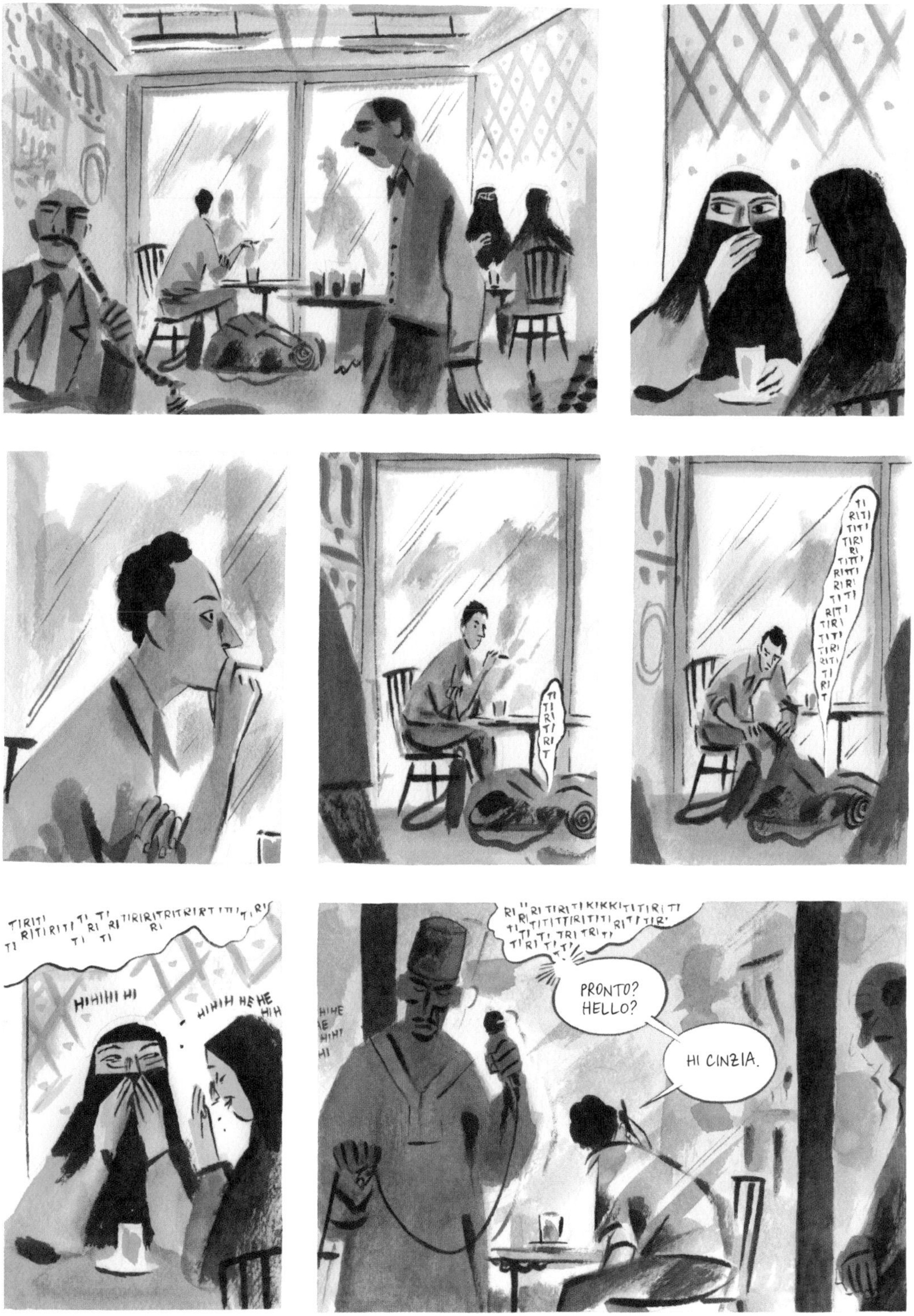
HIHIHI HI
HIHIH HE HE HIH
PRONTO? HELLO?
HI CINZIA.

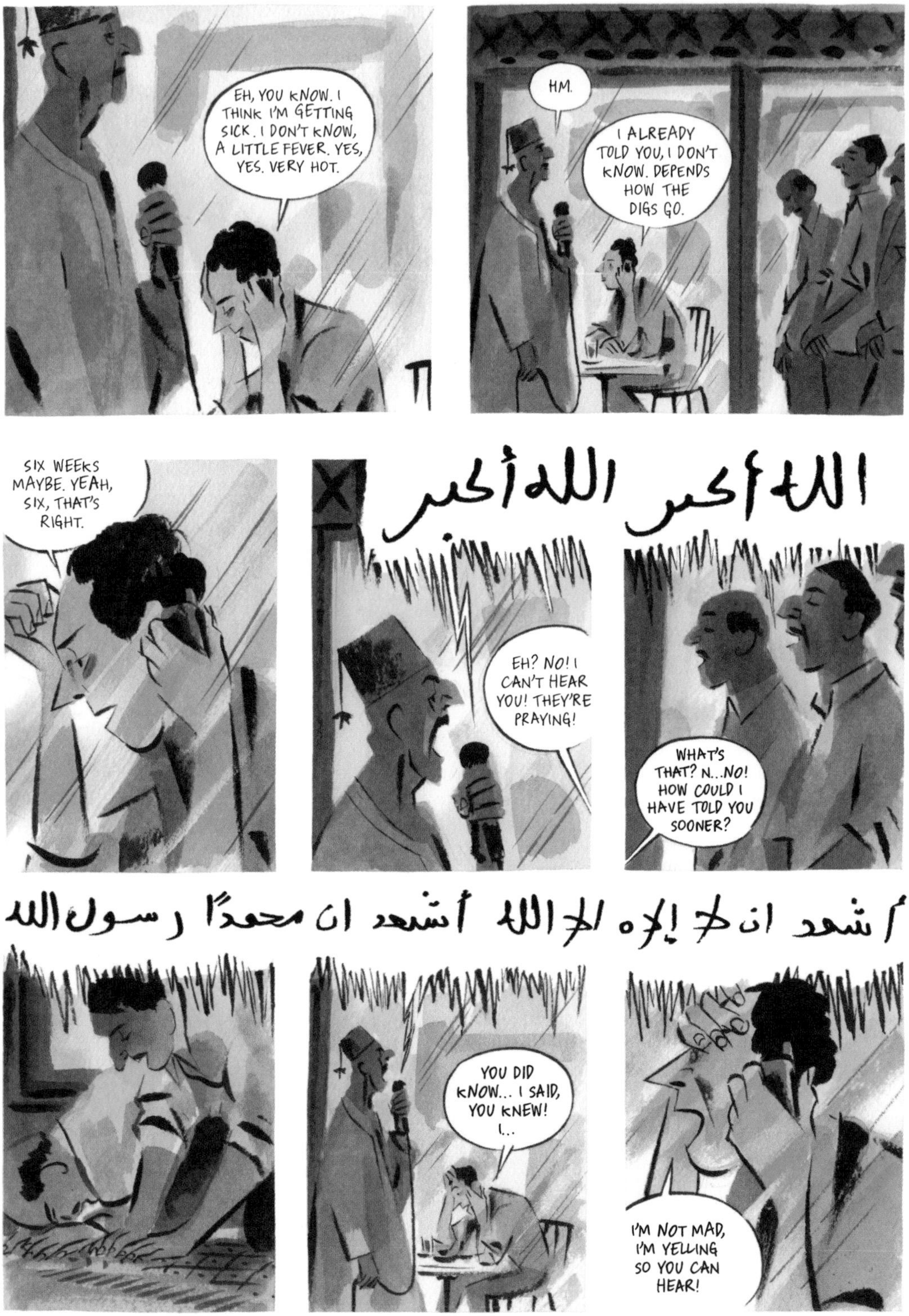
EH, YOU KNOW. I THINK I'M GETTING SICK. I DON'T KNOW, A LITTLE FEVER. YES, YES. VERY HOT.
HM.
I ALREADY TOLD YOU, I DON'T KNOW. DEPENDS HOW THE DIGS GO.
SIX WEEKS MAYBE. YEAH, SIX, THAT'S RIGHT.
الله أكبر الله أكبر
EH? NO! I CAN'T HEAR YOU! THEY'RE PRAYING!
WHAT'S THAT? N...NO! HOW COULD I HAVE TOLD YOU SOONER?
أشهد ان لا إله إلا الله أشهد ان محمداً رسول الله
YOU DID KNOW... I SAID, YOU KNEW! I...
I'M NOT MAD, I'M YELLING SO YOU CAN HEAR!

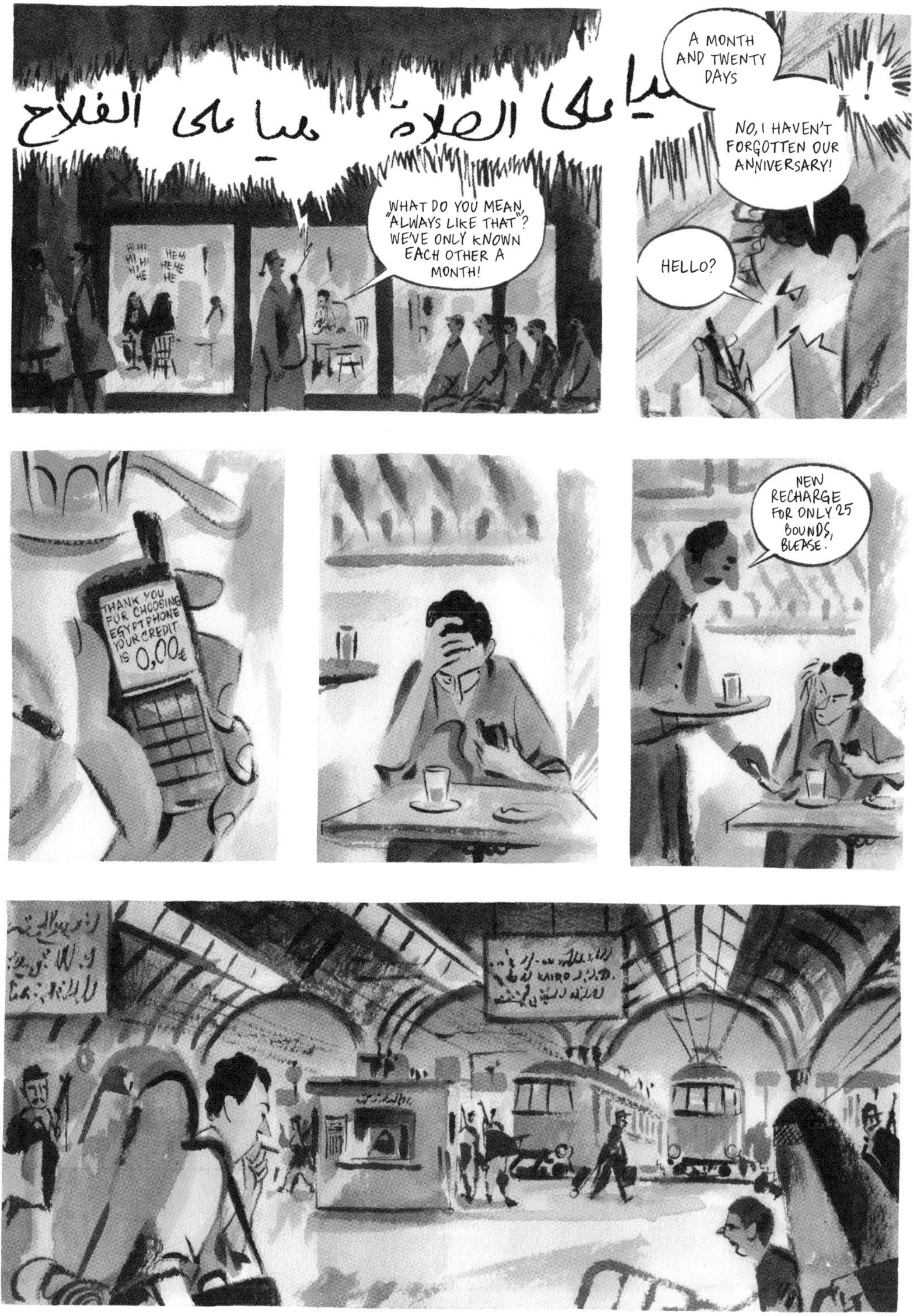

حيا على الصلاة حيا على الفلاح
WHAT DO YOU MEAN, "ALWAYS LIKE THAT"? WE'VE ONLY KNOWN EACH OTHER A MONTH!
A MONTH AND TWENTY DAYS
!
NO, I HAVEN'T FORGOTTEN OUR ANNIVERSARY!
HELLO?
THANK YOU FOR CHOOSING EGYPT PHONE YOUR CREDIT IS 0,00€
NEW RECHARGE FOR ONLY 25 BOUNDS, BLEASE.
KAIRO

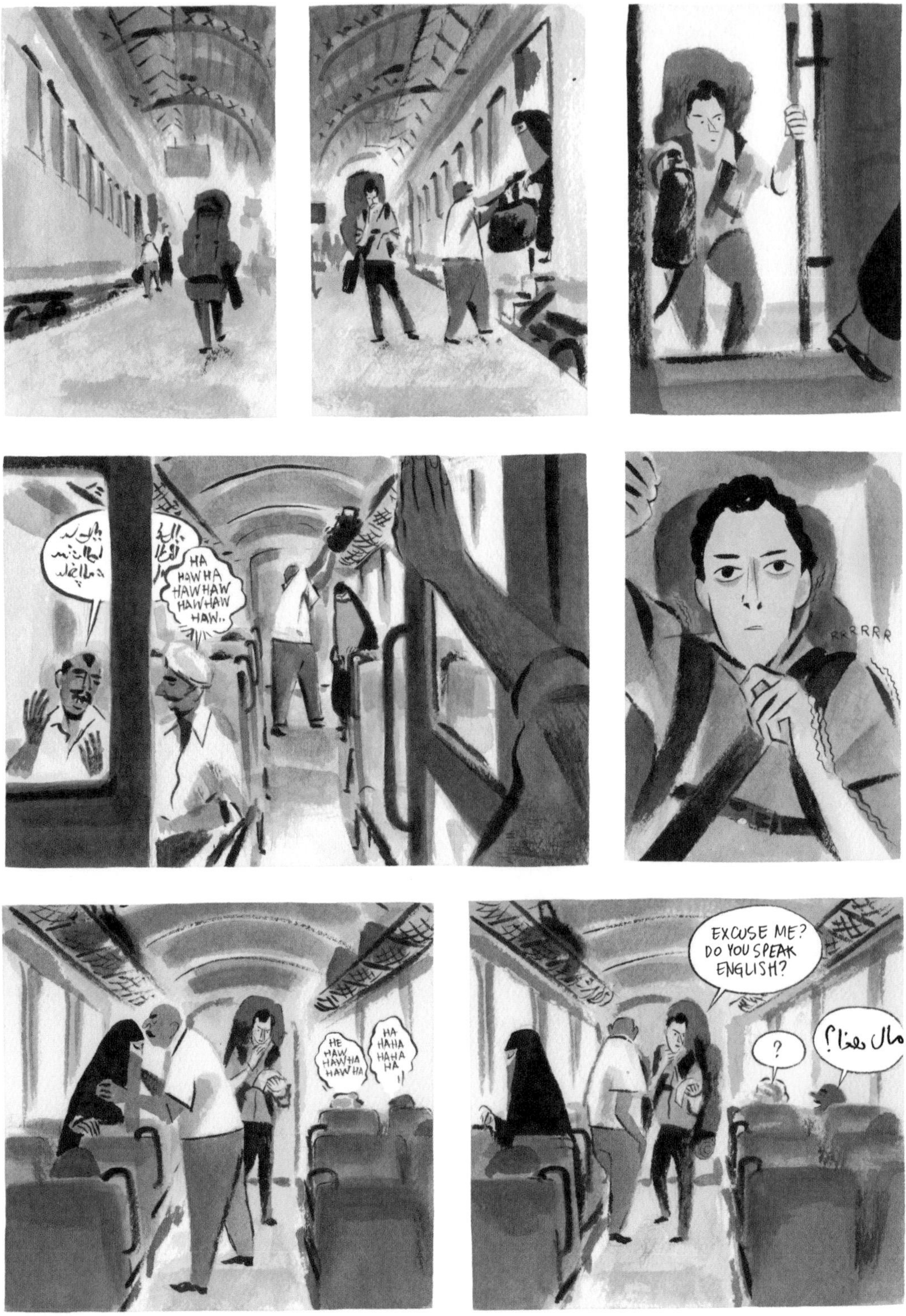
HA HAWHA HAWHAW HAWHAW HAW..
RRRRRR
HE HAW HAWHA HAWHA
HA HAHA HAHA HA
EXCUSE ME? DO YOU SPEAK ENGLISH?
?
مال هذا؟

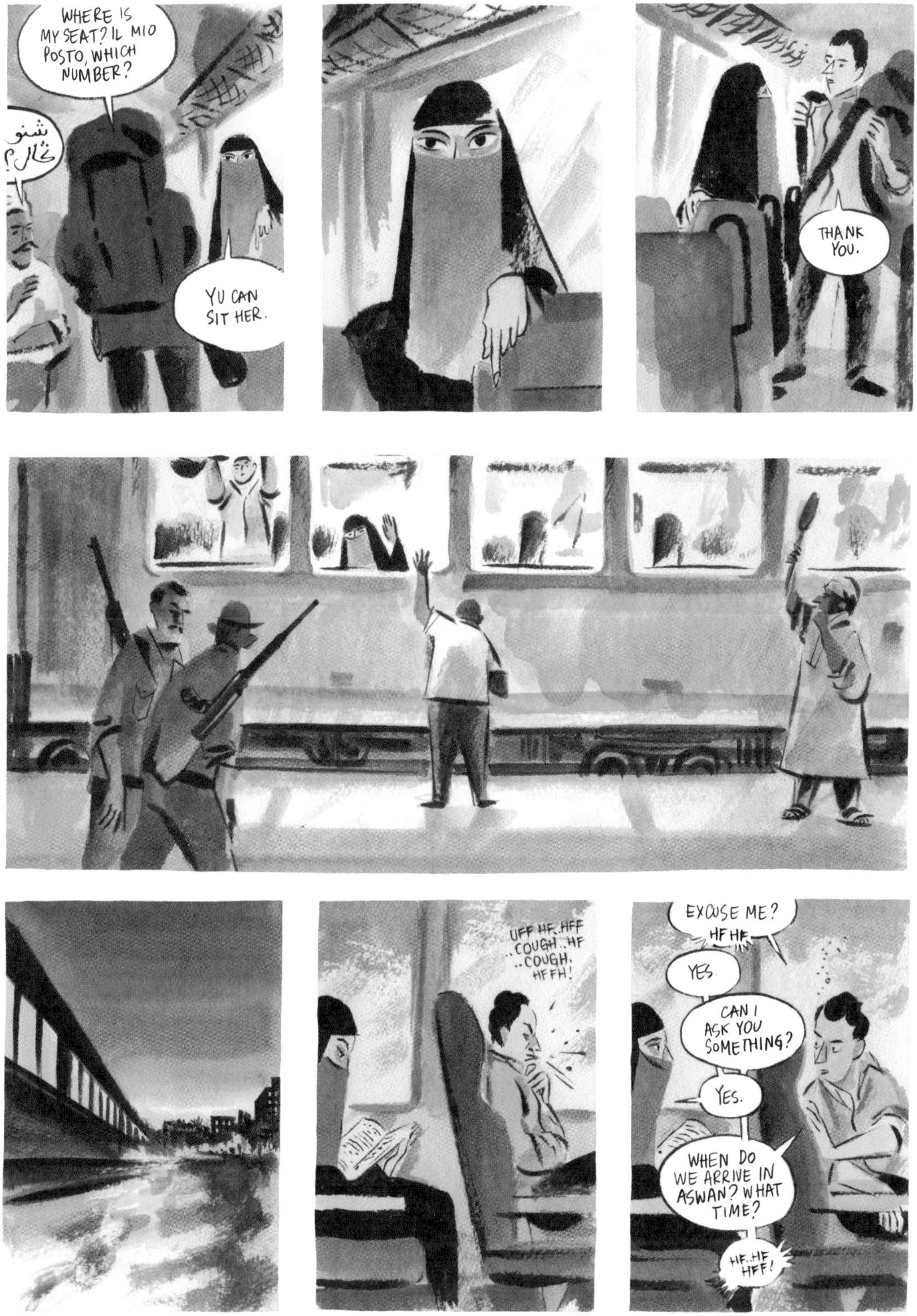
WHERE IS MY SEAT? IL MIO POSTO, WHICH NUMBER?
شنو
YU CAN SIT HER.
THANK YOU.
UFF HF..HFF ..COUGH..HF ..COUGH. HFFH!
EXCUSE ME?
HF HF
YES.
CAN I ASK YOU SOMETHING?
YES.
WHEN DO WE ARRIVE IN ASWAN? WHAT TIME?
HF..HF HFF!

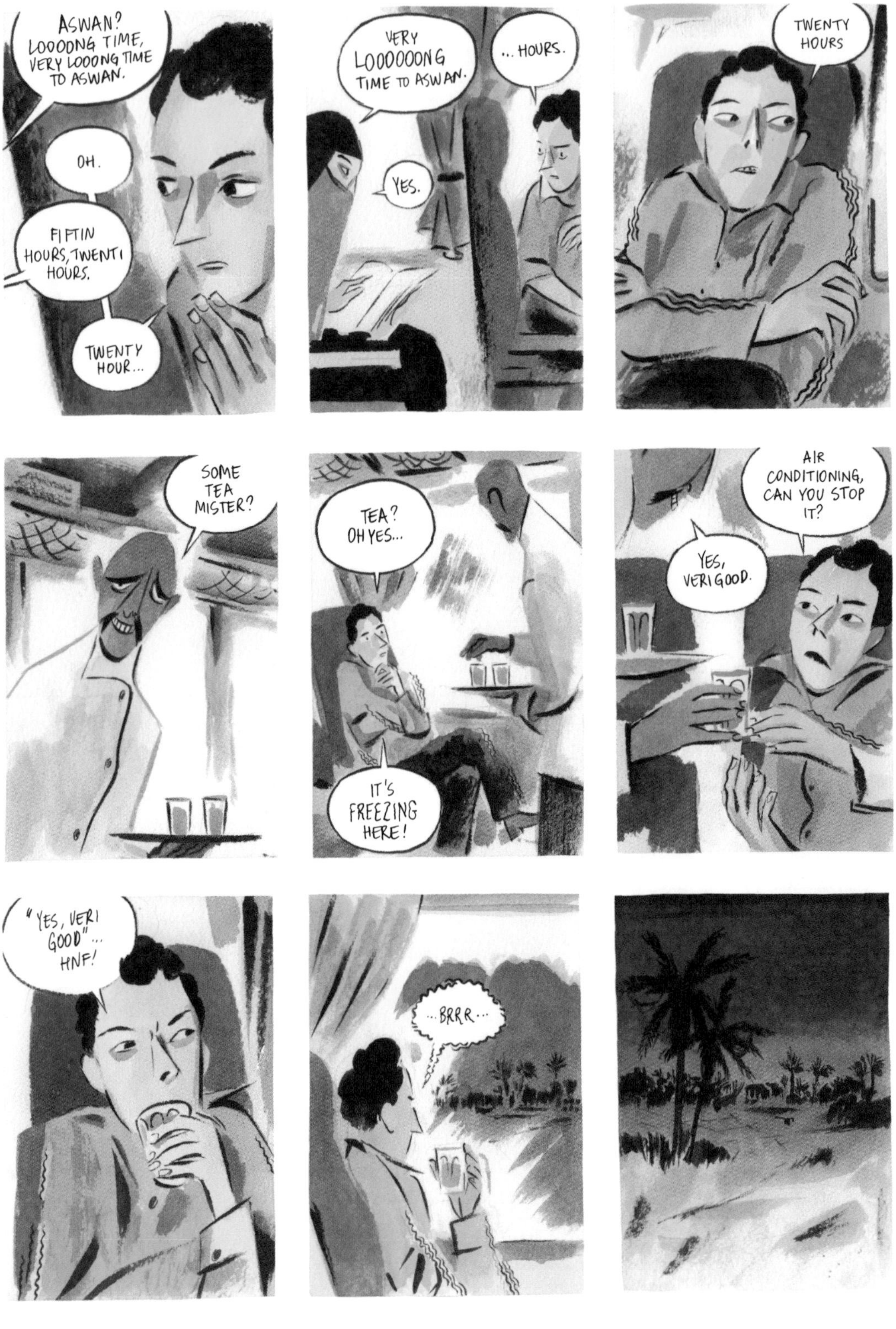
ASWAN? LOOOONG TIME, VERY LOOONG TIME TO ASWAN.
OH.
FIFTIN HOURS, TWENTI HOURS.
TWENTY HOUR...
VERY LOOOOOONG TIME TO ASWAN.
YES.
... HOURS.
TWENTY HOURS
SOME TEA MISTER?
TEA? OH YES...
IT'S FREEZING HERE!
AIR CONDITIONING, CAN YOU STOP IT?
YES, VERI GOOD.
"YES, VERI GOOD"... HNF!
... BRRR ...

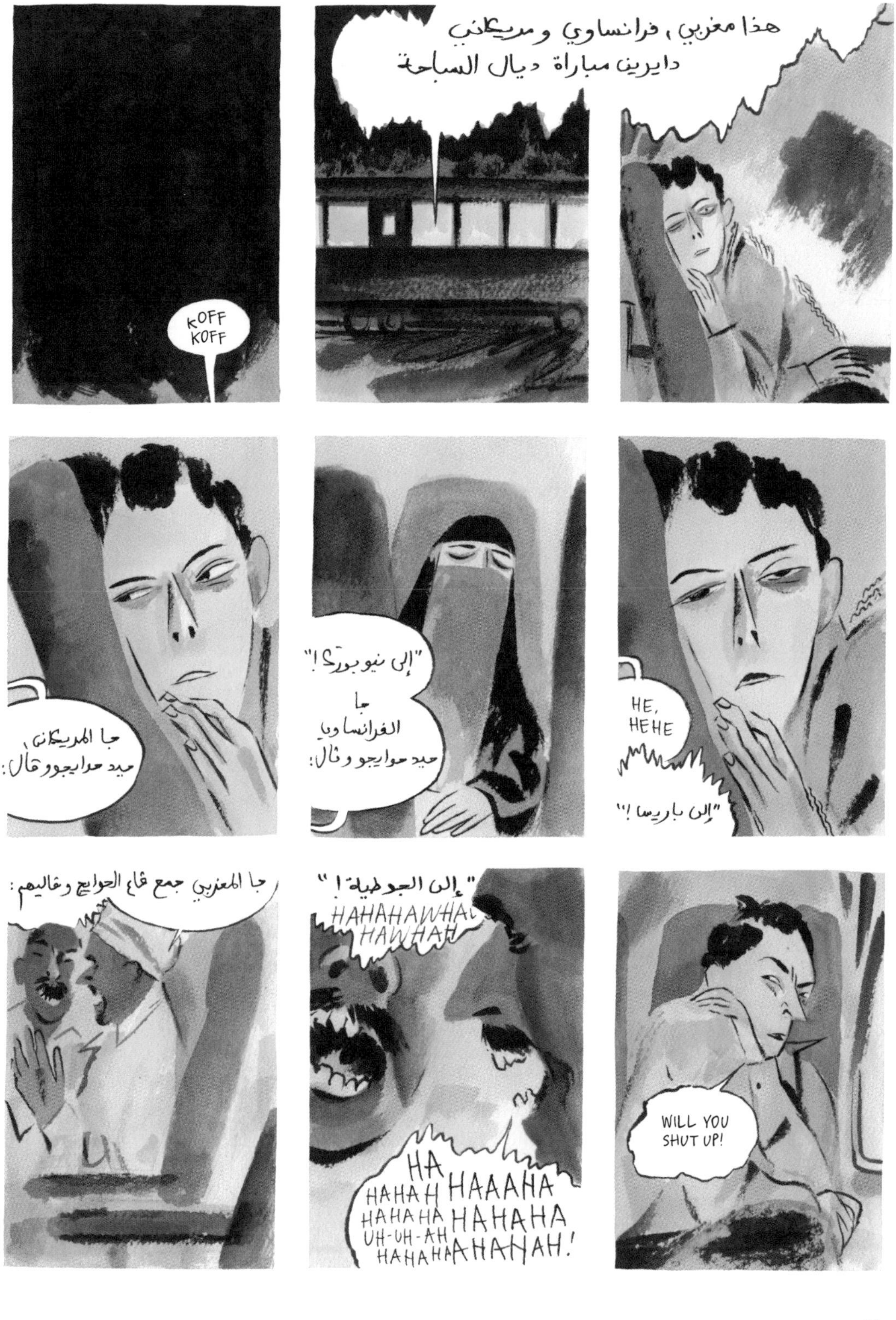
KOFF KOFF
هذا مغربي، فرانساوي ومريكاني
دايرين مباراة ديال السباحة
جا المريكاني، حيد حوايجو وقال:
"إلى نيويورك!"
جا الفرانساوي، حيد حوايجو وقال:
HE, HEHE
"إلى باريس!"
جا المغربي جمع قاع الحوايج وقاليهم:
"إلى الجوطية!"
HAHAHAWHA HAWHAH
HA HAHAH HAAAHA HAHAHA HAHAHA UH-UH-AH HAHAHAAHAHAH!
WILL YOU SHUT UP!

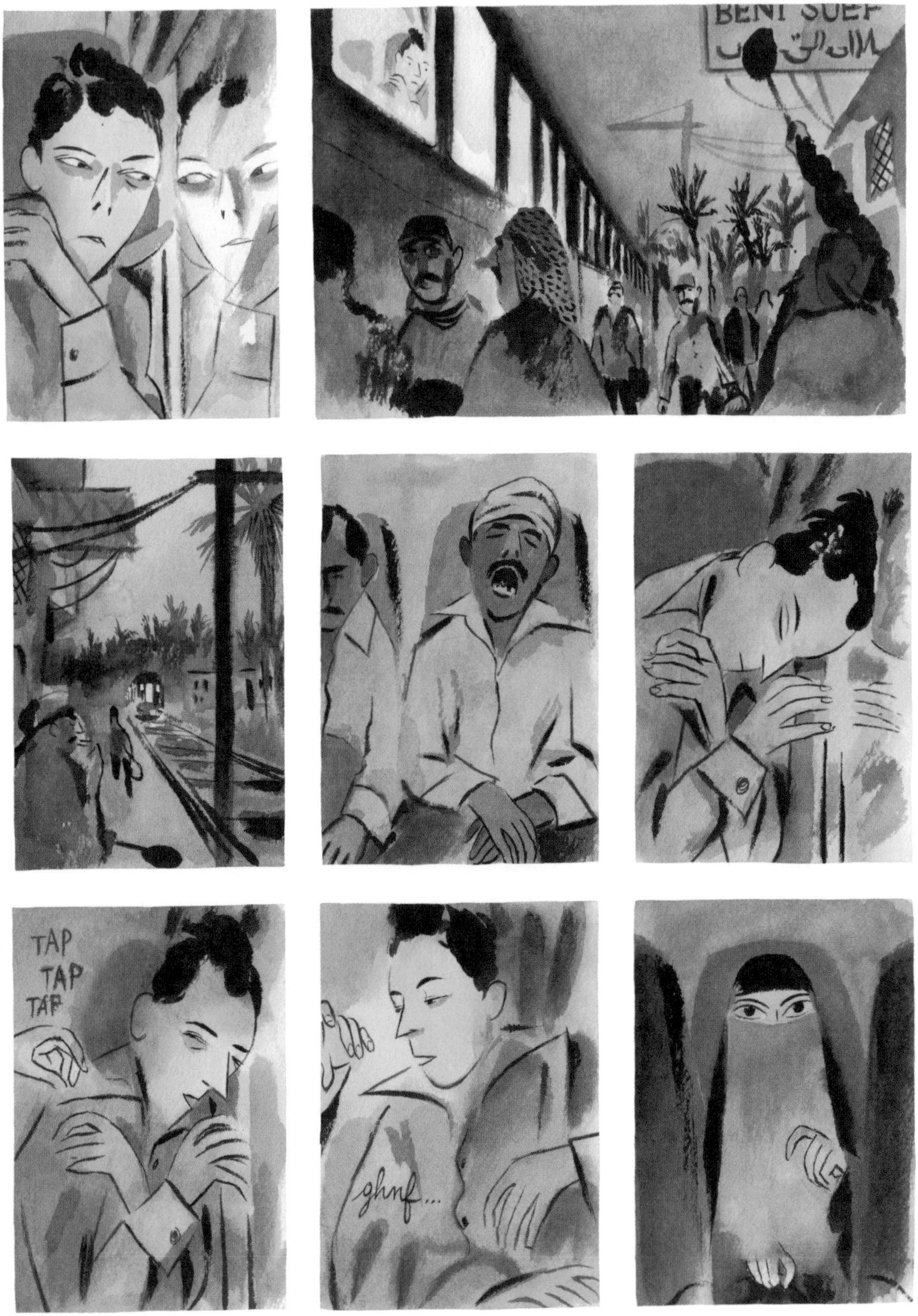
BENI SUEF
TAP
TAP
TAP
ghnf...

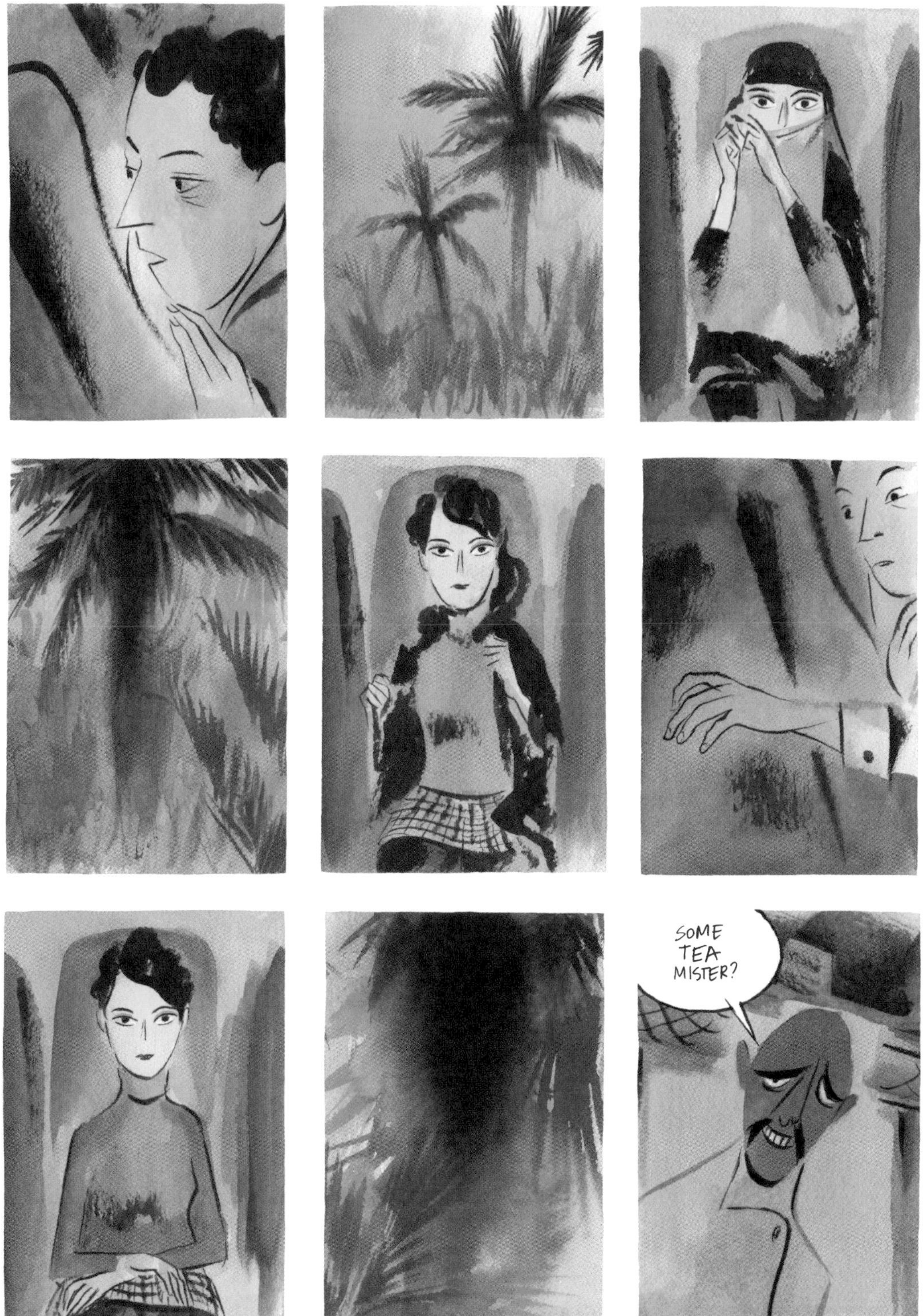
SOME TEA MISTER?

WHAT? TEA? NO, NO.

WHAT WAS I DREAMING?

VRRMMM...

I HAVE A FEVERRRR

LUCY

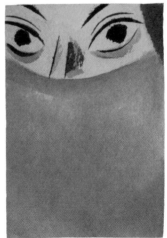

WHAT ARE YOU DOING HERE?

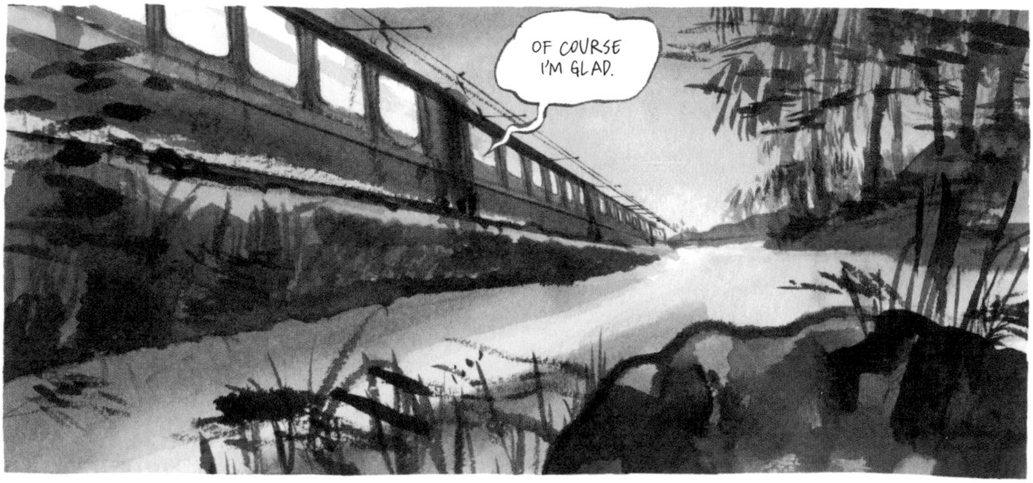
OF COURSE I'M GLAD.

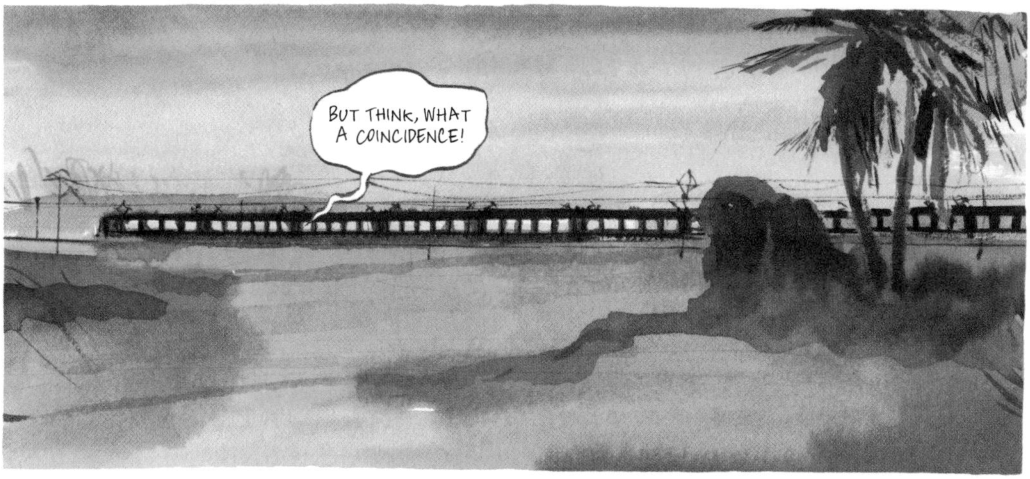
BUT THINK, WHAT A COINCIDENCE!

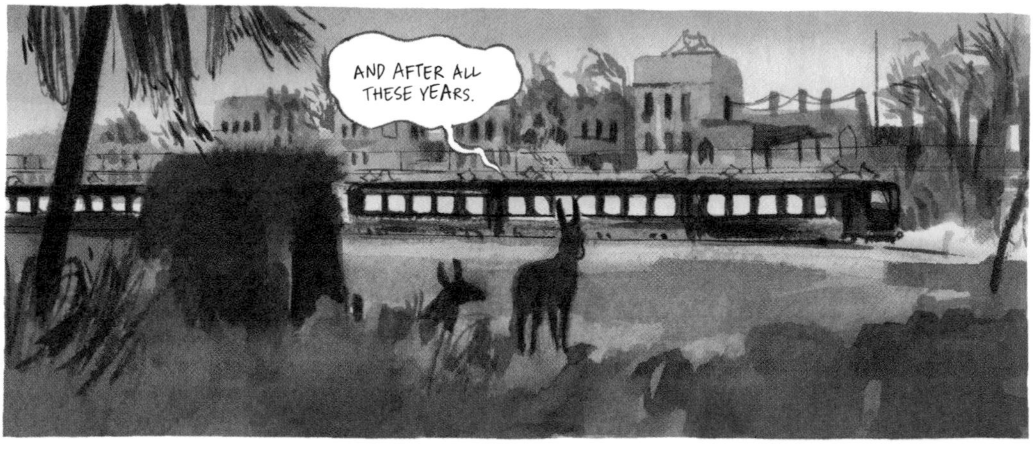
AND AFTER ALL THESE YEARS.

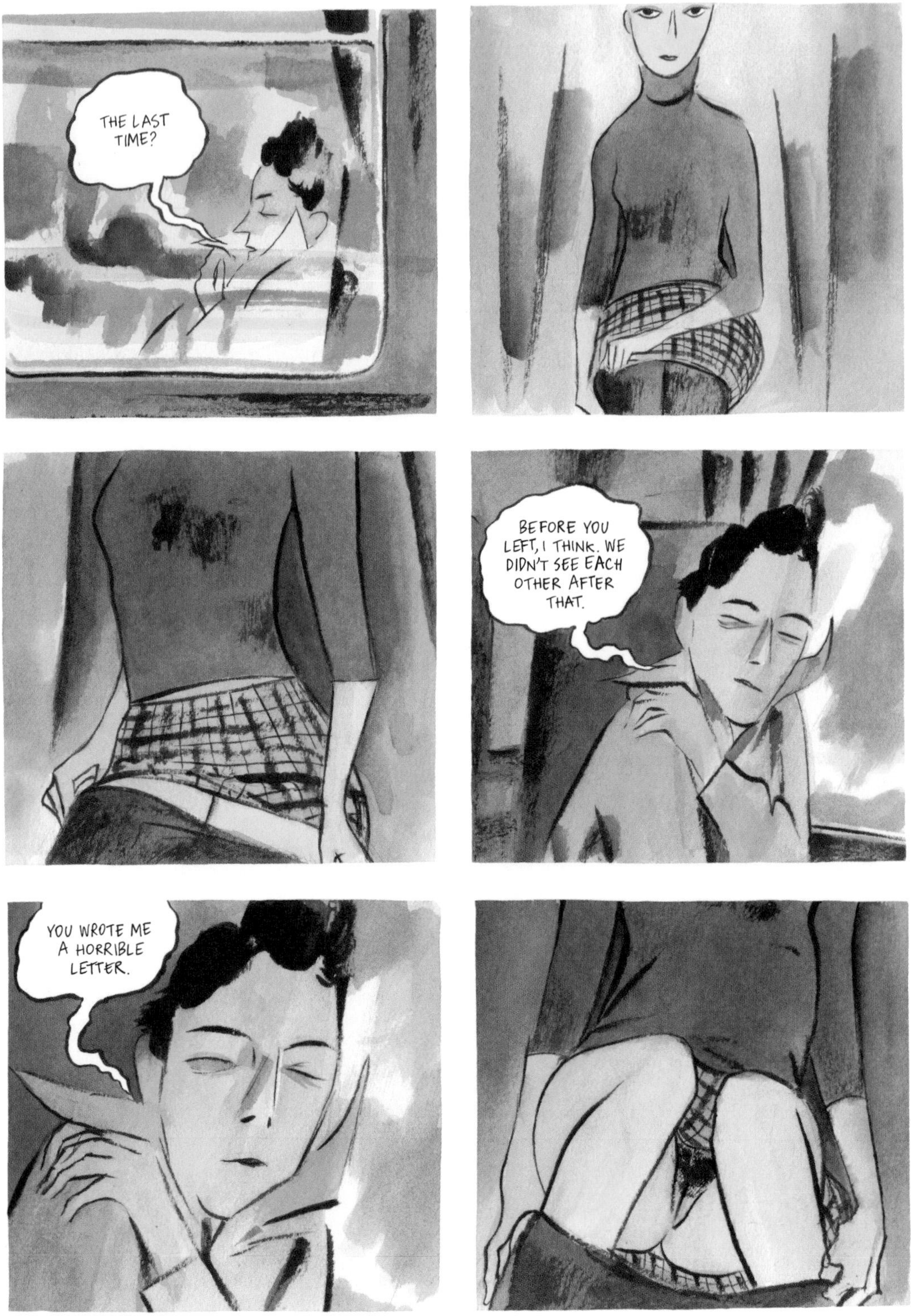
THE LAST TIME?
BEFORE YOU LEFT, I THINK. WE DIDN'T SEE EACH OTHER AFTER THAT.
YOU WROTE ME A HORRIBLE LETTER.

YEAH, IT'S ALL OVER. LET'S FORGET ABOUT IT.

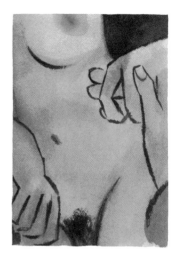

COME HERE, LET ME GIVE YOU A HUG. WHO WOULD'VE THOUGHT, EH?

ويليا مع هذا!...

اسد فمكا!

YOU'RE SO WARM...

WHERE'D SHE GO?

LUCY?

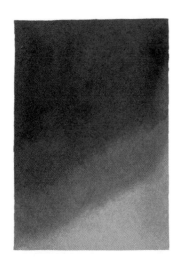

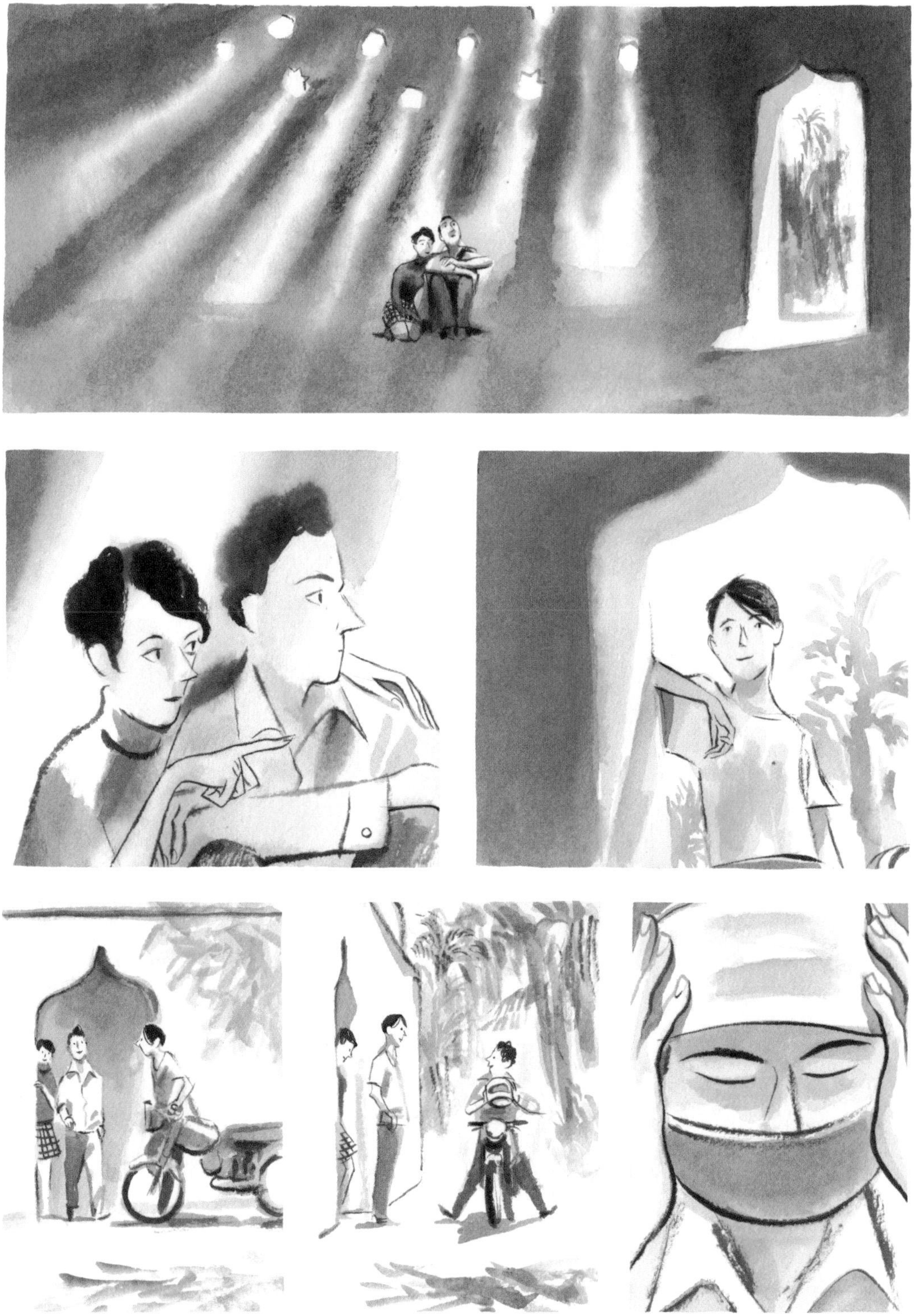

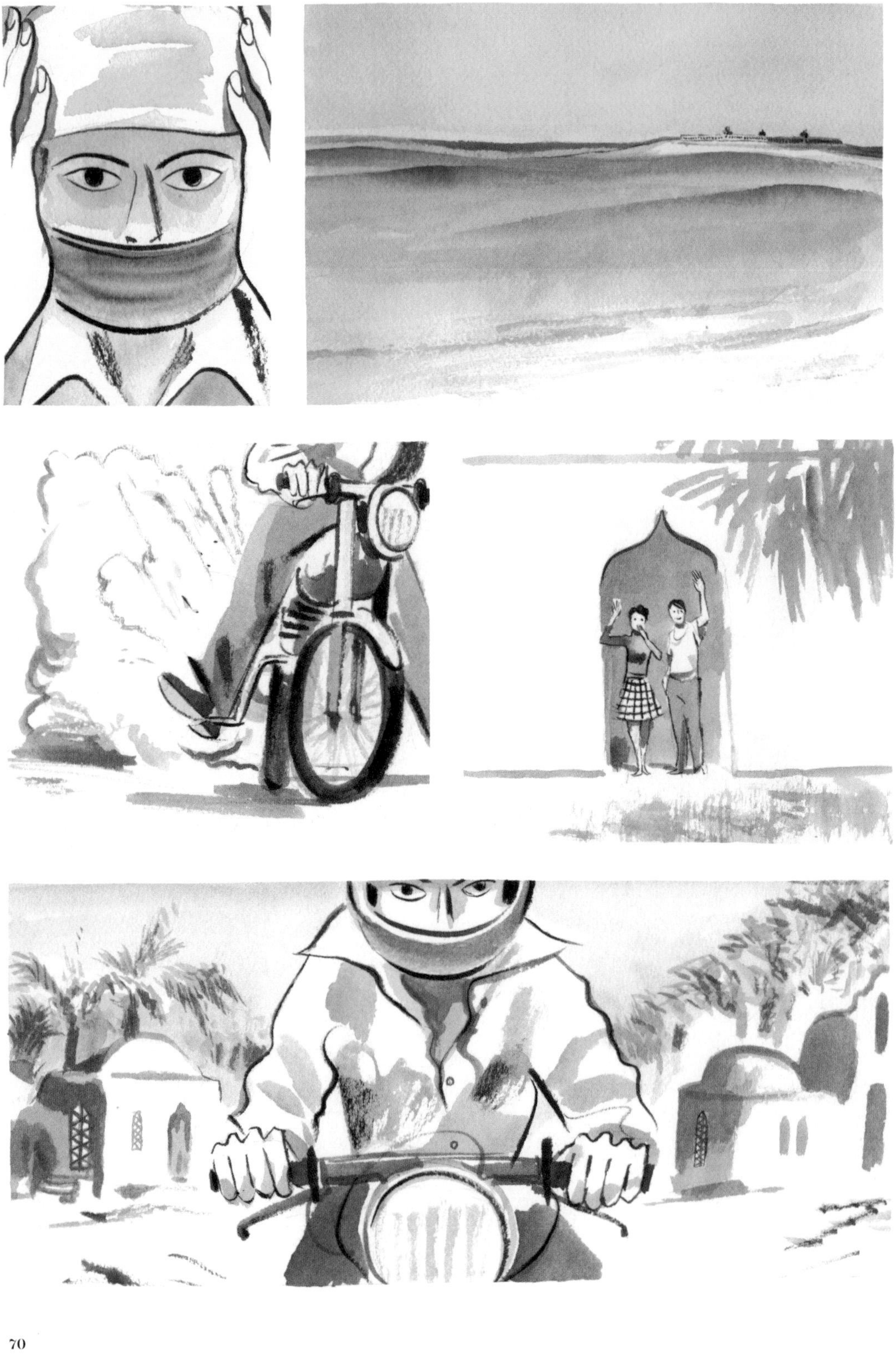

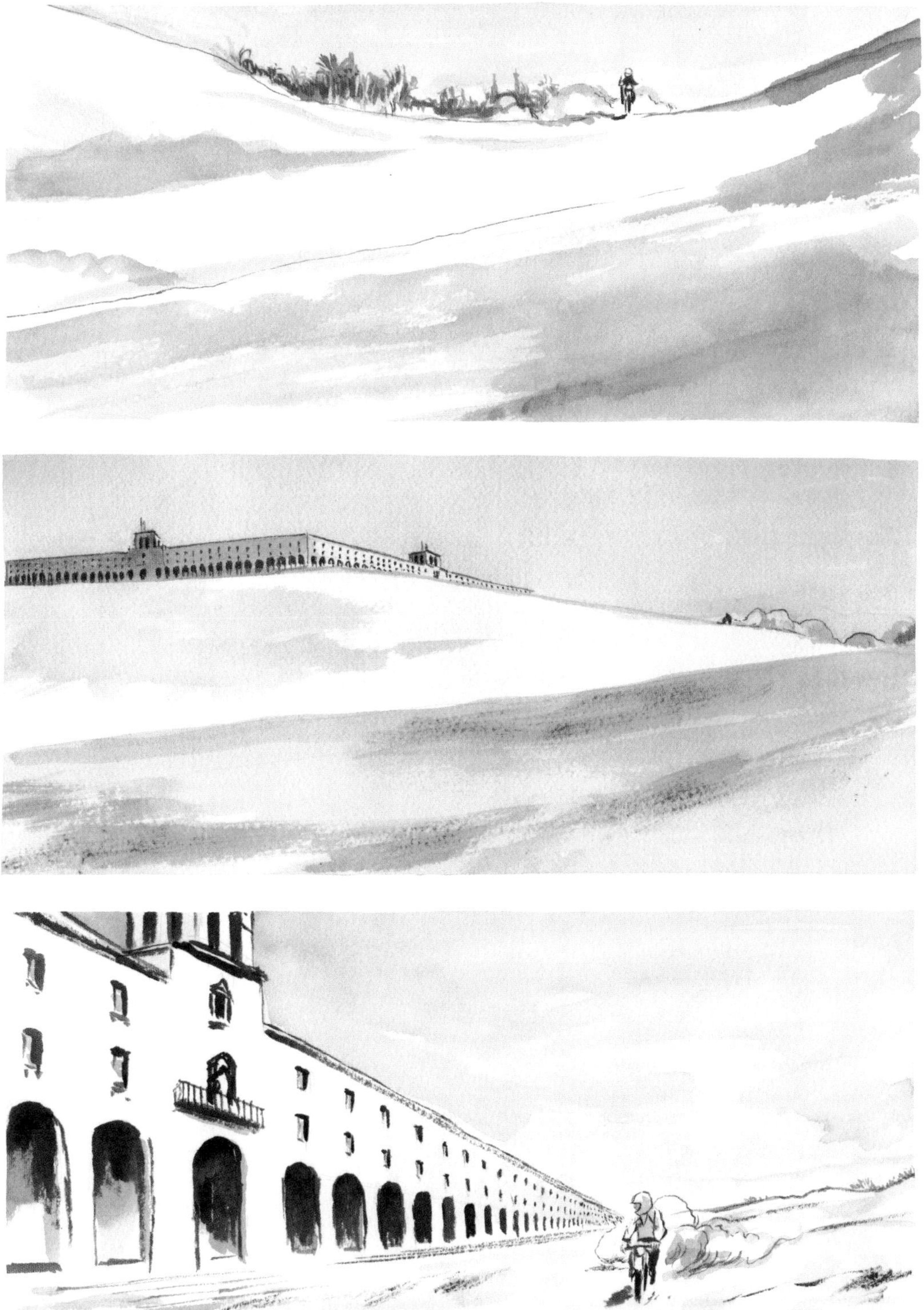

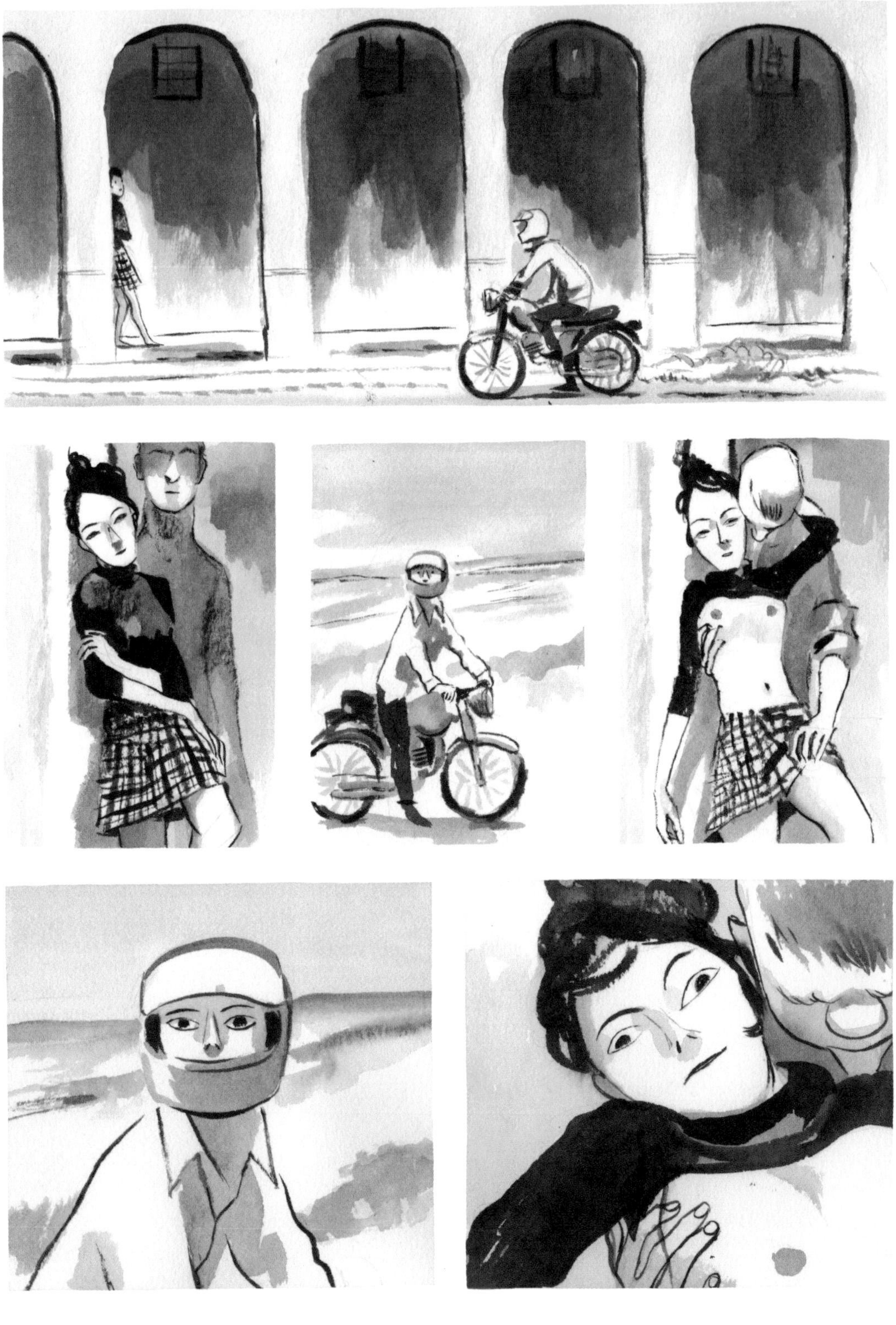

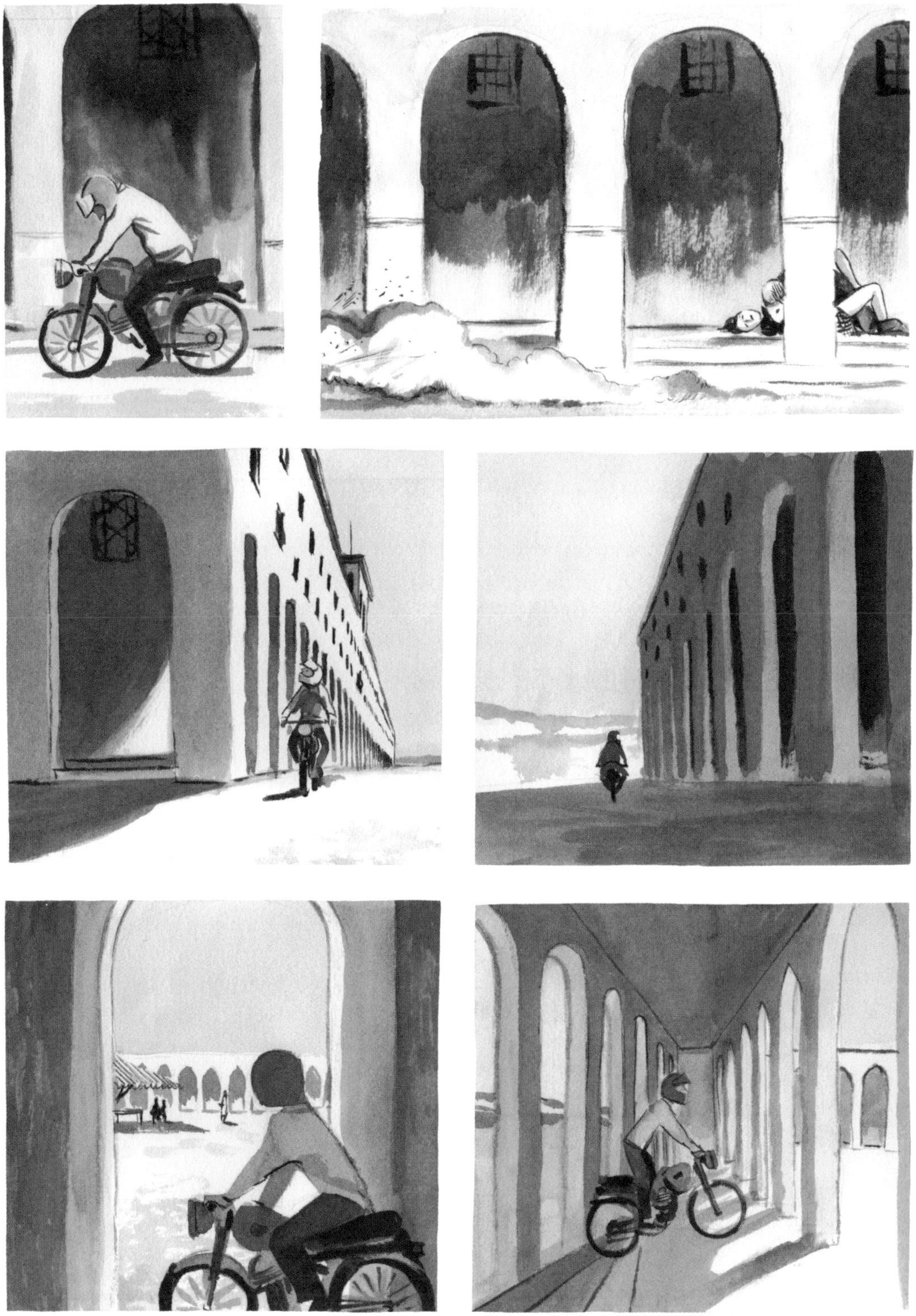

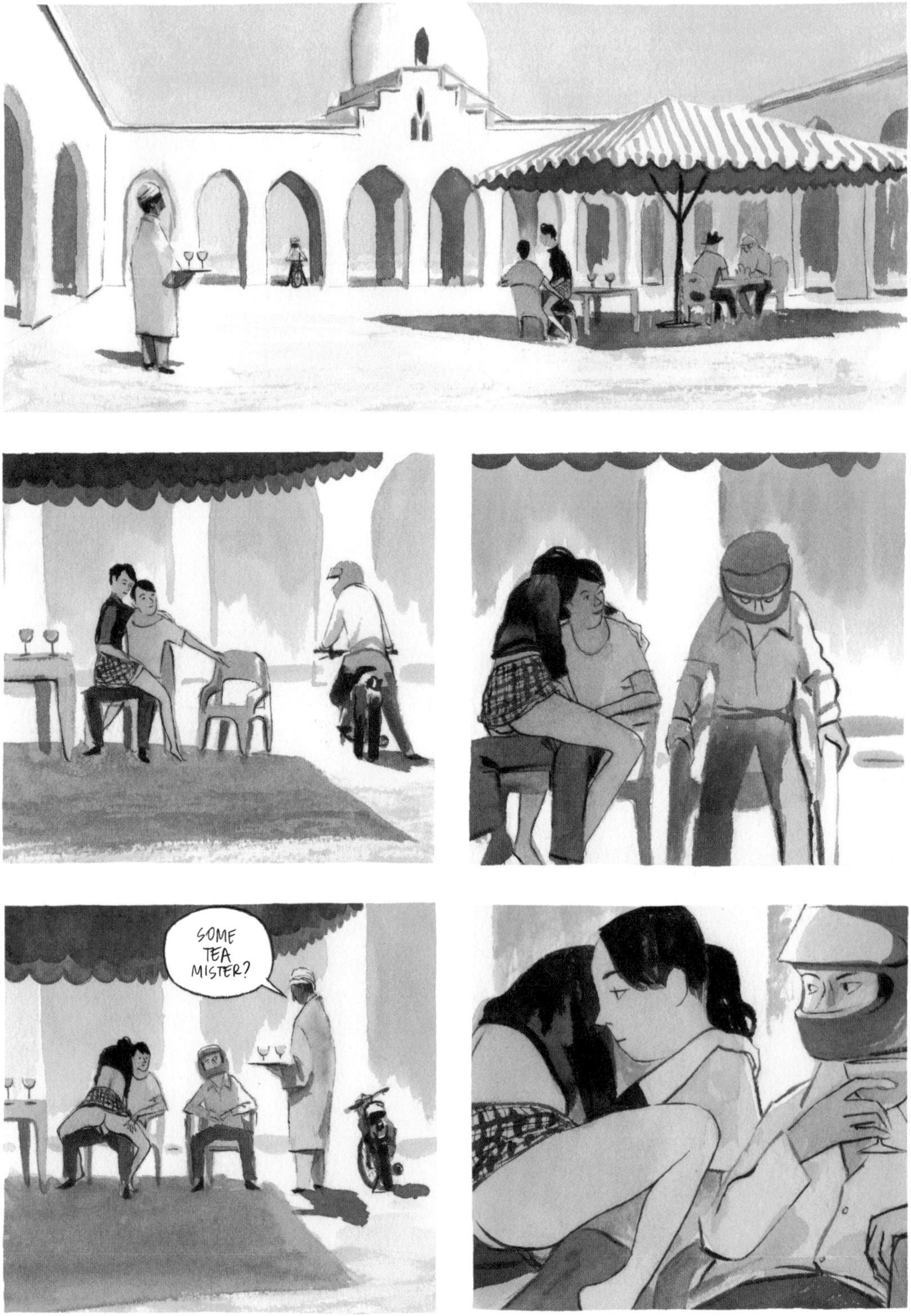
SOME TEA MISTER?

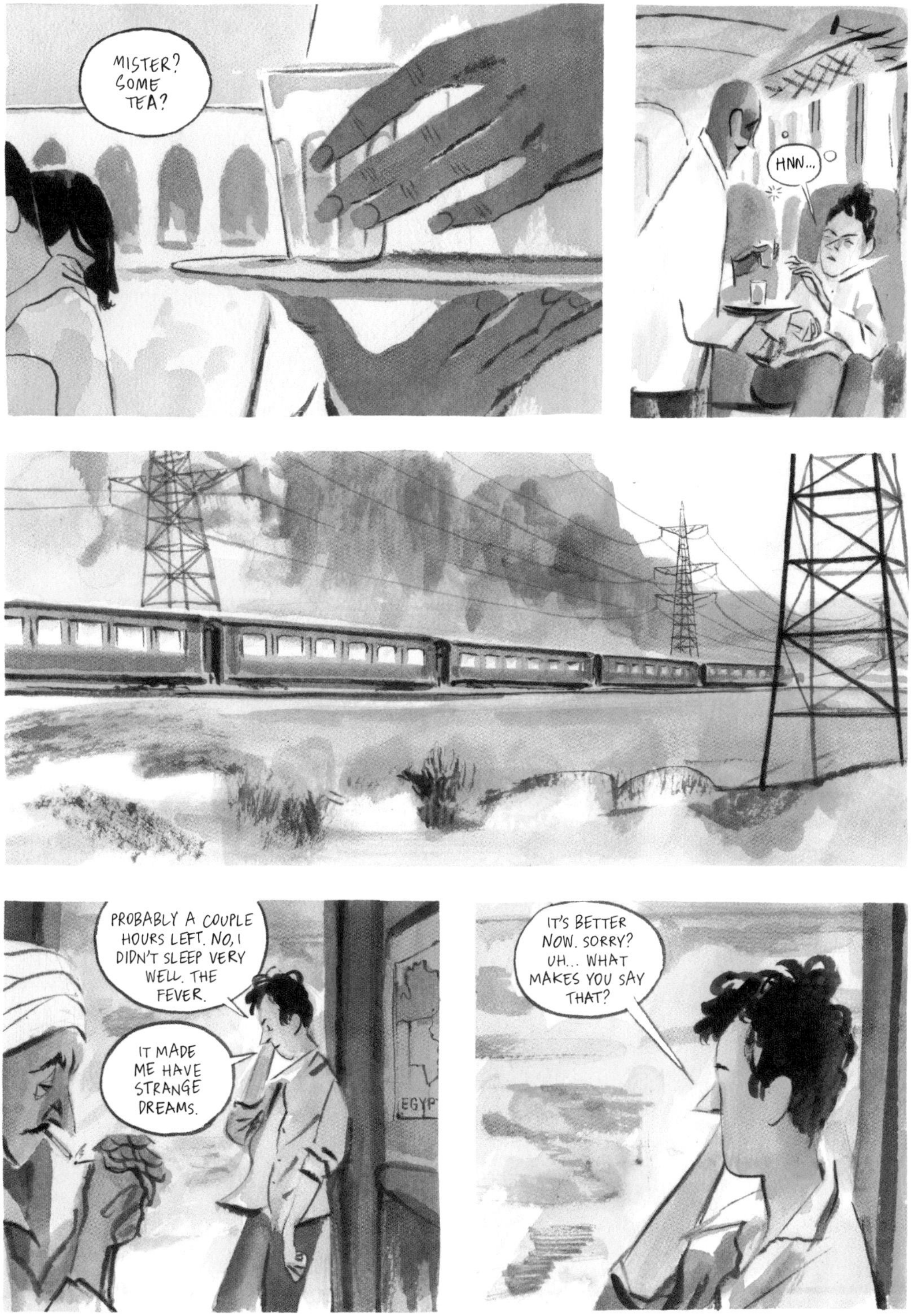
MISTER? SOME TEA?
HNN...
PROBABLY A COUPLE HOURS LEFT. NO, I DIDN'T SLEEP VERY WELL. THE FEVER.
IT MADE ME HAVE STRANGE DREAMS.
EGYP
IT'S BETTER NOW. SORRY? UH... WHAT MAKES YOU SAY THAT?

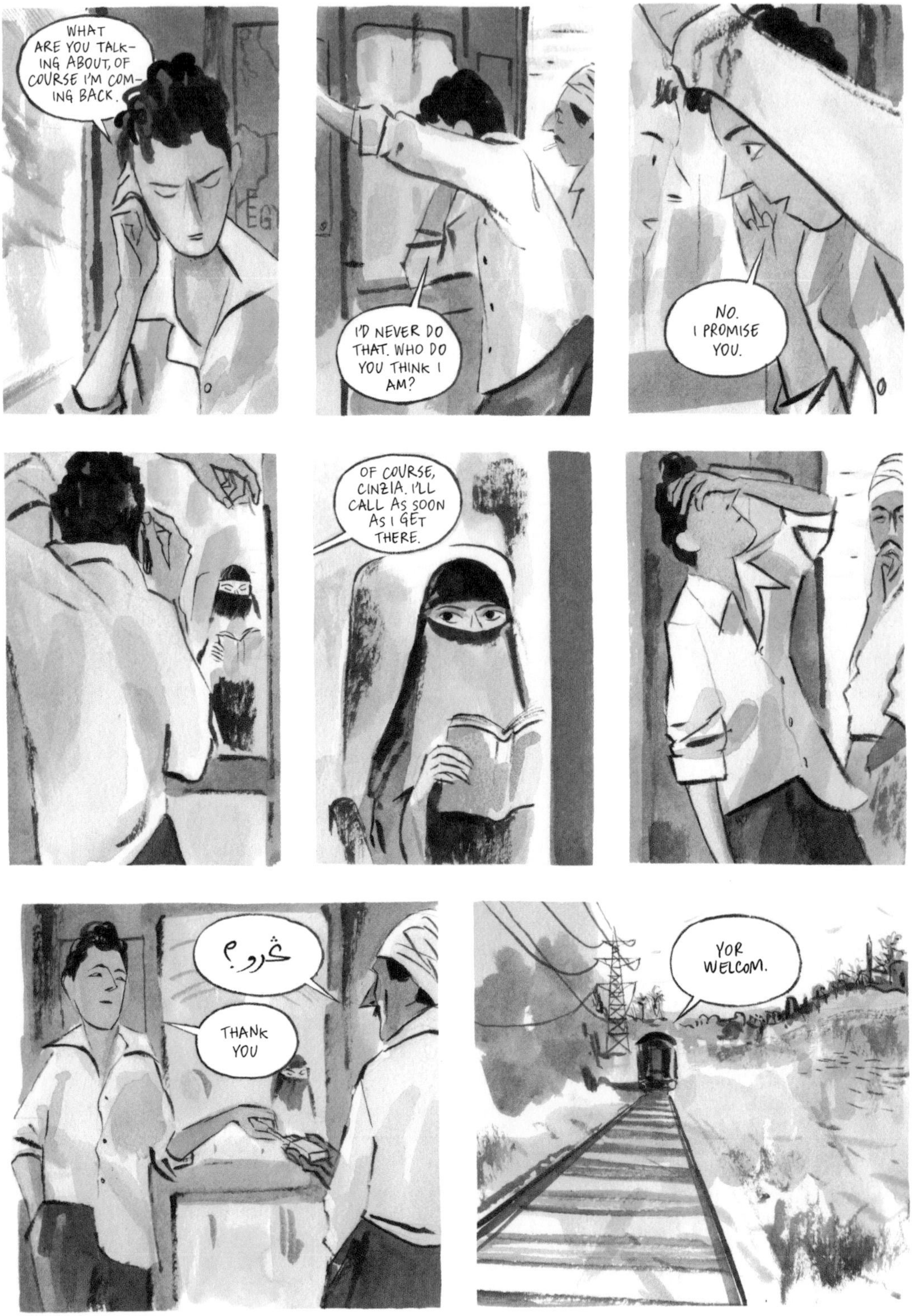
WHAT ARE YOU TALK-ING ABOUT, OF COURSE I'M COM-ING BACK.
I'D NEVER DO THAT. WHO DO YOU THINK I AM?
NO. I PROMISE YOU.
OF COURSE, CINZIA. I'LL CALL AS SOON AS I GET THERE.
THANK YOU
YOR WELCOM.

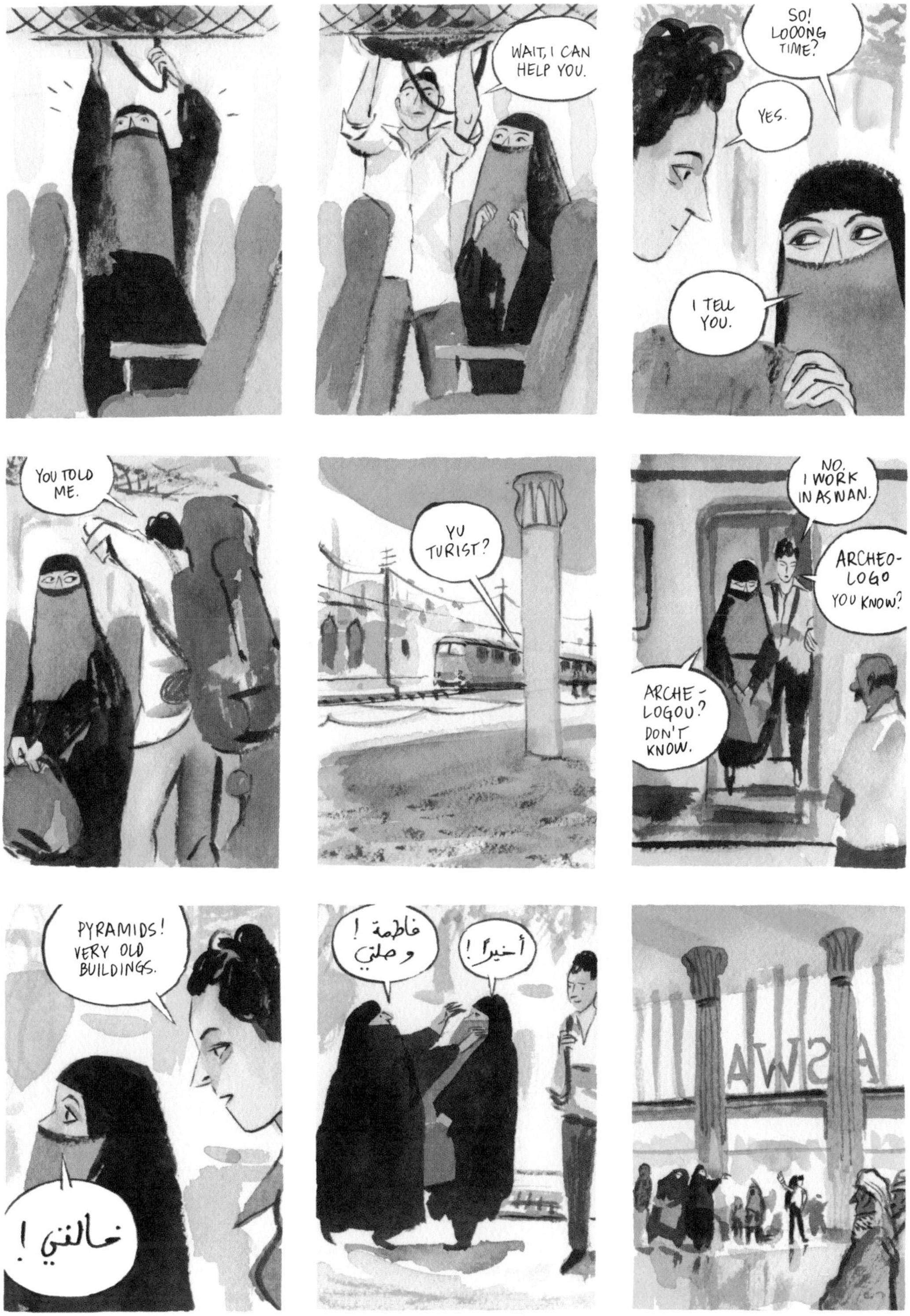
WAIT, I CAN HELP YOU.
SO! LOOONG TIME?
YES.
I TELL YOU.
YOU TOLD ME.
YU TURIST?
NO. I WORK IN ASWAN.
ARCHEO-LOGO YOU KNOW?
ARCHE-LOGOU? DON'T KNOW.
PYRAMIDS! VERY OLD BUILDINGS.
خالتي !
فاطمة ! وصلتي
أخيراً !

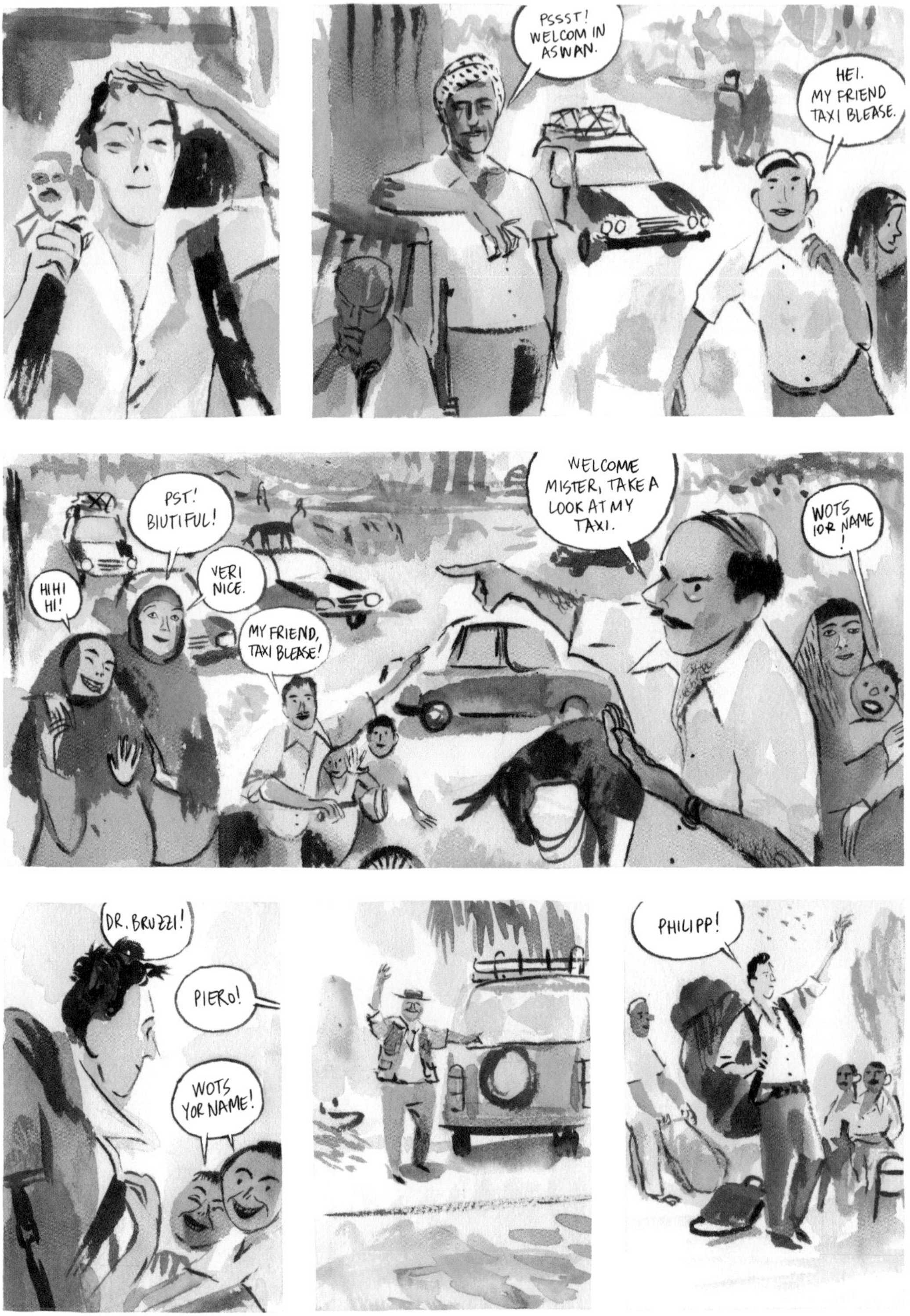
PSSST! WELCOM IN ASWAN.
HEI. MY FRIEND TAXI BLEASE.
HIHI HI!
PST! BIUTIFUL!
VERI NICE.
MY FRIEND, TAXI BLEASE!
WELCOME MISTER, TAKE A LOOK AT MY TAXI.
WOTS IOR NAME!
DR. BRUZZI!
PIERO!
WOTS YOR NAME!
PHILIPP!

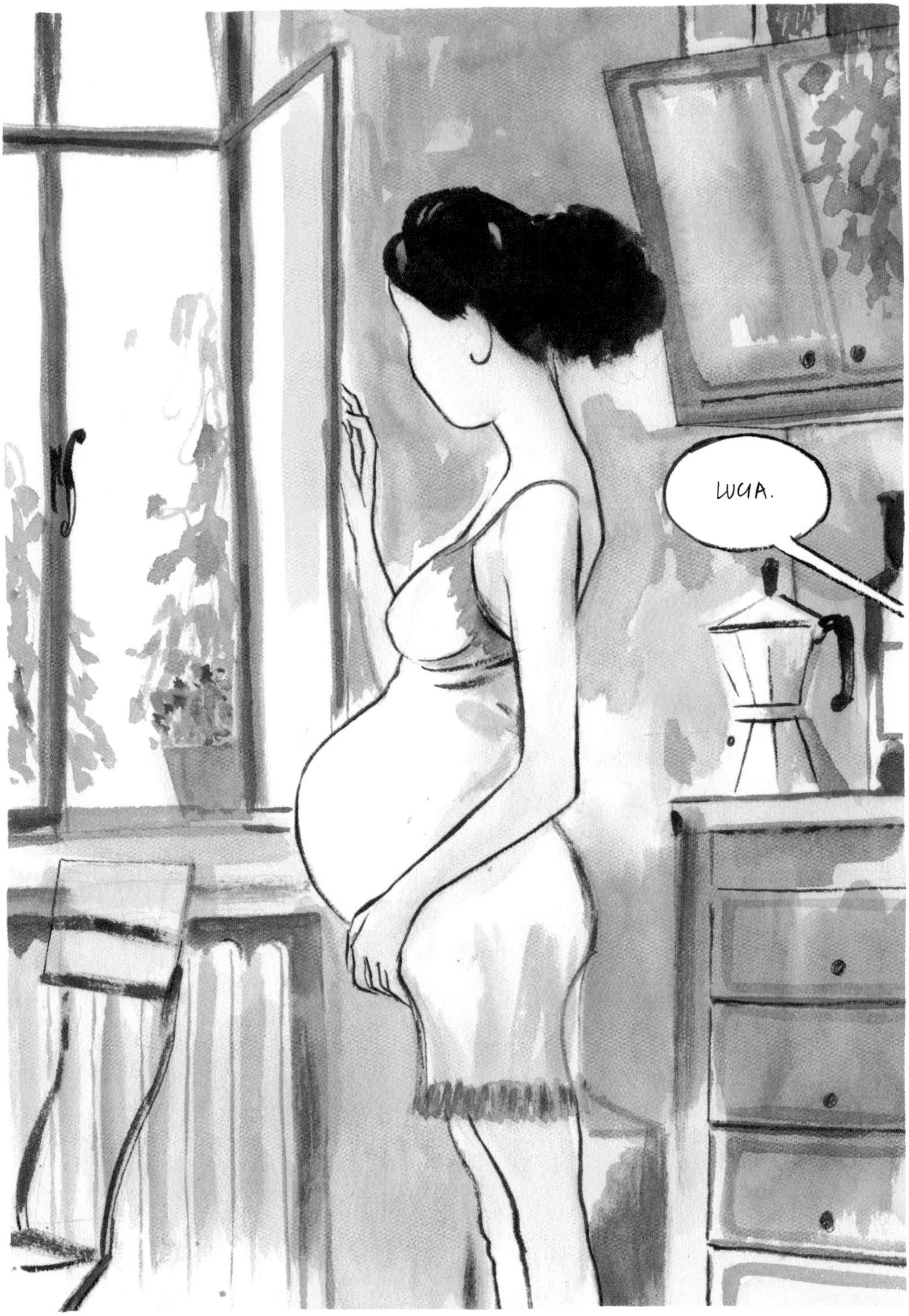
LUCIA.

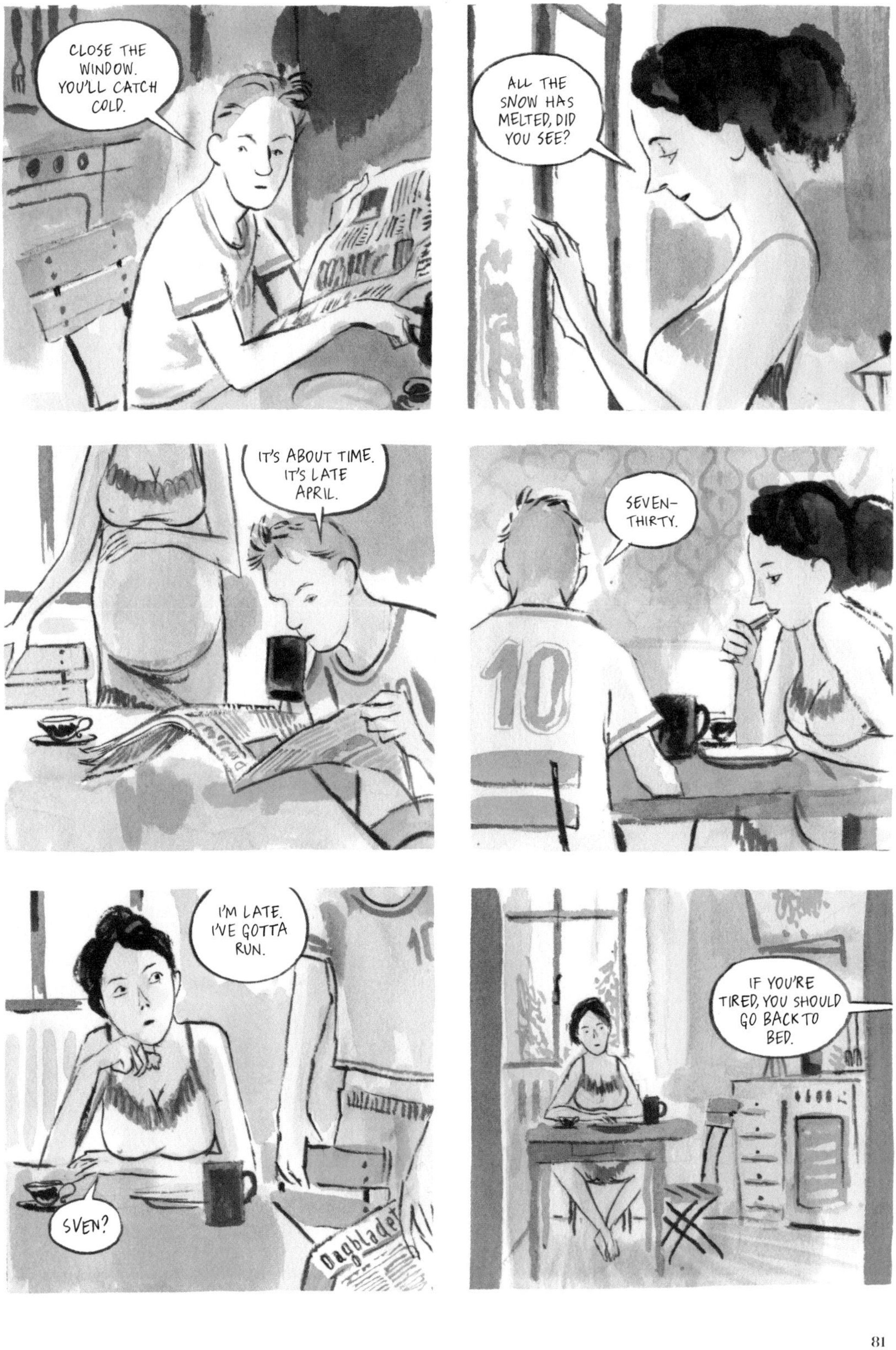
CLOSE THE WINDOW. YOU'LL CATCH COLD.
ALL THE SNOW HAS MELTED, DID YOU SEE?
IT'S ABOUT TIME. IT'S LATE APRIL.
SEVEN-THIRTY.
I'M LATE. I'VE GOTTA RUN.
SVEN?
Dagbladet
IF YOU'RE TIRED, YOU SHOULD GO BACK TO BED.

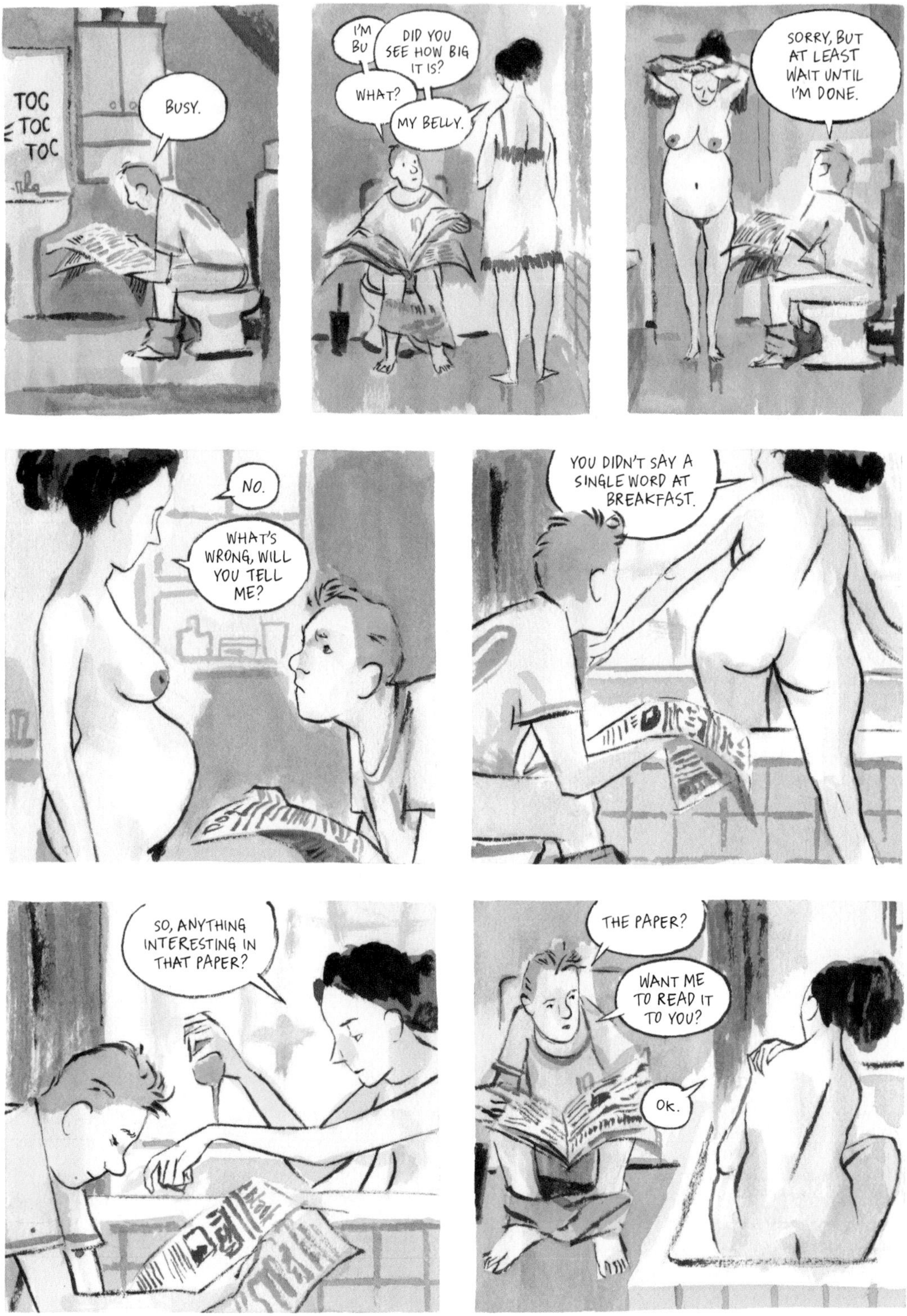
TOC
TOC
TOC
BUSY.
I'M BU
DID YOU SEE HOW BIG IT IS?
WHAT?
MY BELLY.
SORRY, BUT AT LEAST WAIT UNTIL I'M DONE.
NO.
WHAT'S WRONG, WILL YOU TELL ME?
YOU DIDN'T SAY A SINGLE WORD AT BREAKFAST.
SO, ANYTHING INTERESTING IN THAT PAPER?
THE PAPER?
WANT ME TO READ IT TO YOU?
OK.

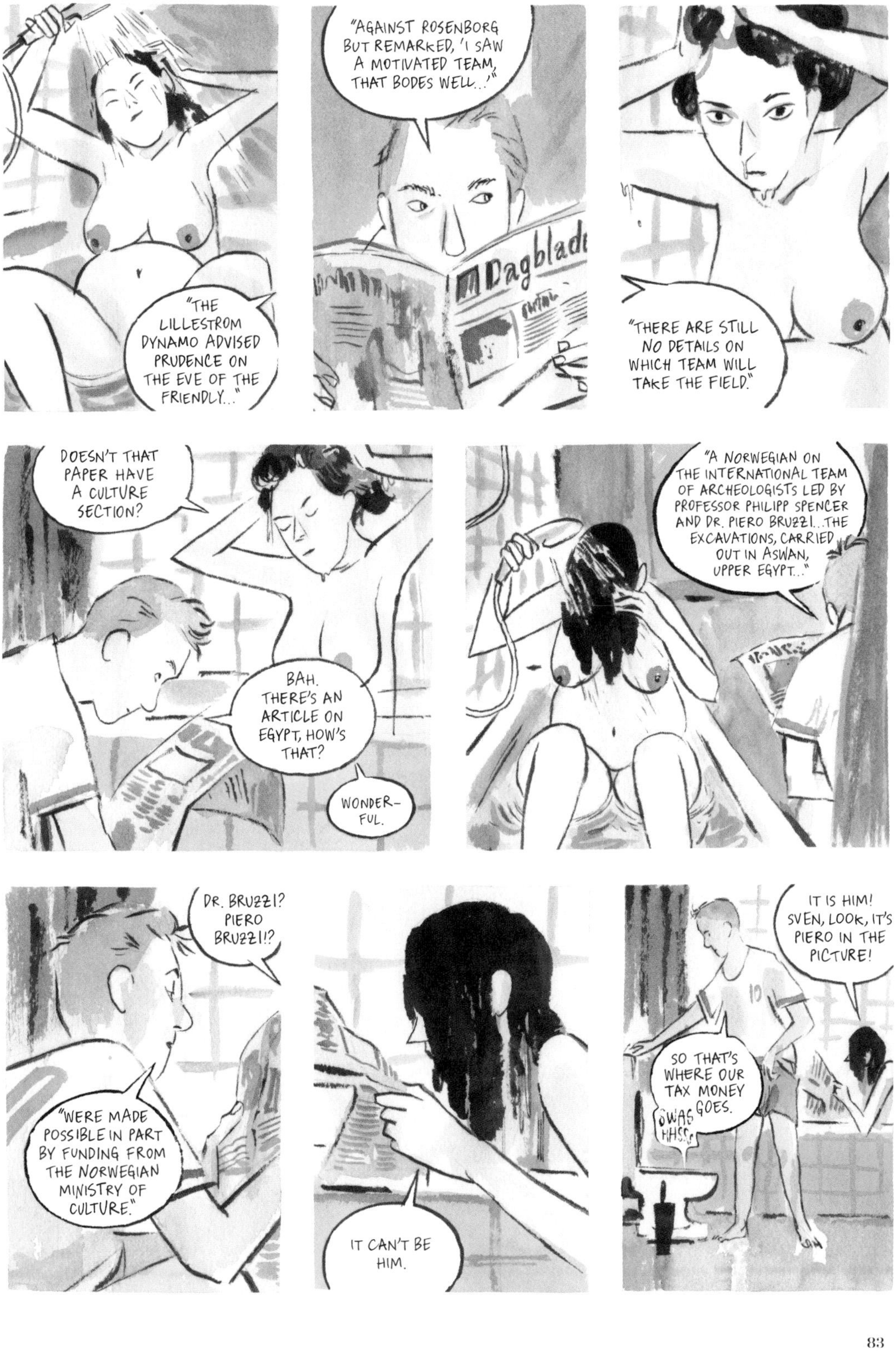
"THE LILLESTROM DYNAMO ADVISED PRUDENCE ON THE EVE OF THE FRIENDLY..."
"AGAINST ROSENBORG BUT REMARKED, 'I SAW A MOTIVATED TEAM, THAT BODES WELL...'"
Dagblad
"THERE ARE STILL NO DETAILS ON WHICH TEAM WILL TAKE THE FIELD."
DOESN'T THAT PAPER HAVE A CULTURE SECTION?
BAH. THERE'S AN ARTICLE ON EGYPT, HOW'S THAT?
WONDER-FUL.
"A NORWEGIAN ON THE INTERNATIONAL TEAM OF ARCHEOLOGISTS LED BY PROFESSOR PHILIPP SPENCER AND DR. PIERO BRUZZI...THE EXCAVATIONS, CARRIED OUT IN ASWAN, UPPER EGYPT..."
DR. BRUZZI? PIERO BRUZZI!?
"WERE MADE POSSIBLE IN PART BY FUNDING FROM THE NORWEGIAN MINISTRY OF CULTURE."
IT CAN'T BE HIM.
IT IS HIM! SVEN, LOOK, IT'S PIERO IN THE PICTURE!
SO THAT'S WHERE OUR TAX MONEY GOES.
ŌWAS HHSS

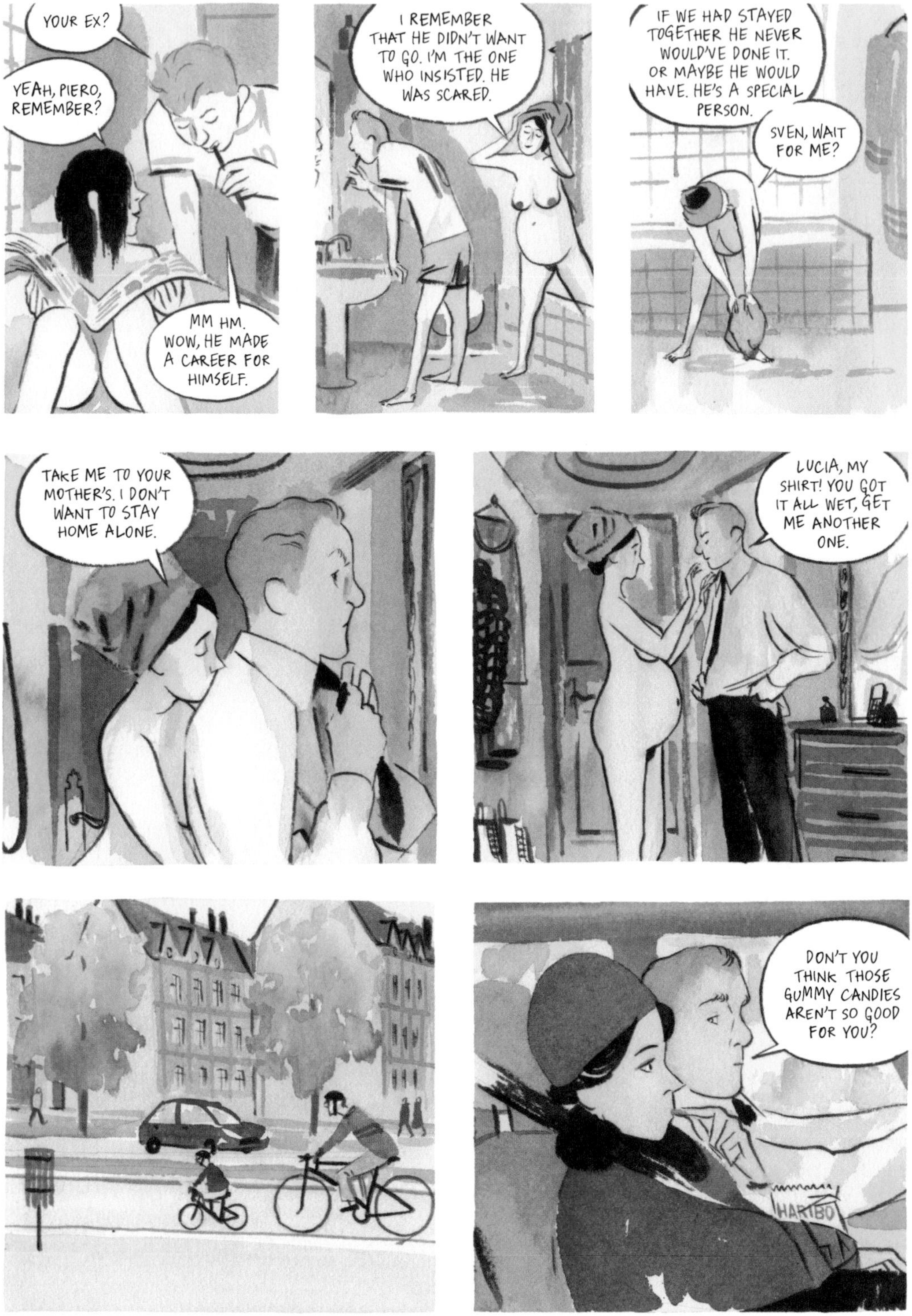
YOUR EX?
YEAH, PIERO, REMEMBER?
MM HM. WOW, HE MADE A CAREER FOR HIMSELF.
I REMEMBER THAT HE DIDN'T WANT TO GO. I'M THE ONE WHO INSISTED. HE WAS SCARED.
IF WE HAD STAYED TOGETHER HE NEVER WOULD'VE DONE IT. OR MAYBE HE WOULD HAVE. HE'S A SPECIAL PERSON.
SVEN, WAIT FOR ME?
TAKE ME TO YOUR MOTHER'S. I DON'T WANT TO STAY HOME ALONE.
LUCIA, MY SHIRT! YOU GOT IT ALL WET, GET ME ANOTHER ONE.
DON'T YOU THINK THOSE GUMMY CANDIES AREN'T SO GOOD FOR YOU?
HARIBO

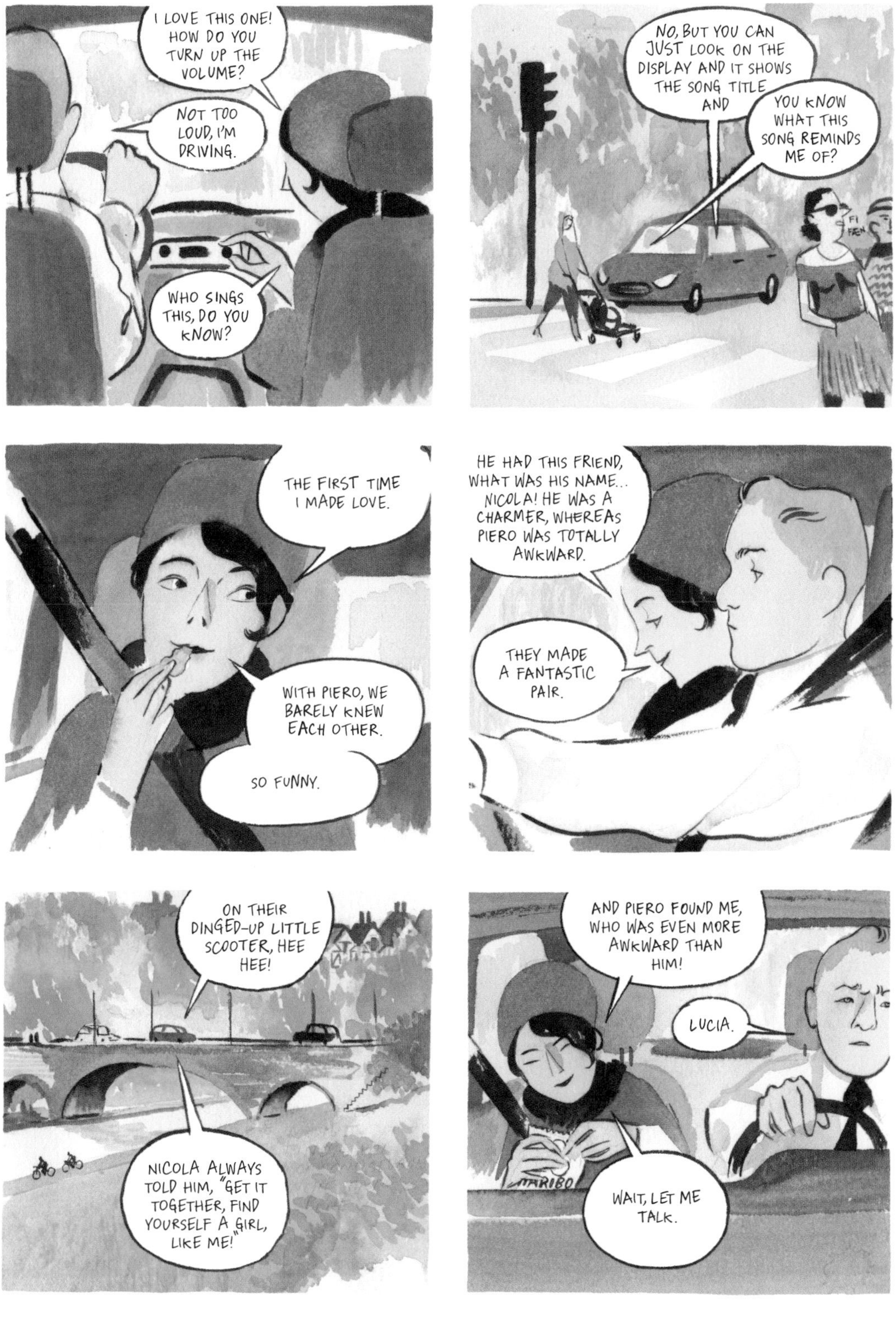
I LOVE THIS ONE! HOW DO YOU TURN UP THE VOLUME?
NOT TOO LOUD, I'M DRIVING.
WHO SINGS THIS, DO YOU KNOW?
NO, BUT YOU CAN JUST LOOK ON THE DISPLAY AND IT SHOWS THE SONG TITLE AND
YOU KNOW WHAT THIS SONG REMINDS ME OF?
THE FIRST TIME I MADE LOVE.
WITH PIERO, WE BARELY KNEW EACH OTHER.
SO FUNNY.
HE HAD THIS FRIEND, WHAT WAS HIS NAME... NICOLA! HE WAS A CHARMER, WHEREAS PIERO WAS TOTALLY AWKWARD.
THEY MADE A FANTASTIC PAIR.
ON THEIR DINGED-UP LITTLE SCOOTER, HEE HEE!
NICOLA ALWAYS TOLD HIM, "GET IT TOGETHER, FIND YOURSELF A GIRL, LIKE ME!"
AND PIERO FOUND ME, WHO WAS EVEN MORE AWKWARD THAN HIM!
LUCIA.
WAIT, LET ME TALK.

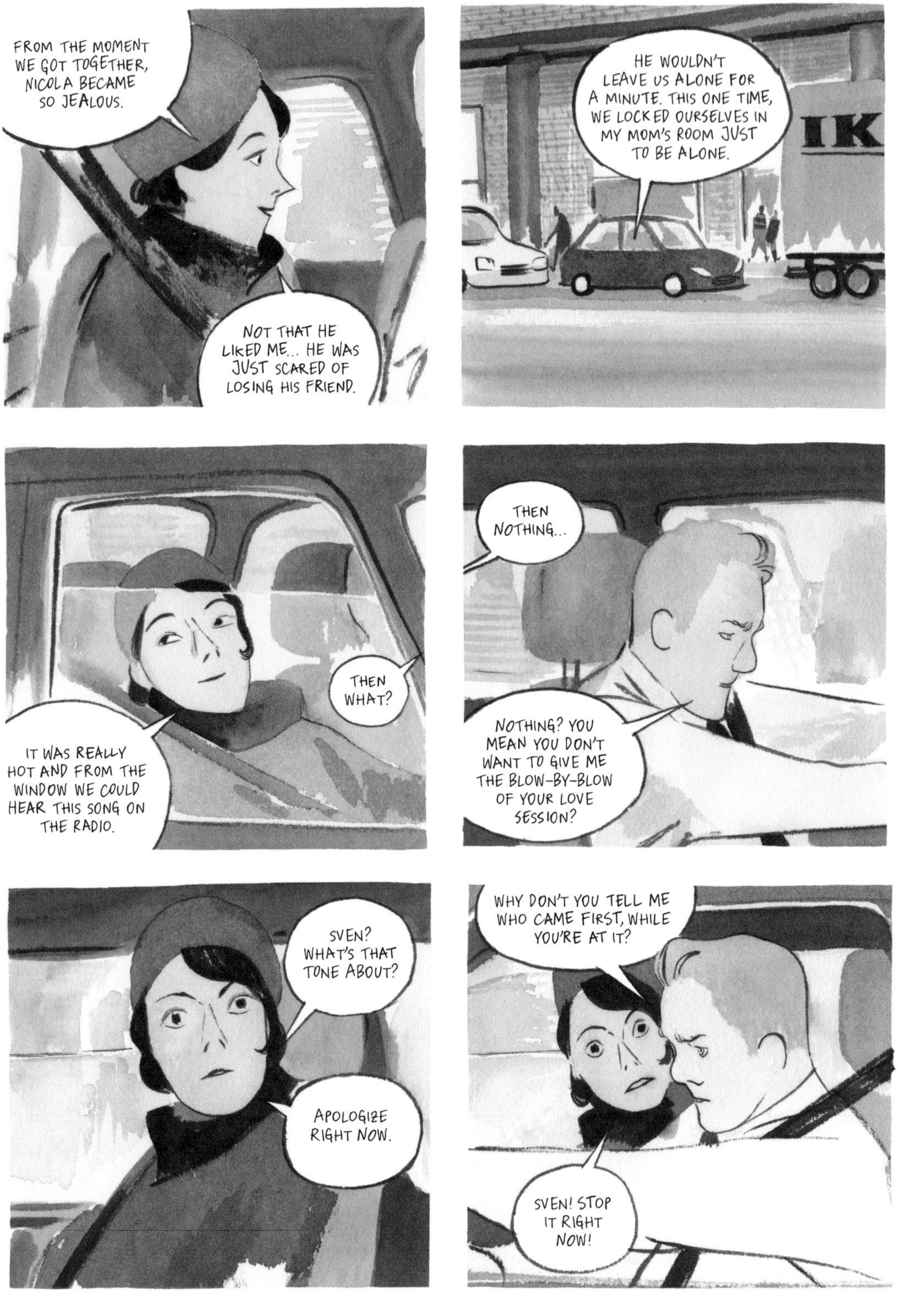
FROM THE MOMENT WE GOT TOGETHER, NICOLA BECAME SO JEALOUS.
NOT THAT HE LIKED ME... HE WAS JUST SCARED OF LOSING HIS FRIEND.
HE WOULDN'T LEAVE US ALONE FOR A MINUTE. THIS ONE TIME, WE LOCKED OURSELVES IN MY MOM'S ROOM JUST TO BE ALONE.
IK
THEN WHAT?
IT WAS REALLY HOT AND FROM THE WINDOW WE COULD HEAR THIS SONG ON THE RADIO.
THEN NOTHING...
NOTHING? YOU MEAN YOU DON'T WANT TO GIVE ME THE BLOW-BY-BLOW OF YOUR LOVE SESSION?
SVEN? WHAT'S THAT TONE ABOUT?
APOLOGIZE RIGHT NOW.
WHY DON'T YOU TELL ME WHO CAME FIRST, WHILE YOU'RE AT IT?
SVEN! STOP IT RIGHT NOW!

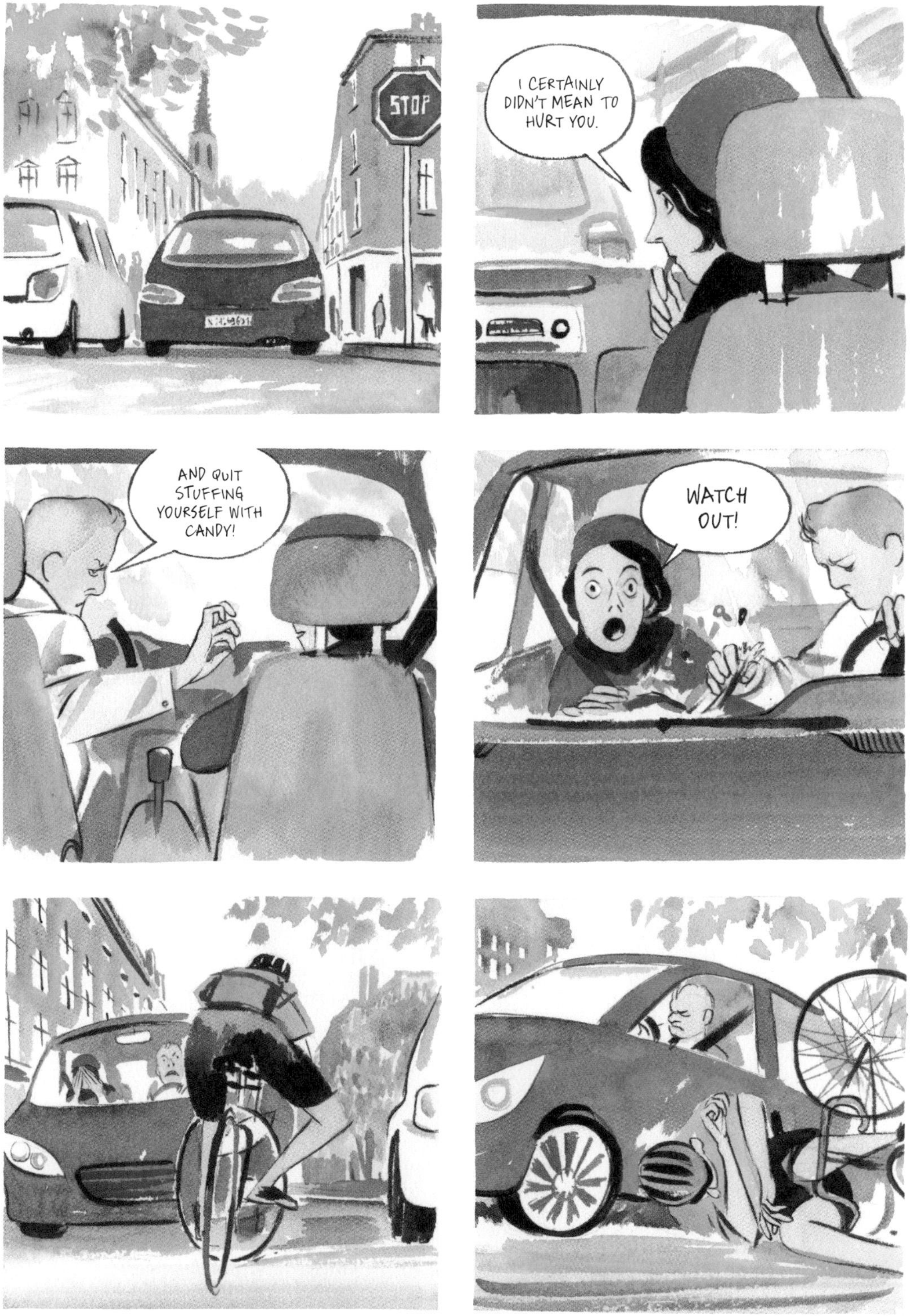
STOP
I CERTAINLY DIDN'T MEAN TO HURT YOU.
AND QUIT STUFFING YOURSELF WITH CANDY!
WATCH OUT!

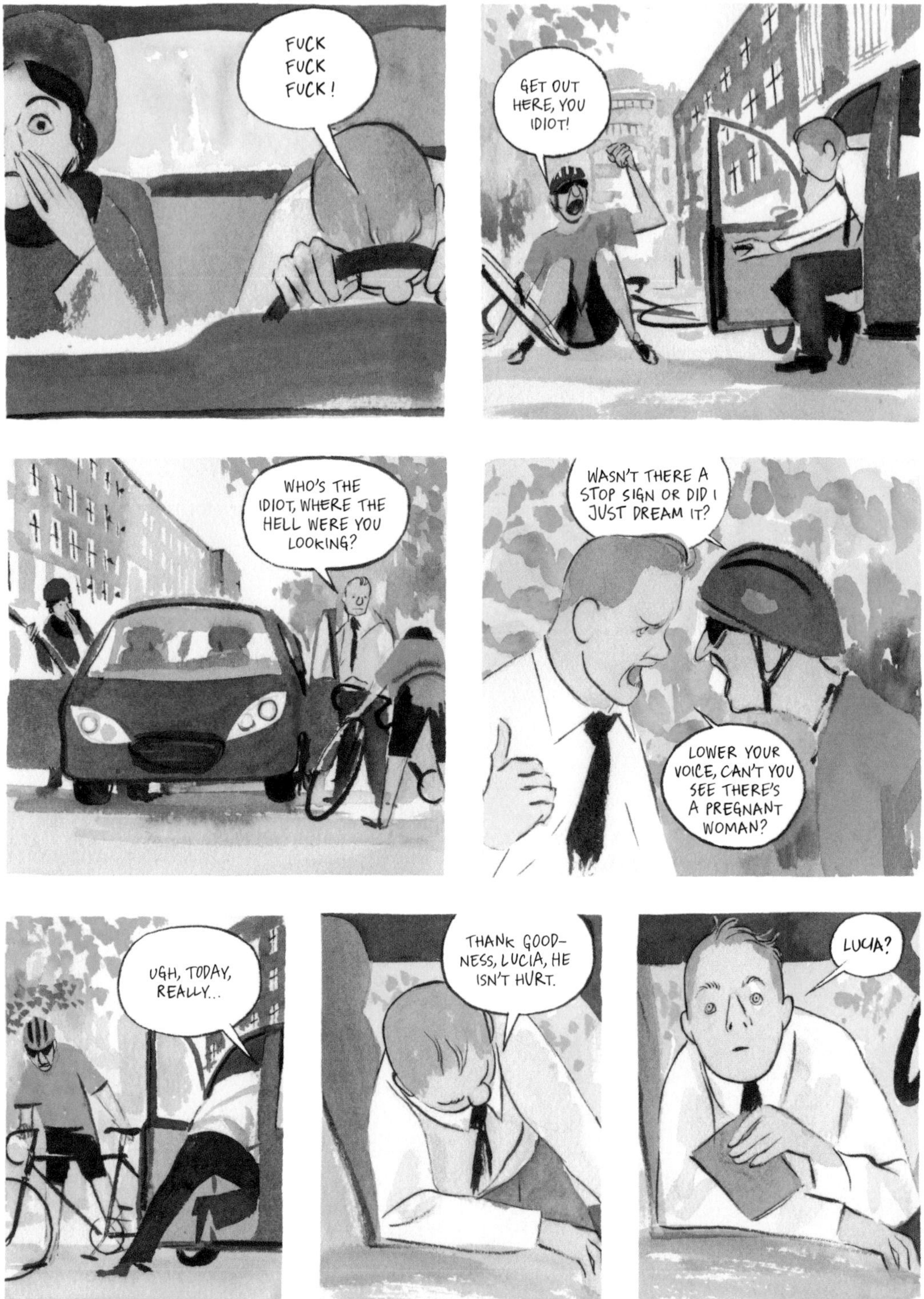
FUCK
FUCK
FUCK!
GET OUT HERE, YOU IDIOT!
WHO'S THE IDIOT, WHERE THE HELL WERE YOU LOOKING?
WASN'T THERE A STOP SIGN OR DID I JUST DREAM IT?
LOWER YOUR VOICE, CAN'T YOU SEE THERE'S A PREGNANT WOMAN?
UGH, TODAY, REALLY...
THANK GOOD-NESS, LUCIA, HE ISN'T HURT.
LUCIA?

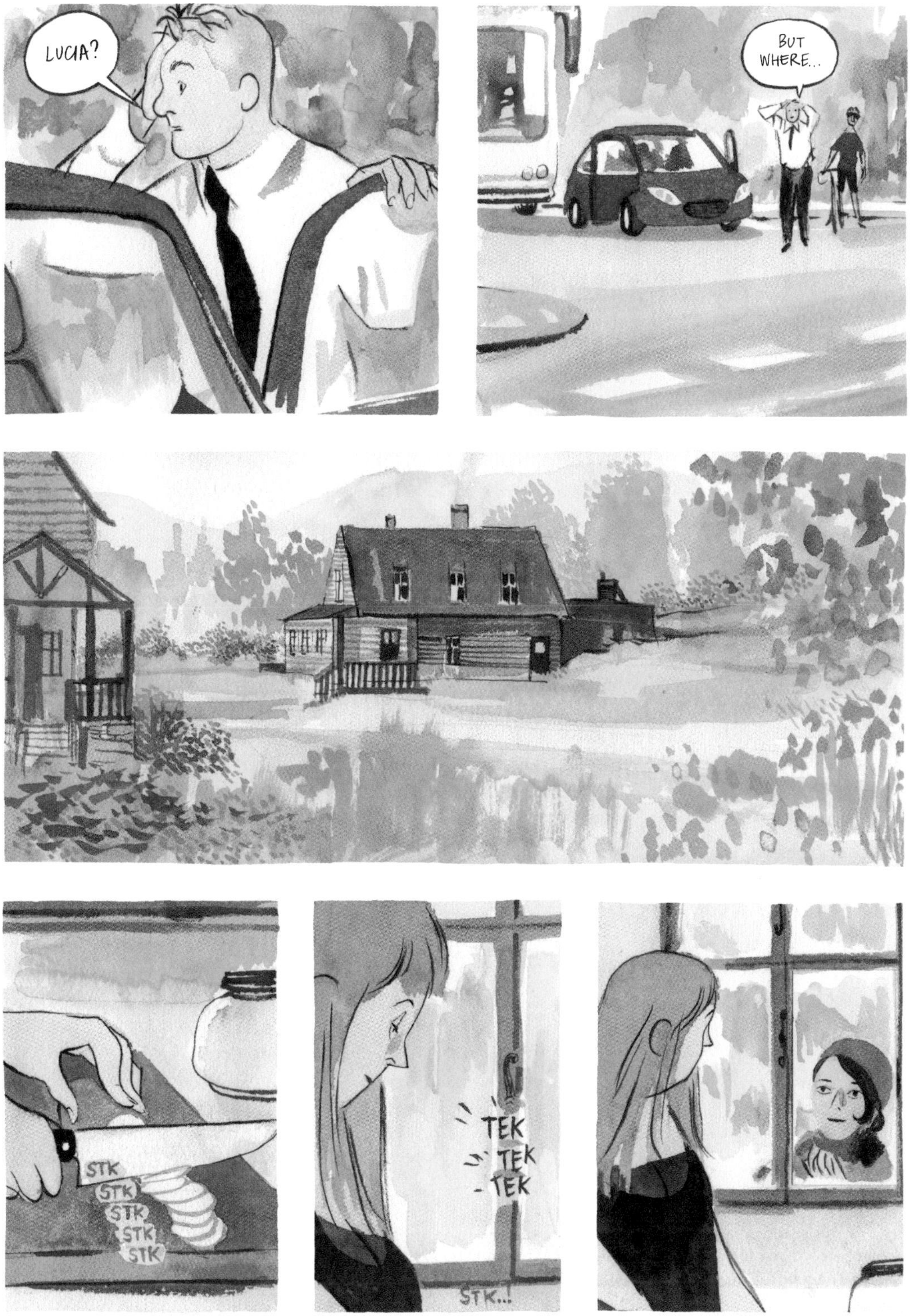
LUCIA?
BUT WHERE...
STK
STK
STK
STK
STK
TEK
TEK
TEK
STK..!

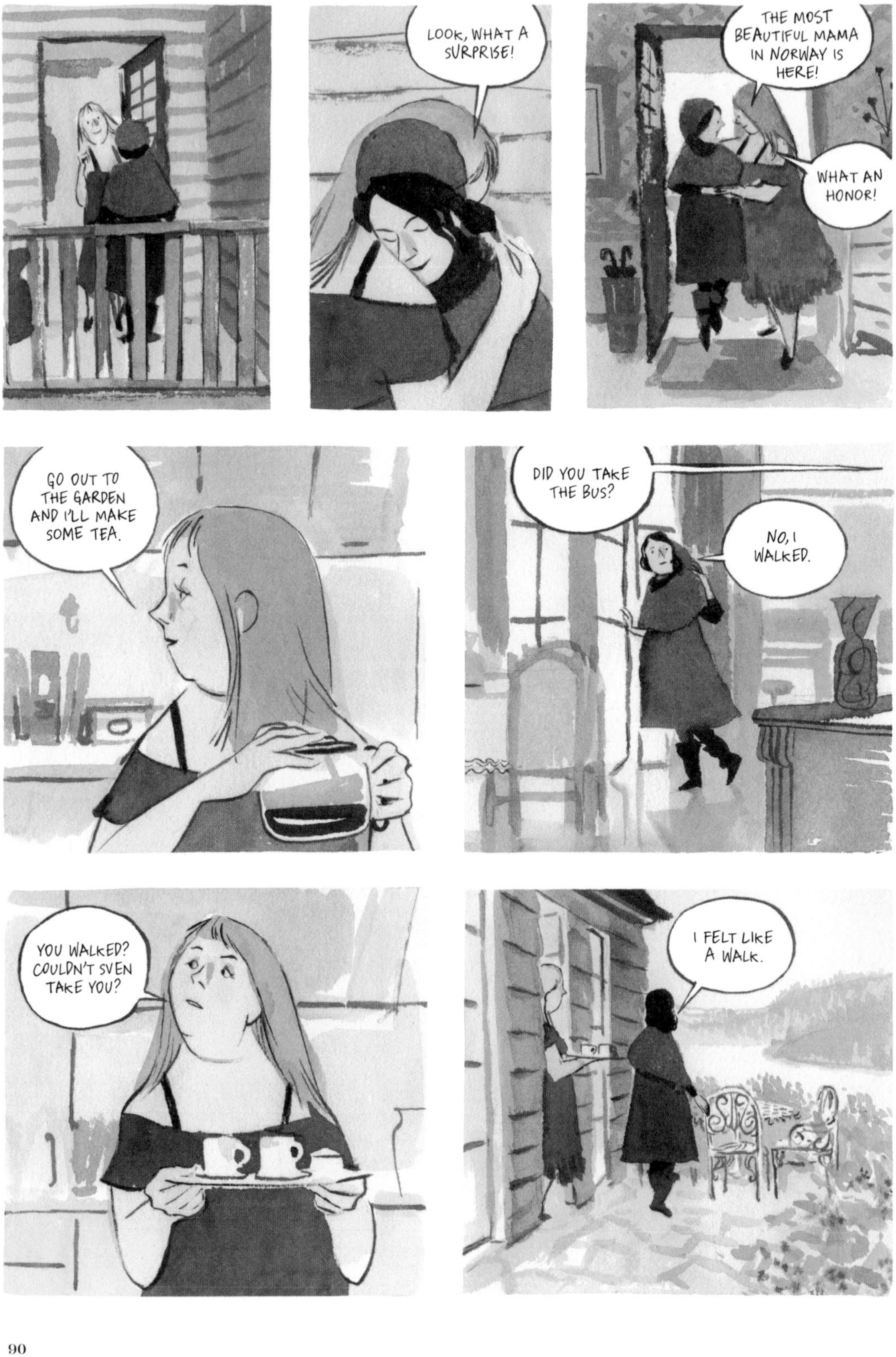

LOOK, WHAT A SURPRISE!
THE MOST BEAUTIFUL MAMA IN NORWAY IS HERE!
WHAT AN HONOR!
GO OUT TO THE GARDEN AND I'LL MAKE SOME TEA.
DID YOU TAKE THE BUS?
NO, I WALKED.
YOU WALKED? COULDN'T SVEN TAKE YOU?
I FELT LIKE A WALK.

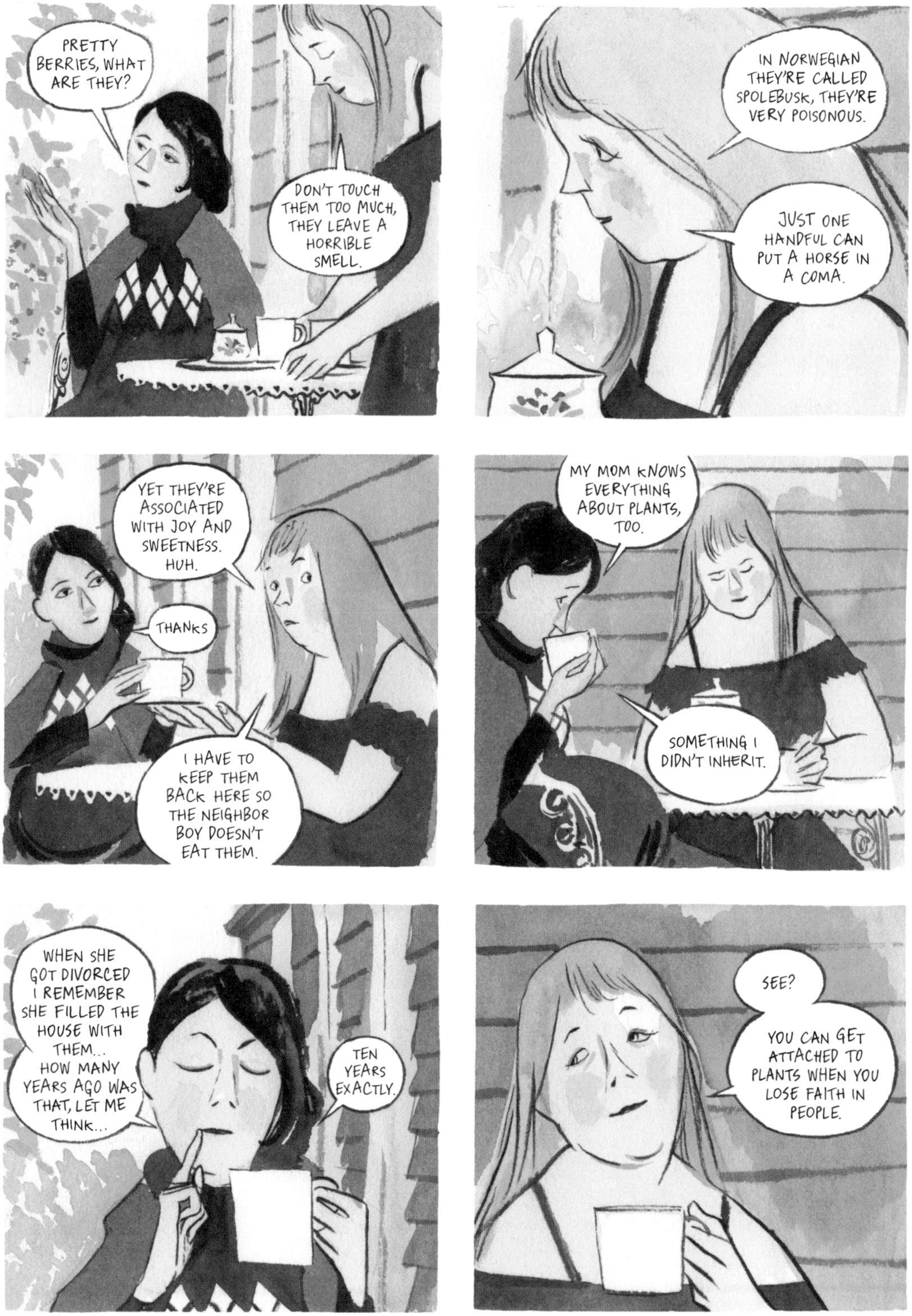
PRETTY BERRIES, WHAT ARE THEY?
DON'T TOUCH THEM TOO MUCH, THEY LEAVE A HORRIBLE SMELL.
IN NORWEGIAN THEY'RE CALLED SPOLEBUSK, THEY'RE VERY POISONOUS.
JUST ONE HANDFUL CAN PUT A HORSE IN A COMA.
YET THEY'RE ASSOCIATED WITH JOY AND SWEETNESS. HUH.
THANKS
I HAVE TO KEEP THEM BACK HERE SO THE NEIGHBOR BOY DOESN'T EAT THEM.
MY MOM KNOWS EVERYTHING ABOUT PLANTS, TOO.
SOMETHING I DIDN'T INHERIT.
WHEN SHE GOT DIVORCED I REMEMBER SHE FILLED THE HOUSE WITH THEM... HOW MANY YEARS AGO WAS THAT, LET ME THINK...
TEN YEARS EXACTLY.
SEE?
YOU CAN GET ATTACHED TO PLANTS WHEN YOU LOSE FAITH IN PEOPLE.

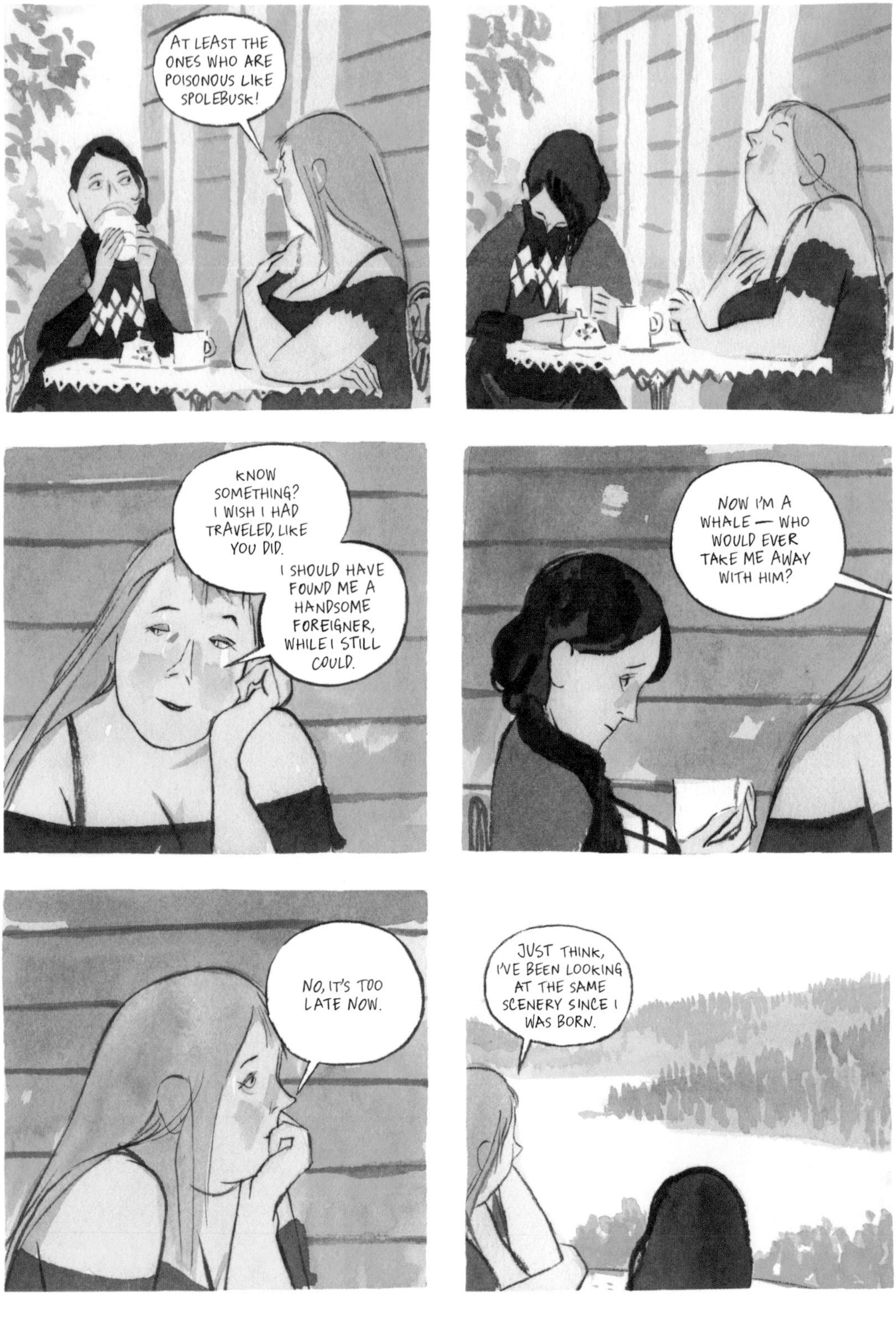
AT LEAST THE ONES WHO ARE POISONOUS LIKE SPOLEBUSK!
KNOW SOMETHING? I WISH I HAD TRAVELED, LIKE YOU DID.
I SHOULD HAVE FOUND ME A HANDSOME FOREIGNER, WHILE I STILL COULD.
NOW I'M A WHALE — WHO WOULD EVER TAKE ME AWAY WITH HIM?
NO, IT'S TOO LATE NOW.
JUST THINK, I'VE BEEN LOOKING AT THE SAME SCENERY SINCE I WAS BORN.

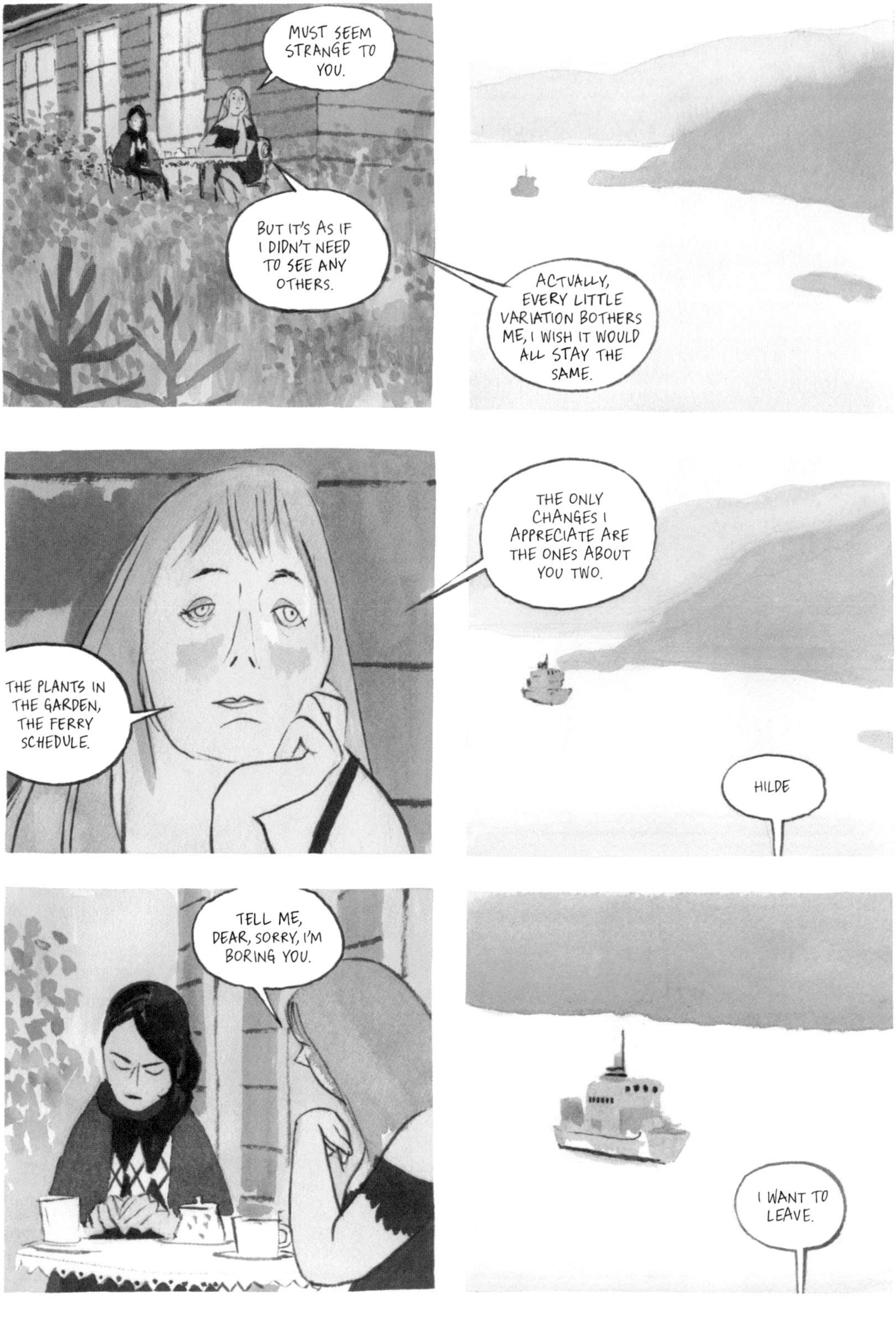
MUST SEEM STRANGE TO YOU.
BUT IT'S AS IF I DIDN'T NEED TO SEE ANY OTHERS.
ACTUALLY, EVERY LITTLE VARIATION BOTHERS ME, I WISH IT WOULD ALL STAY THE SAME.
THE ONLY CHANGES I APPRECIATE ARE THE ONES ABOUT YOU TWO.
THE PLANTS IN THE GARDEN, THE FERRY SCHEDULE.
HILDE
TELL ME, DEAR, SORRY, I'M BORING YOU.
I WANT TO LEAVE.

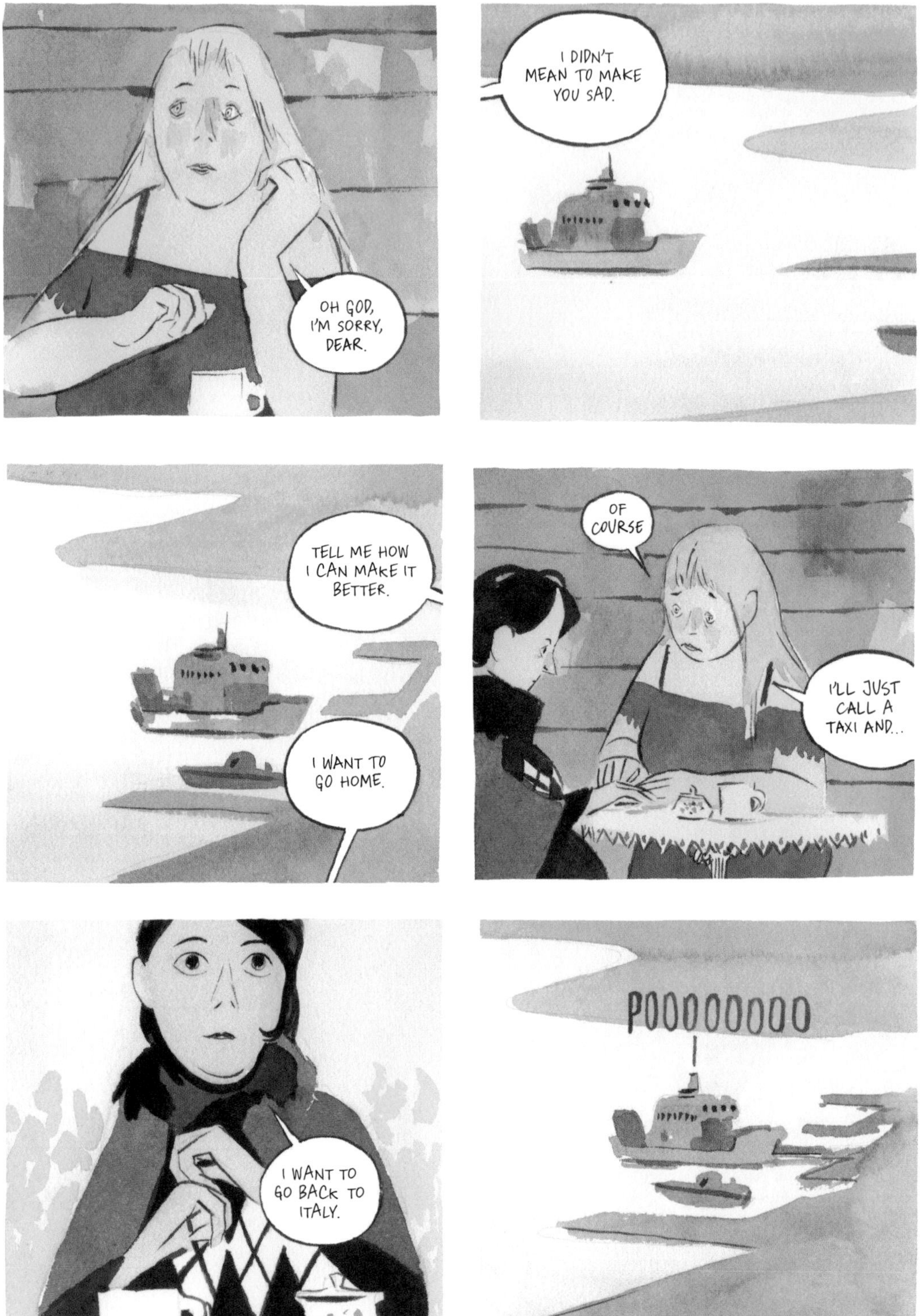
OH GOD, I'M SORRY, DEAR.
I DIDN'T MEAN TO MAKE YOU SAD.
TELL ME HOW I CAN MAKE IT BETTER.
I WANT TO GO HOME.
OF COURSE
I'LL JUST CALL A TAXI AND...
I WANT TO GO BACK TO ITALY.
POOOOOOOO

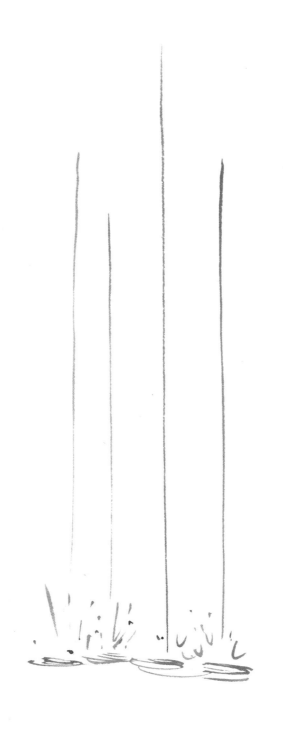

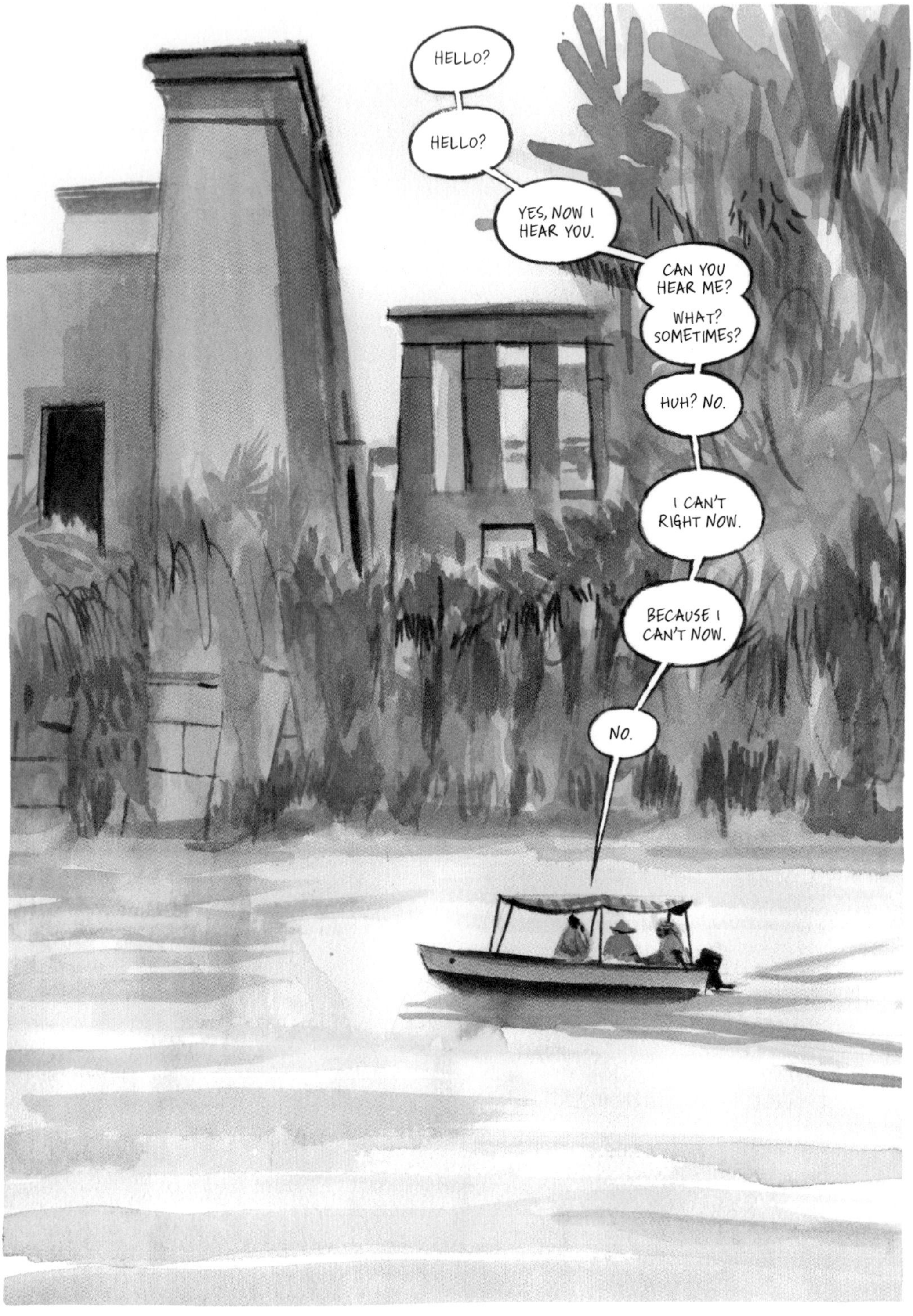
HELLO?
HELLO?
YES, NOW I HEAR YOU.
CAN YOU HEAR ME?
WHAT? SOMETIMES?
HUH? NO.
I CAN'T RIGHT NOW.
BECAUSE I CAN'T NOW.
NO.

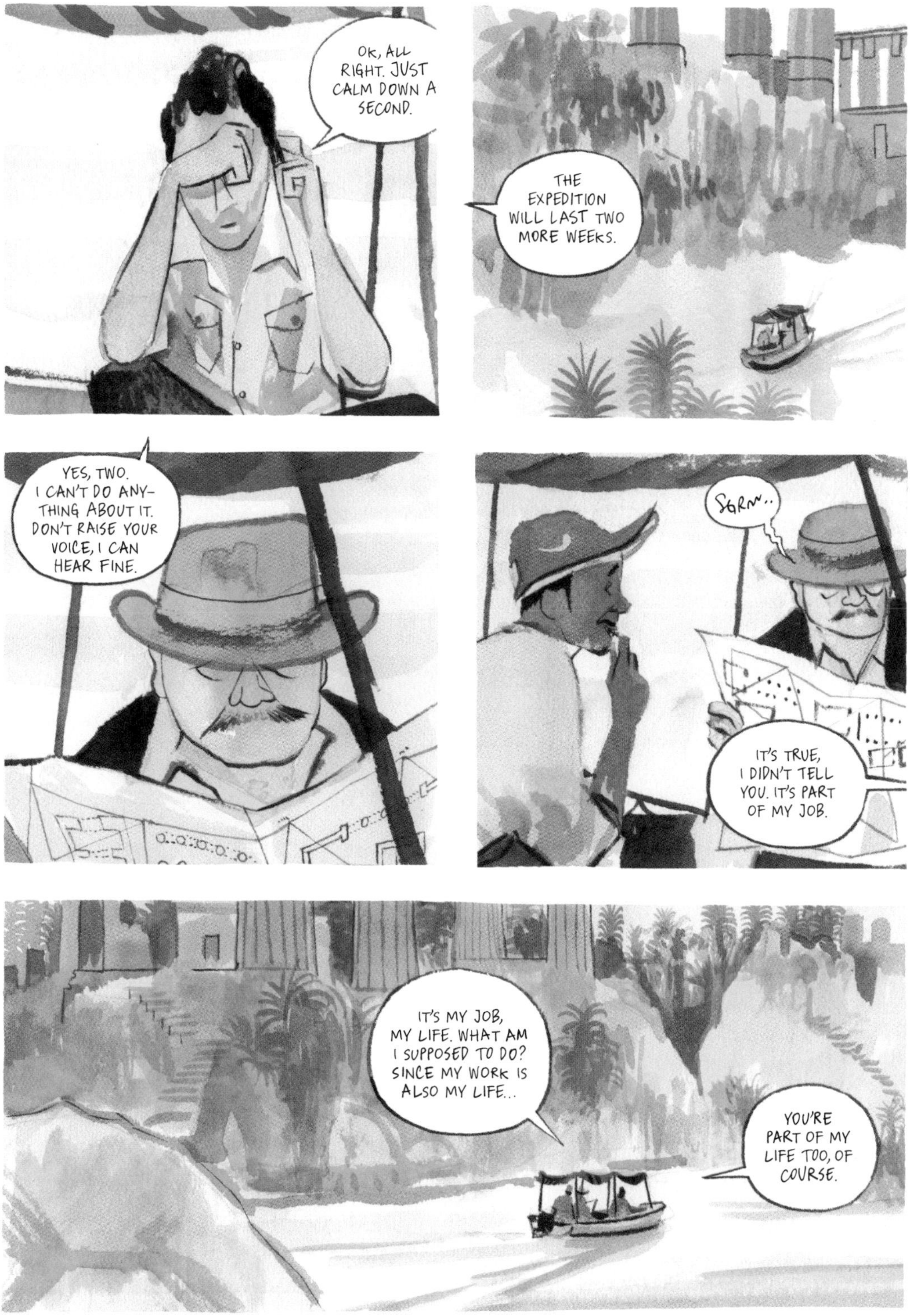
OK, ALL RIGHT. JUST CALM DOWN A SECOND.
THE EXPEDITION WILL LAST TWO MORE WEEKS.
YES, TWO. I CAN'T DO ANYTHING ABOUT IT. DON'T RAISE YOUR VOICE, I CAN HEAR FINE.
SGRM..
IT'S TRUE, I DIDN'T TELL YOU. IT'S PART OF MY JOB.
IT'S MY JOB, MY LIFE. WHAT AM I SUPPOSED TO DO? SINCE MY WORK IS ALSO MY LIFE...
YOU'RE PART OF MY LIFE TOO, OF COURSE.

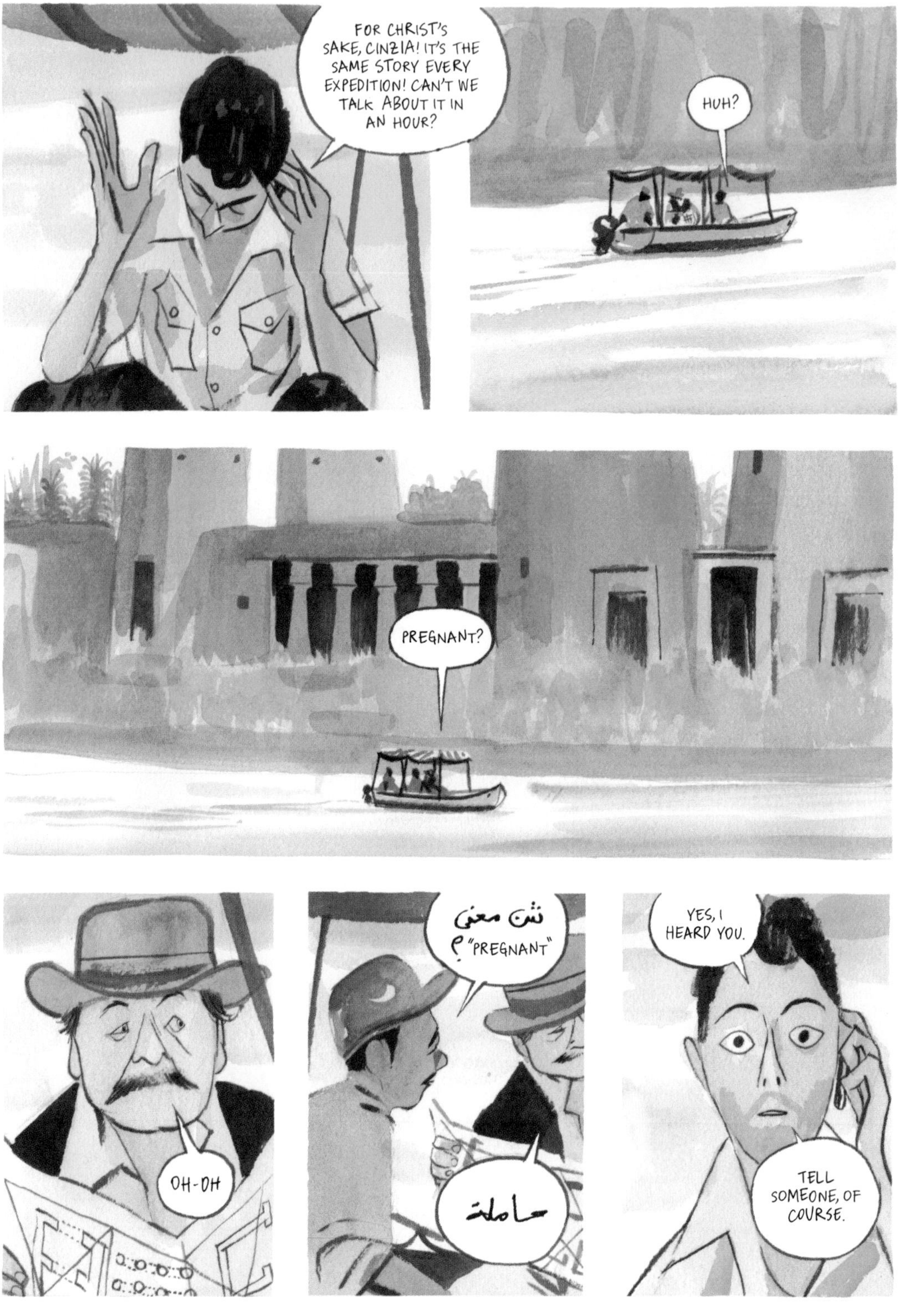

FOR CHRIST'S SAKE, CINZIA! IT'S THE SAME STORY EVERY EXPEDITION! CAN'T WE TALK ABOUT IT IN AN HOUR?
HUH?
PREGNANT?
OH-OH
شن معنى "PREGNANT" ؟
حاملة
YES, I HEARD YOU.
TELL SOMEONE, OF COURSE.

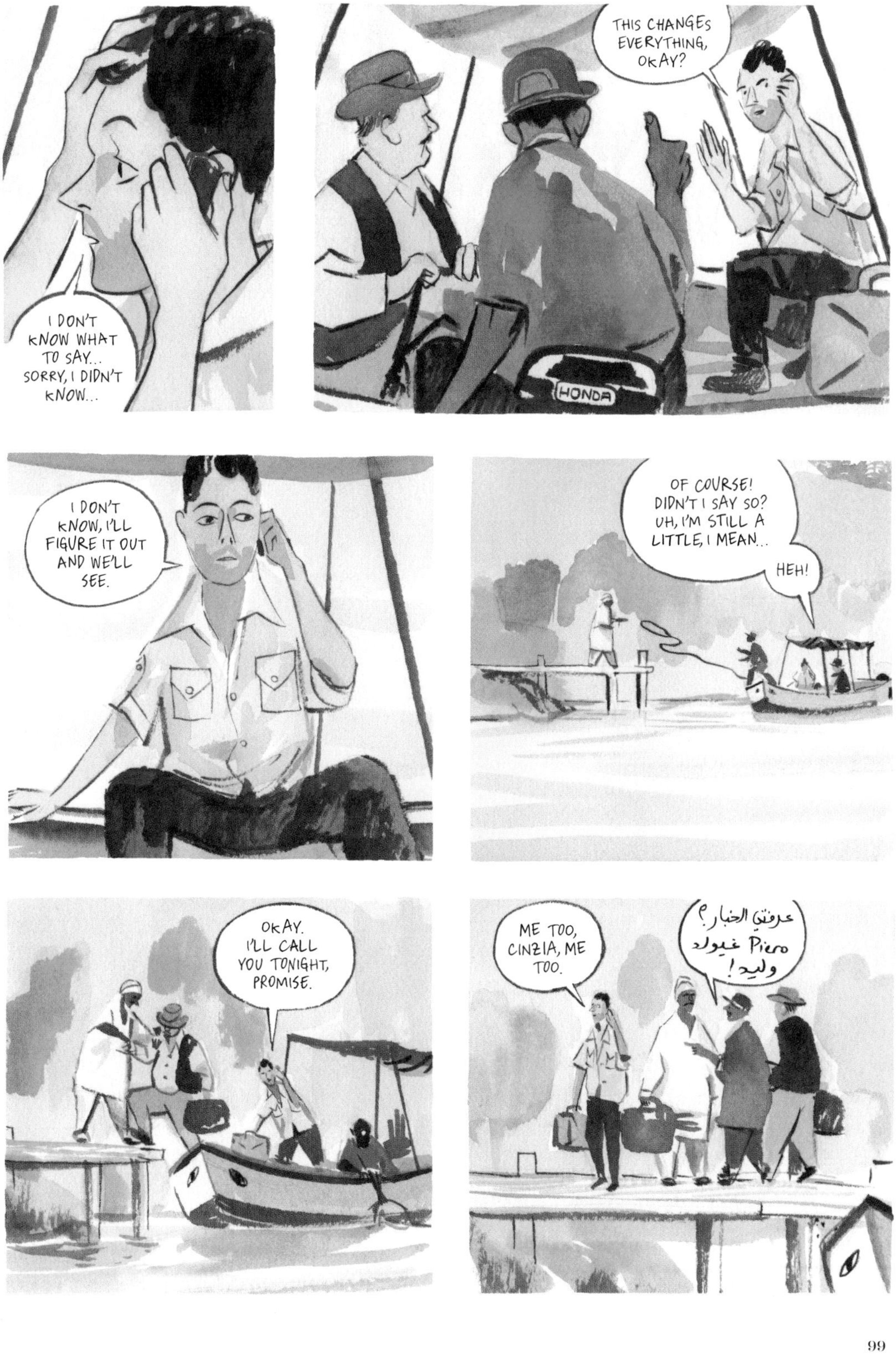
I DON'T KNOW WHAT TO SAY... SORRY, I DIDN'T KNOW...
THIS CHANGES EVERYTHING, OKAY?
HONDA
I DON'T KNOW, I'LL FIGURE IT OUT AND WE'LL SEE.
OF COURSE! DIDN'T I SAY SO? UH, I'M STILL A LITTLE, I MEAN...
HEH!
OKAY. I'LL CALL YOU TONIGHT, PROMISE.
ME TOO, CINZIA, ME TOO.
عرفتي الخبار؟ Piero غيولد وليد!

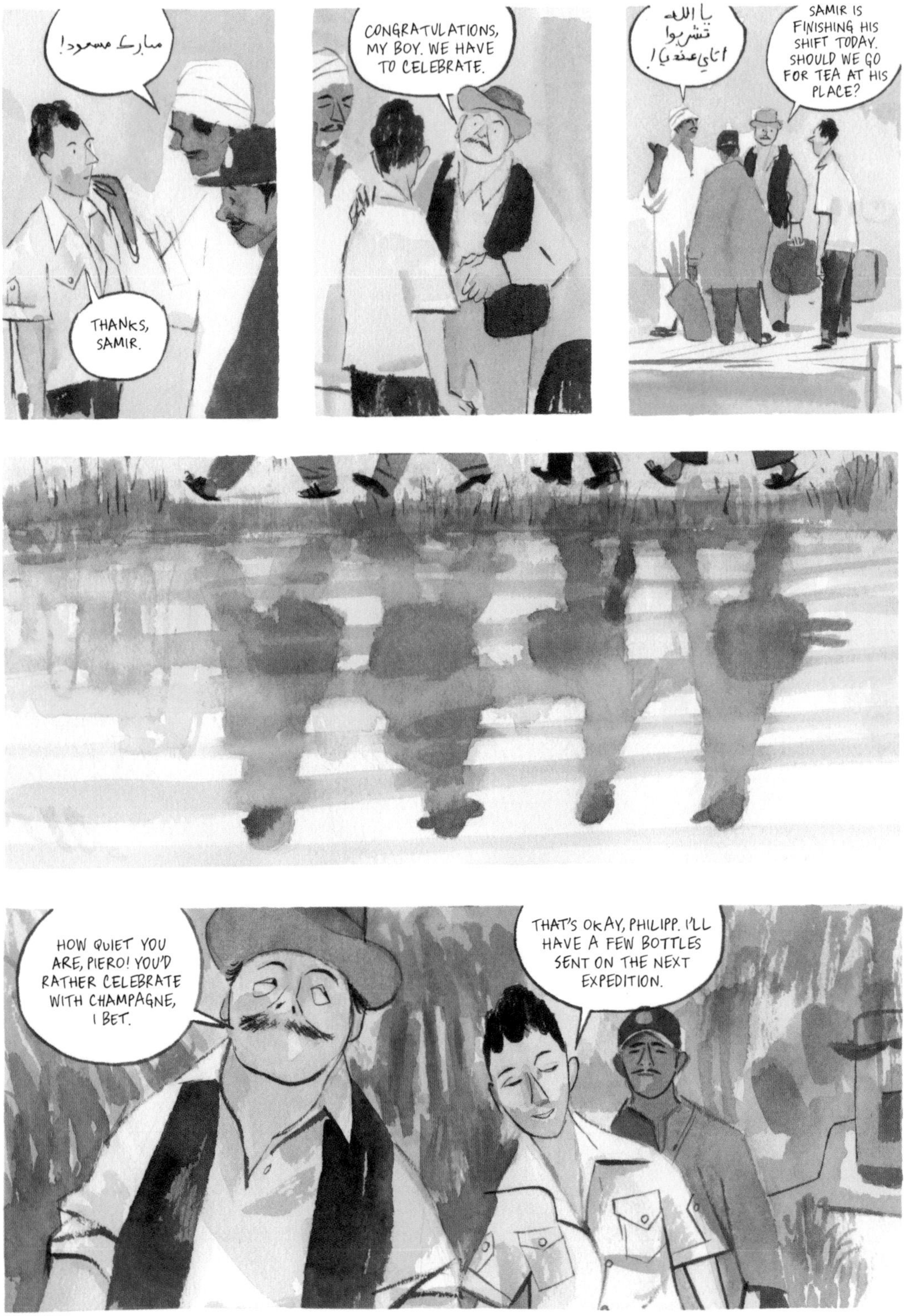
مبارك مسعود!
CONGRATULATIONS, MY BOY. WE HAVE TO CELEBRATE.
THANKS, SAMIR.
يا الله تشربوا اتاي عندي!
SAMIR IS FINISHING HIS SHIFT TODAY. SHOULD WE GO FOR TEA AT HIS PLACE?
HOW QUIET YOU ARE, PIERO! YOU'D RATHER CELEBRATE WITH CHAMPAGNE, I BET.
THAT'S OKAY, PHILIPP. I'LL HAVE A FEW BOTTLES SENT ON THE NEXT EXPEDITION.

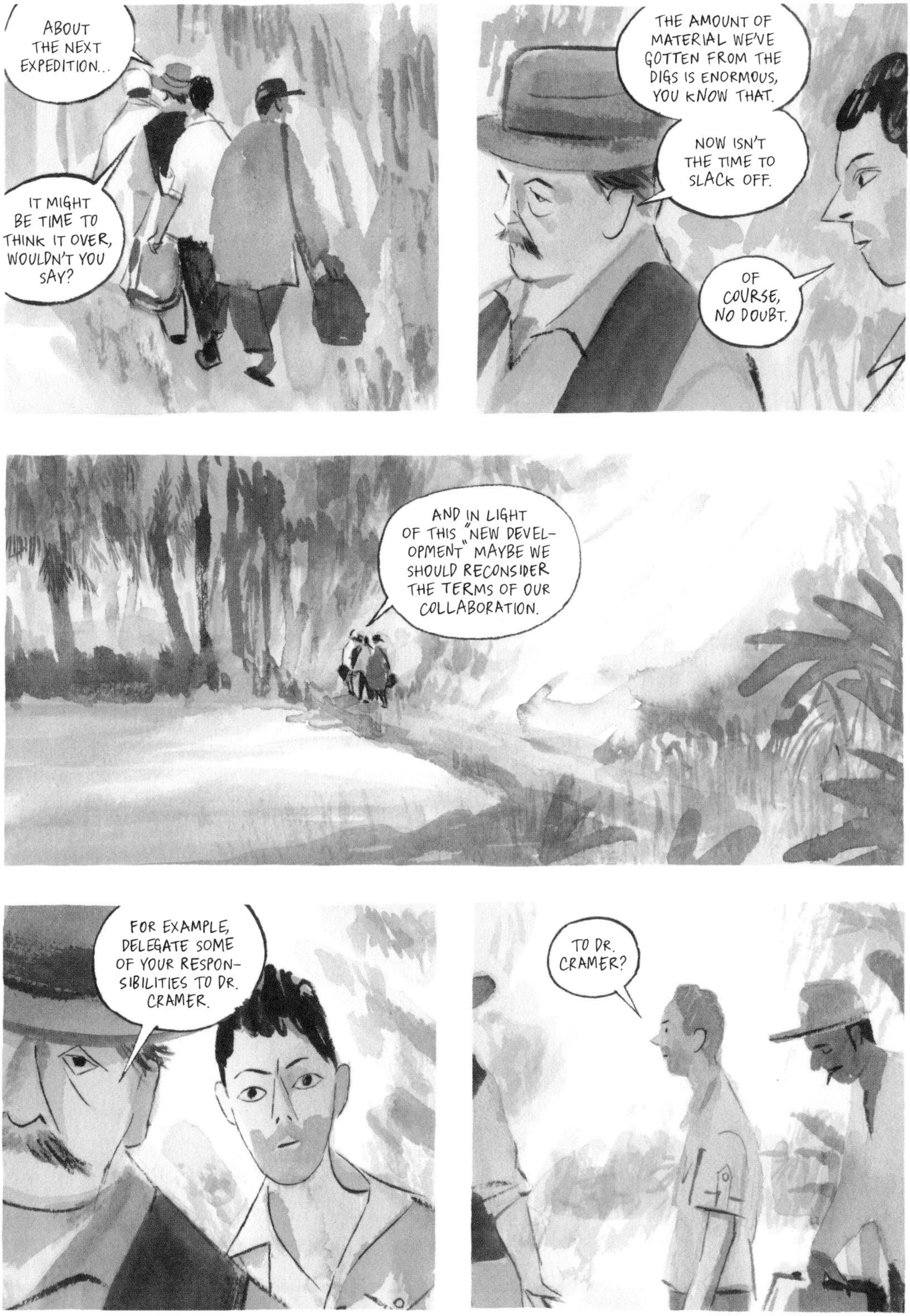
ABOUT THE NEXT EXPEDITION...
IT MIGHT BE TIME TO THINK IT OVER, WOULDN'T YOU SAY?
THE AMOUNT OF MATERIAL WE'VE GOTTEN FROM THE DIGS IS ENORMOUS, YOU KNOW THAT.
NOW ISN'T THE TIME TO SLACK OFF.
OF COURSE, NO DOUBT.
AND IN LIGHT OF THIS "NEW DEVELOPMENT" MAYBE WE SHOULD RECONSIDER THE TERMS OF OUR COLLABORATION.
FOR EXAMPLE, DELEGATE SOME OF YOUR RESPONSIBILITIES TO DR. CRAMER.
TO DR. CRAMER?

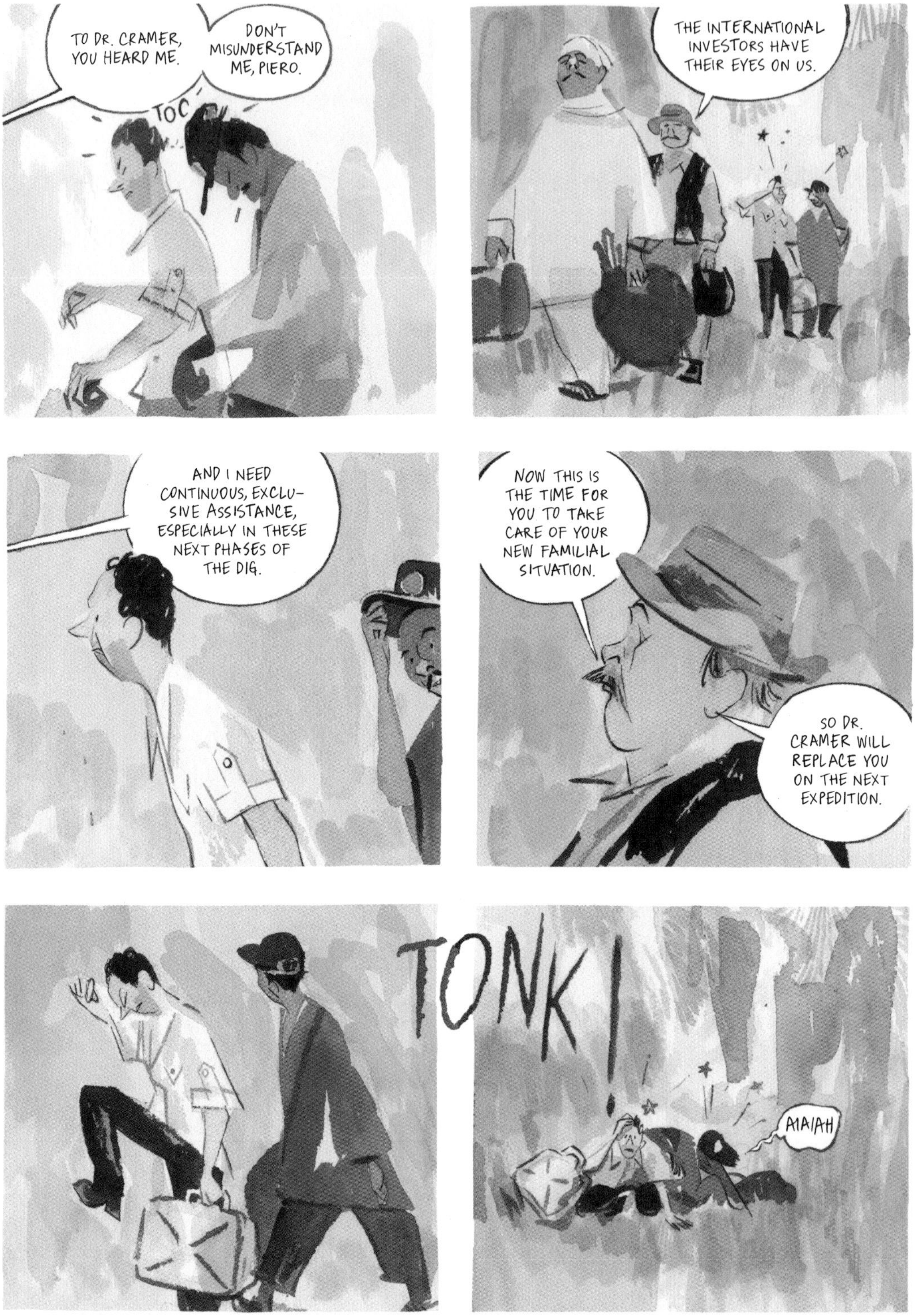
TO DR. CRAMER, YOU HEARD ME.
DON'T MISUNDERSTAND ME, PIERO.
TOC
THE INTERNATIONAL INVESTORS HAVE THEIR EYES ON US.
AND I NEED CONTINUOUS, EXCLUSIVE ASSISTANCE, ESPECIALLY IN THESE NEXT PHASES OF THE DIG.
NOW THIS IS THE TIME FOR YOU TO TAKE CARE OF YOUR NEW FAMILIAL SITUATION.
SO DR. CRAMER WILL REPLACE YOU ON THE NEXT EXPEDITION.
TONK!
AIAIAH

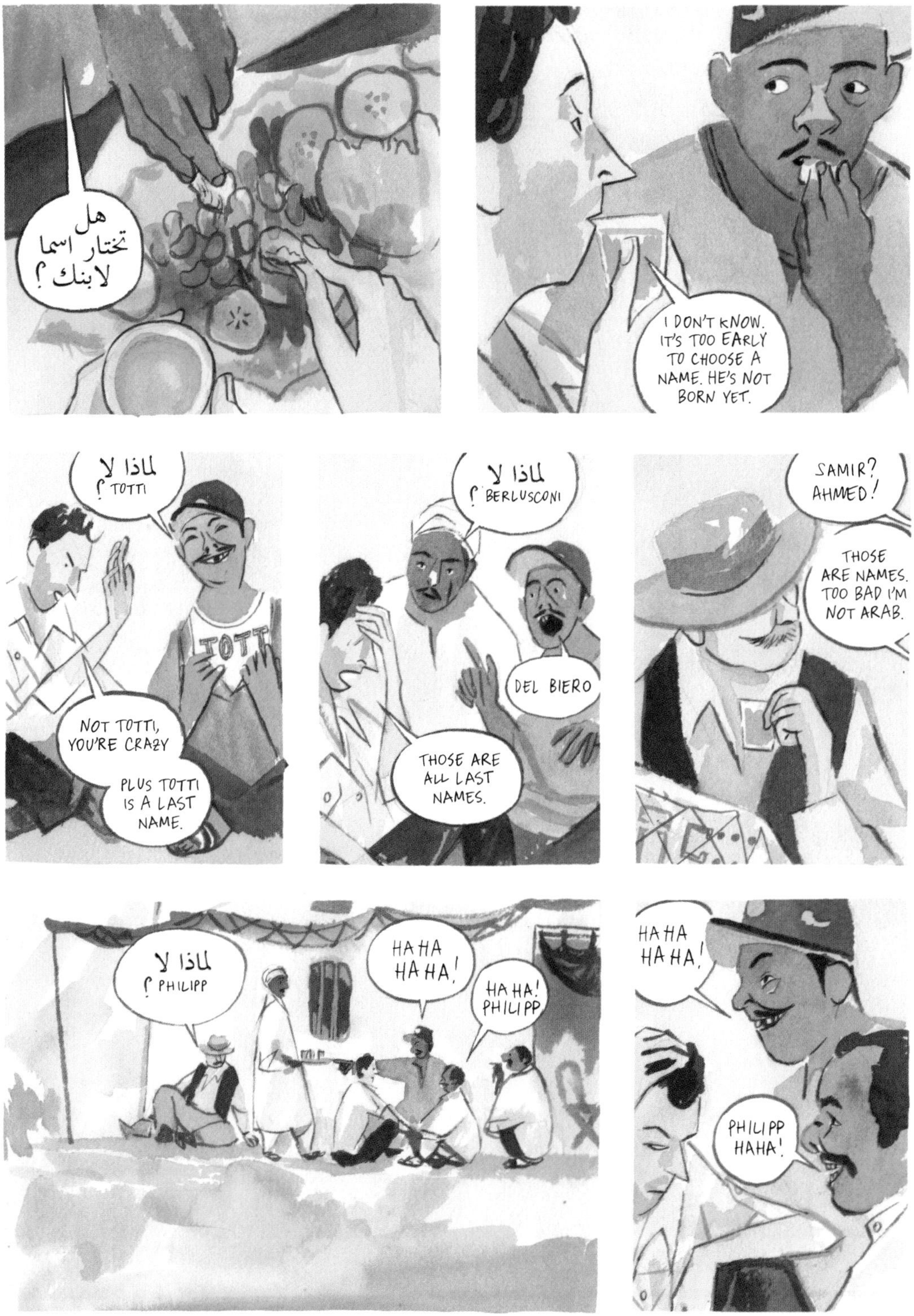
هل تختار اسما لابنك ؟
I DON'T KNOW. IT'S TOO EARLY TO CHOOSE A NAME. HE'S NOT BORN YET.
لماذا لا TOTTI ؟
NOT TOTTI, YOU'RE CRAZY
PLUS TOTTI IS A LAST NAME.
لماذا لا BERLUSCONI ؟
DEL BIERO
THOSE ARE ALL LAST NAMES.
SAMIR? AHMED!
THOSE ARE NAMES. TOO BAD I'M NOT ARAB.
لماذا لا PHILIPP ؟
HA HA HA HA!
HA HA! PHILIPP
HA HA HA HA!
PHILIPP HAHA!

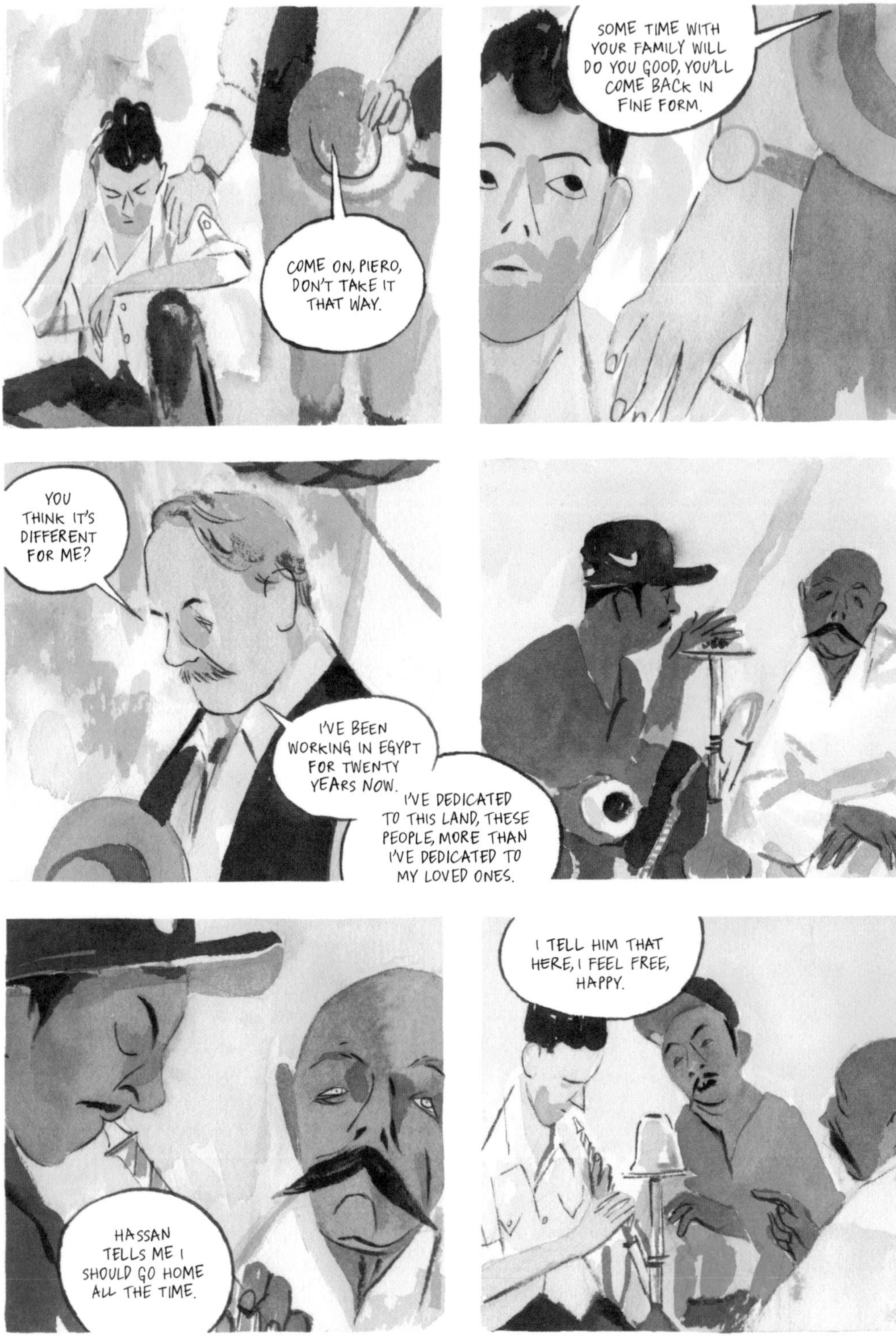
COME ON, PIERO, DON'T TAKE IT THAT WAY.
SOME TIME WITH YOUR FAMILY WILL DO YOU GOOD, YOU'LL COME BACK IN FINE FORM.
YOU THINK IT'S DIFFERENT FOR ME?
I'VE BEEN WORKING IN EGYPT FOR TWENTY YEARS NOW.
I'VE DEDICATED TO THIS LAND, THESE PEOPLE, MORE THAN I'VE DEDICATED TO MY LOVED ONES.
HASSAN TELLS ME I SHOULD GO HOME ALL THE TIME.
I TELL HIM THAT HERE, I FEEL FREE, HAPPY.

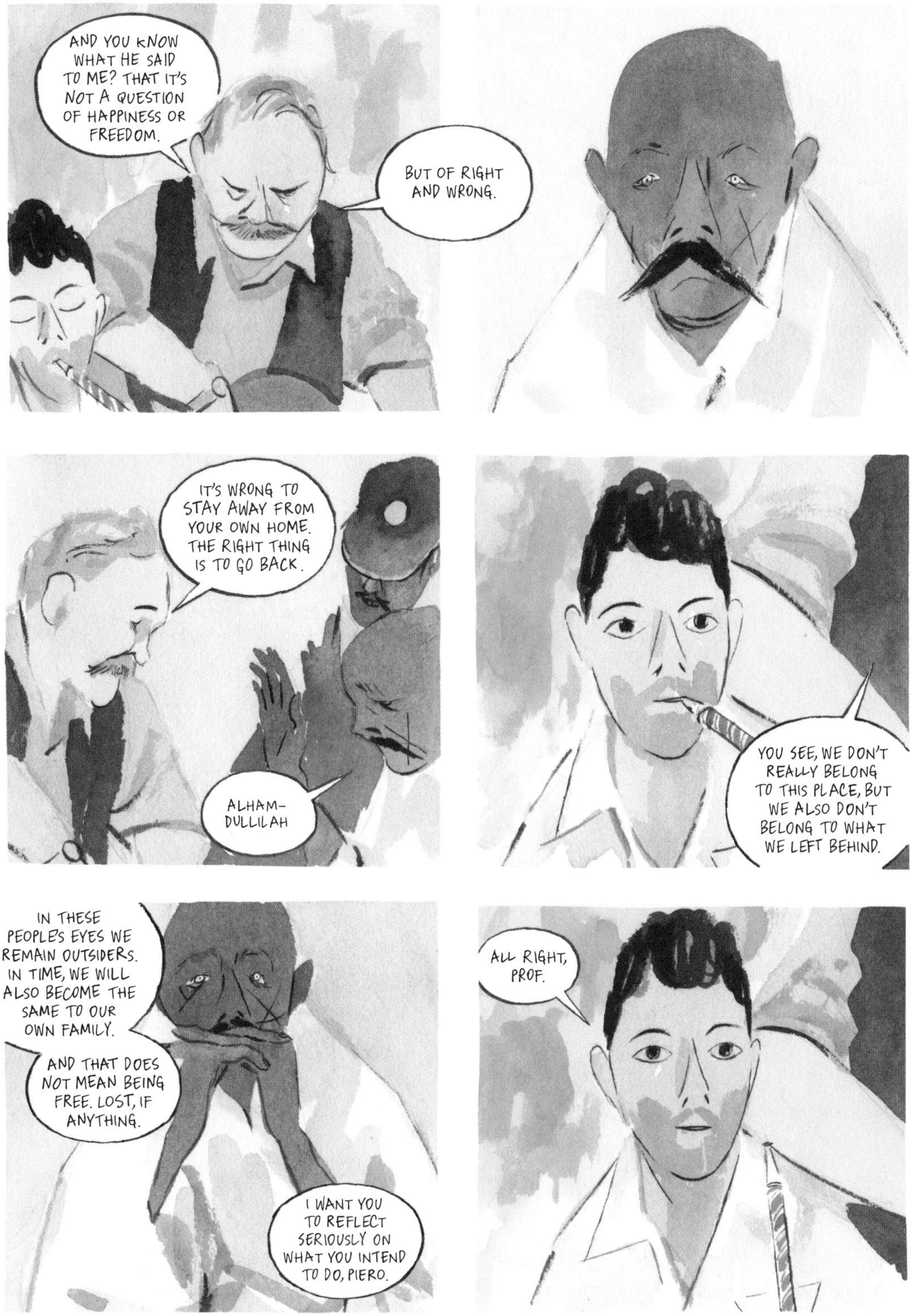
AND YOU KNOW WHAT HE SAID TO ME? THAT IT'S NOT A QUESTION OF HAPPINESS OR FREEDOM.
BUT OF RIGHT AND WRONG.
IT'S WRONG TO STAY AWAY FROM YOUR OWN HOME. THE RIGHT THING IS TO GO BACK.
ALHAM-DULLILAH
YOU SEE, WE DON'T REALLY BELONG TO THIS PLACE, BUT WE ALSO DON'T BELONG TO WHAT WE LEFT BEHIND.
IN THESE PEOPLE'S EYES WE REMAIN OUTSIDERS. IN TIME, WE WILL ALSO BECOME THE SAME TO OUR OWN FAMILY.
AND THAT DOES NOT MEAN BEING FREE. LOST, IF ANYTHING.
I WANT YOU TO REFLECT SERIOUSLY ON WHAT YOU INTEND TO DO, PIERO.
ALL RIGHT, PROF.

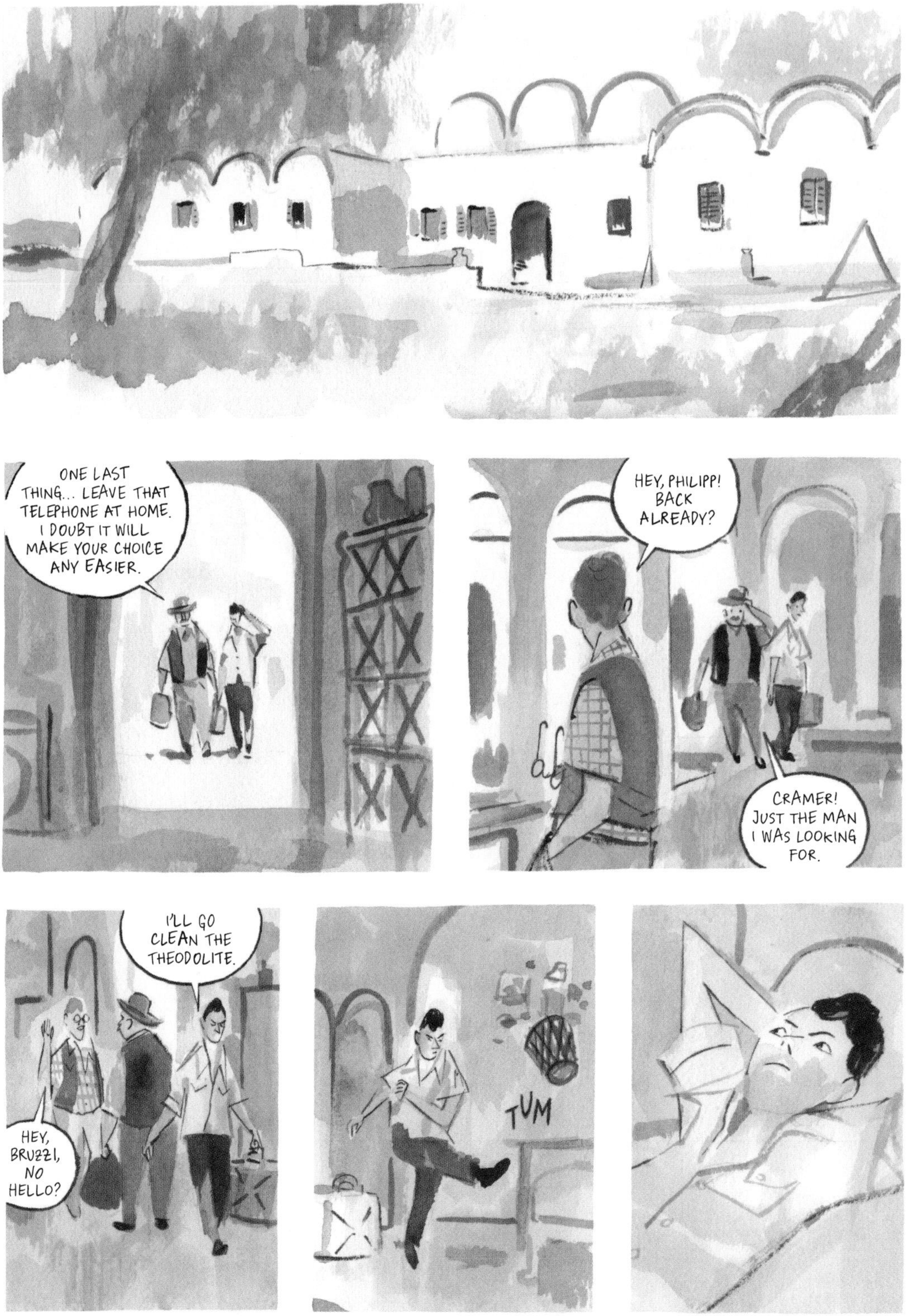
ONE LAST THING... LEAVE THAT TELEPHONE AT HOME. I DOUBT IT WILL MAKE YOUR CHOICE ANY EASIER.
HEY, PHILIPP! BACK ALREADY?
CRAMER! JUST THE MAN I WAS LOOKING FOR.
I'LL GO CLEAN THE THEODOLITE.
HEY, BRUZZI, NO HELLO?
TUM

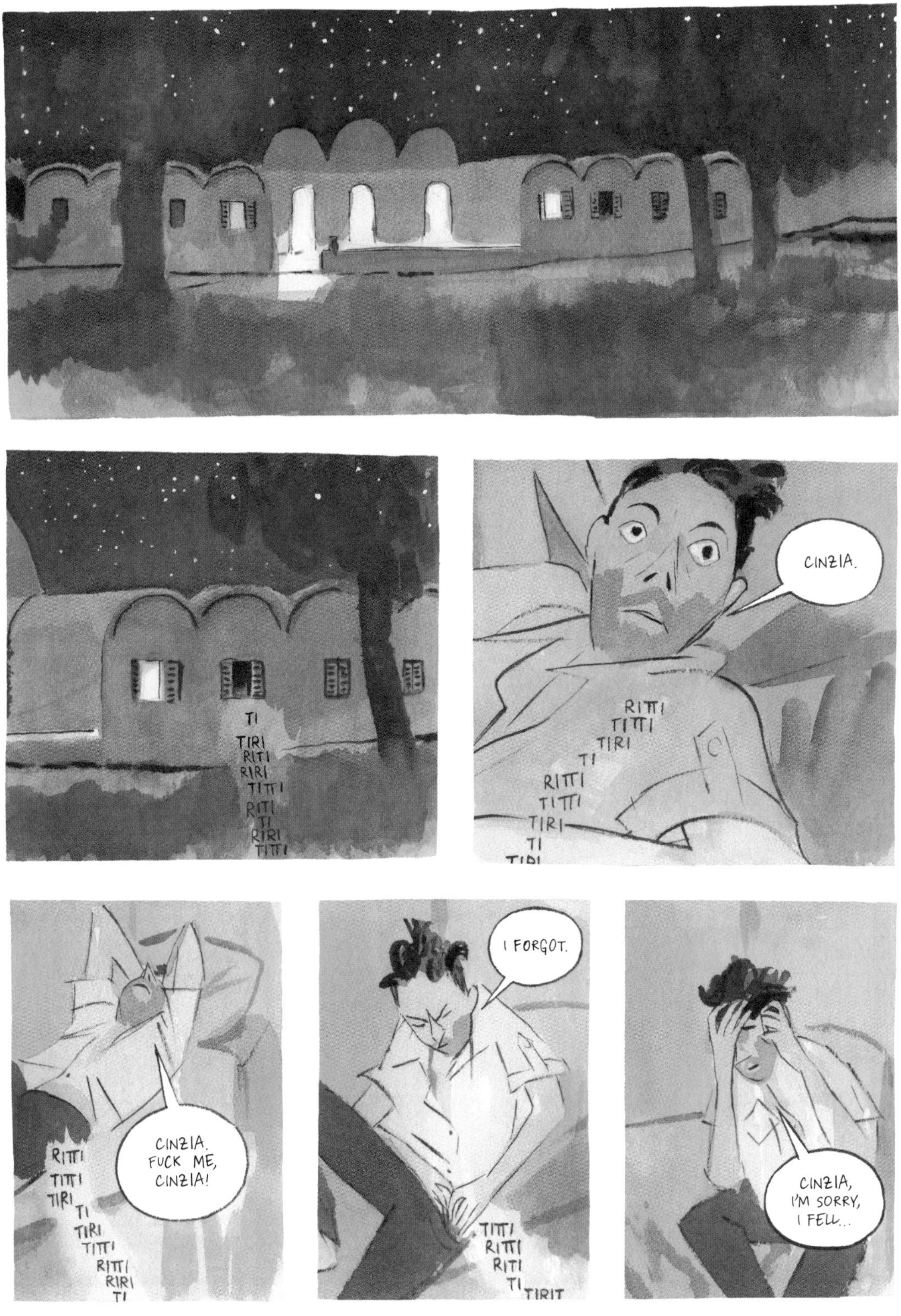

TI
TIRI
RITI
RIRI
TITTI
RITI
TI
RIRI
TITTI
CINZIA.
RITTI
TITTI
TIRI
TI
RITTI
TITTI
TIRI
TI
RITTI
TITTI
TIRI
TI
TIRI
TITTI
RITTI
RIRI
TI
CINZIA. FUCK ME, CINZIA!
I FORGOT.
TITTI
RITTI
RITI
TI
TIRIT
CINZIA, I'M SORRY, I FELL...

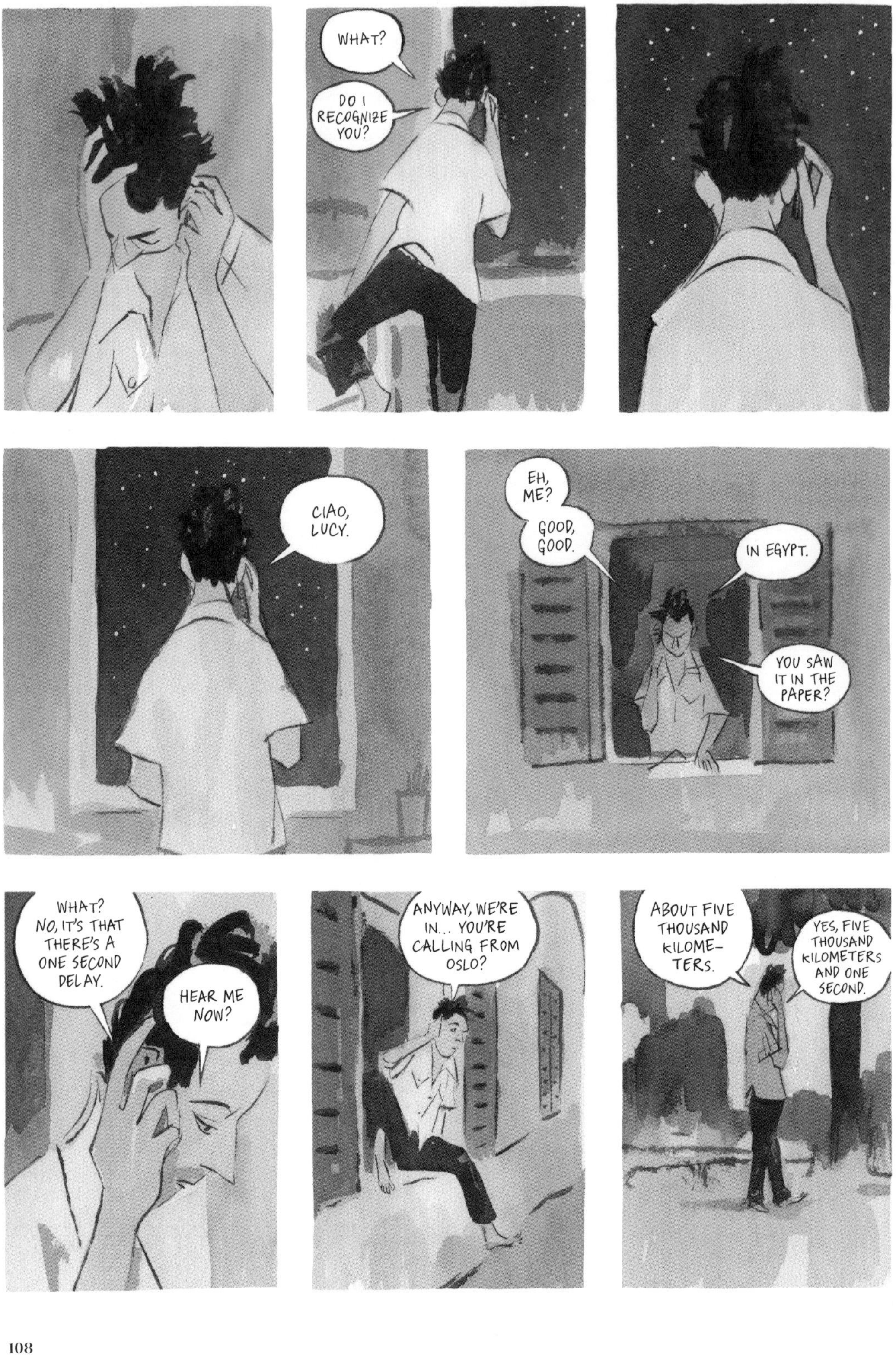
WHAT?
DO I RECOGNIZE YOU?
CIAO, LUCY.
EH, ME?
GOOD, GOOD.
IN EGYPT.
YOU SAW IT IN THE PAPER?
WHAT? NO, IT'S THAT THERE'S A ONE SECOND DELAY.
HEAR ME NOW?
ANYWAY, WE'RE IN... YOU'RE CALLING FROM OSLO?
ABOUT FIVE THOUSAND KILOME-TERS.
YES, FIVE THOUSAND KILOMETERS AND ONE SECOND.

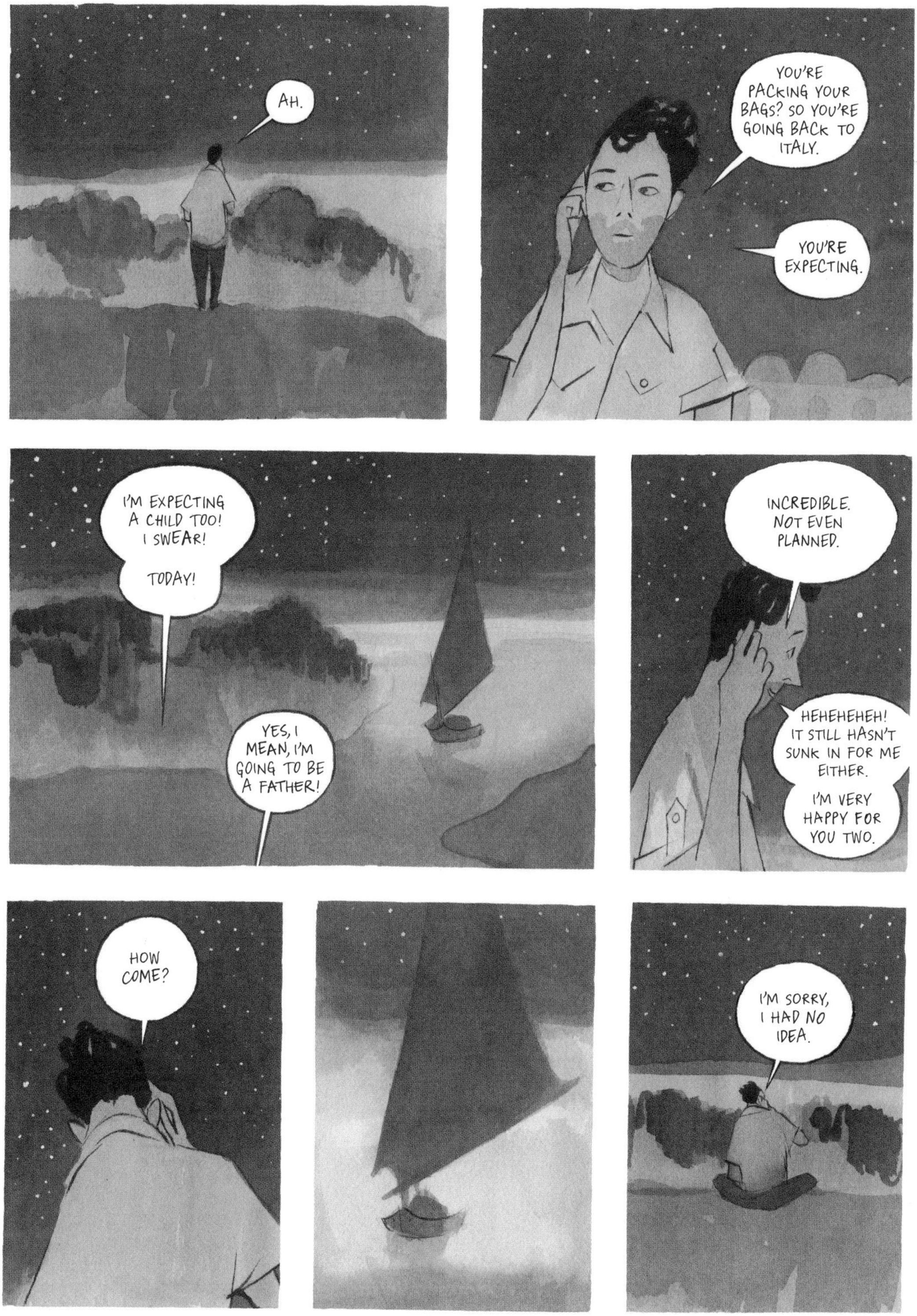
AH.
YOU'RE PACKING YOUR BAGS? SO YOU'RE GOING BACK TO ITALY.
YOU'RE EXPECTING.
I'M EXPECTING A CHILD TOO! I SWEAR!
TODAY!
YES, I MEAN, I'M GOING TO BE A FATHER!
INCREDIBLE. NOT EVEN PLANNED.
HEHEHEHEH! IT STILL HASN'T SUNK IN FOR ME EITHER.
I'M VERY HAPPY FOR YOU TWO.
HOW COME?
I'M SORRY, I HAD NO IDEA.

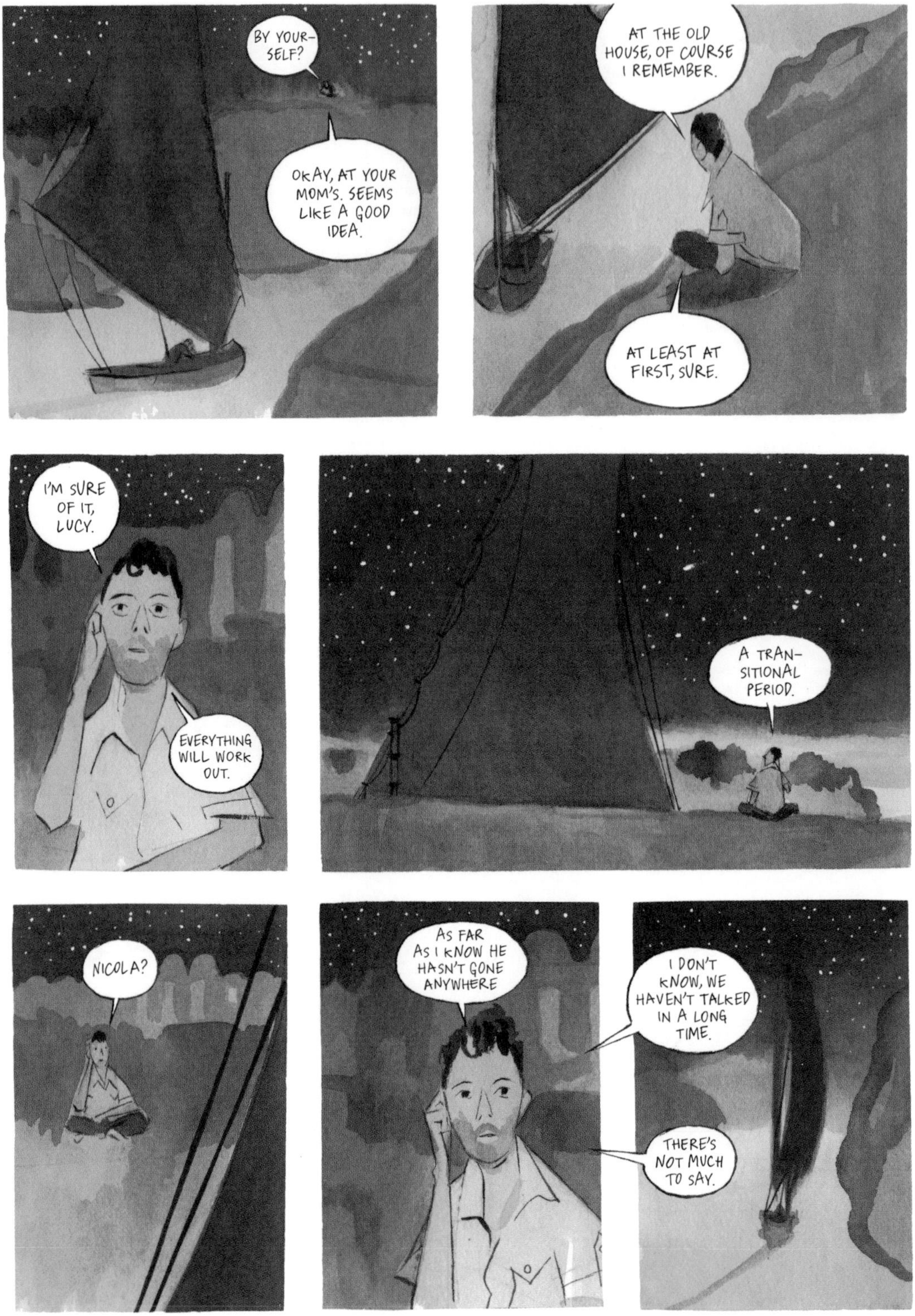
BY YOURSELF?
OKAY, AT YOUR MOM'S. SEEMS LIKE A GOOD IDEA.
AT THE OLD HOUSE, OF COURSE I REMEMBER.
AT LEAST AT FIRST, SURE.
I'M SURE OF IT, LUCY.
EVERYTHING WILL WORK OUT.
A TRANSITIONAL PERIOD.
NICOLA?
AS FAR AS I KNOW HE HASN'T GONE ANYWHERE
I DON'T KNOW, WE HAVEN'T TALKED IN A LONG TIME.
THERE'S NOT MUCH TO SAY.

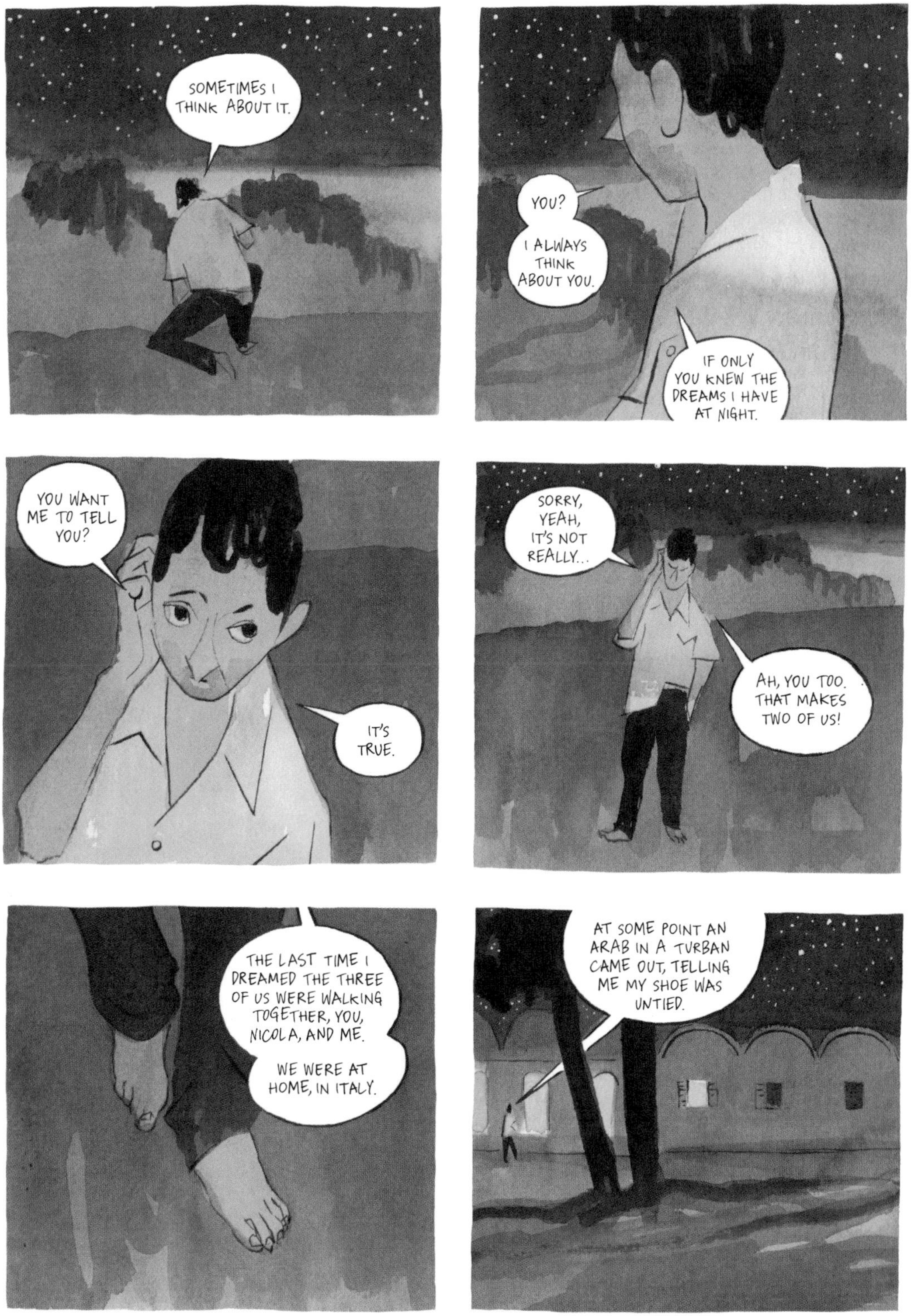
SOMETIMES I THINK ABOUT IT.
YOU?
I ALWAYS THINK ABOUT YOU.
IF ONLY YOU KNEW THE DREAMS I HAVE AT NIGHT.
YOU WANT ME TO TELL YOU?
IT'S TRUE.
SORRY, YEAH, IT'S NOT REALLY...
AH, YOU TOO. THAT MAKES TWO OF US!
THE LAST TIME I DREAMED THE THREE OF US WERE WALKING TOGETHER, YOU, NICOLA, AND ME.
WE WERE AT HOME, IN ITALY.
AT SOME POINT AN ARAB IN A TURBAN CAME OUT, TELLING ME MY SHOE WAS UNTIED.

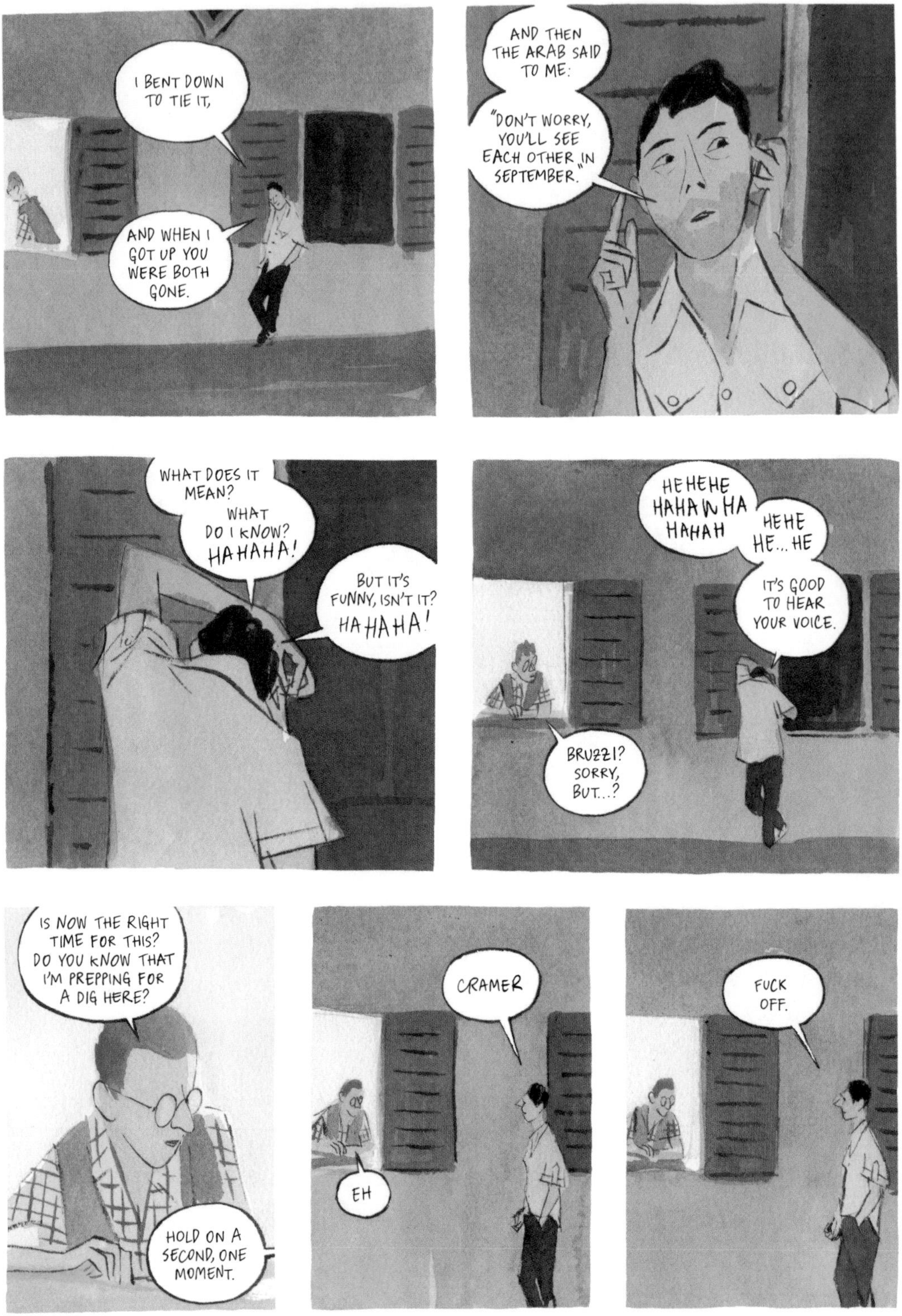
I BENT DOWN TO TIE IT,
AND WHEN I GOT UP YOU WERE BOTH GONE.
AND THEN THE ARAB SAID TO ME:
"DON'T WORRY, YOU'LL SEE EACH OTHER IN SEPTEMBER."
WHAT DOES IT MEAN? WHAT DO I KNOW? HAHAHA!
BUT IT'S FUNNY, ISN'T IT? HAHAHA!
HEHEHE HAHAWHA HAHAH
HEHE HE... HE
IT'S GOOD TO HEAR YOUR VOICE.
BRUZZI? SORRY, BUT...?
IS NOW THE RIGHT TIME FOR THIS? DO YOU KNOW THAT I'M PREPPING FOR A DIG HERE?
HOLD ON A SECOND, ONE MOMENT.
CRAMER
EH
FUCK OFF.

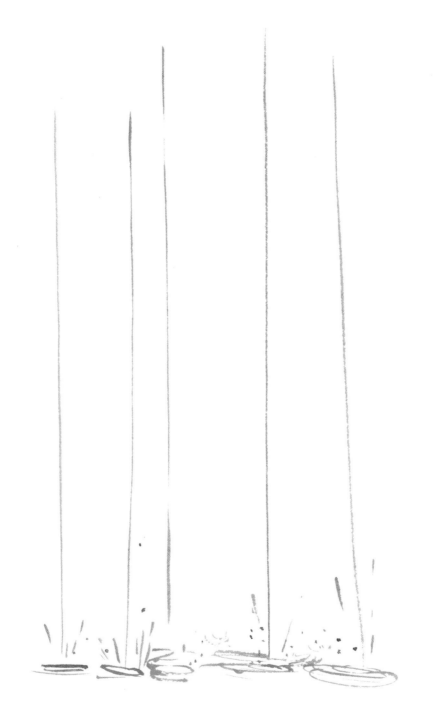

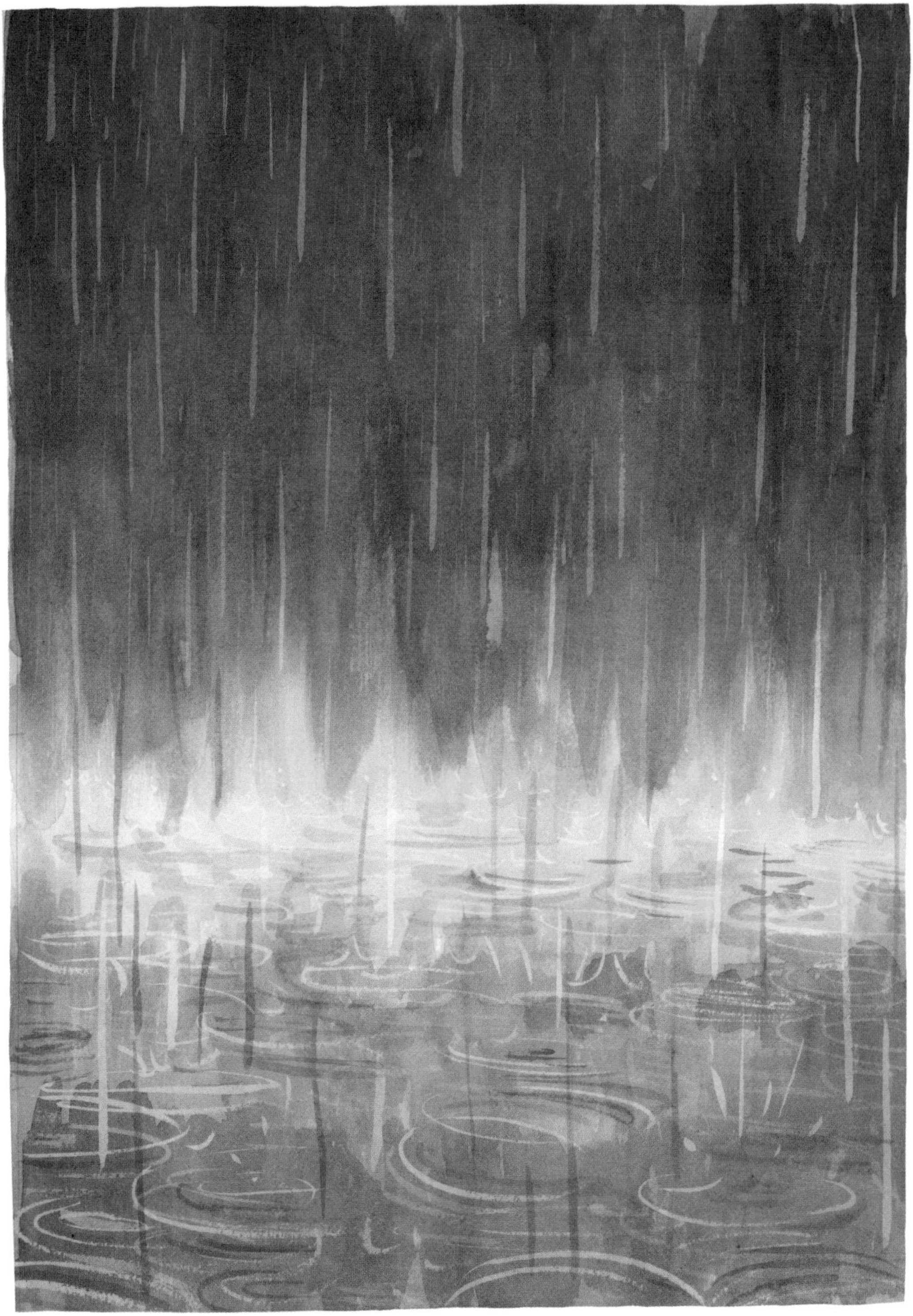

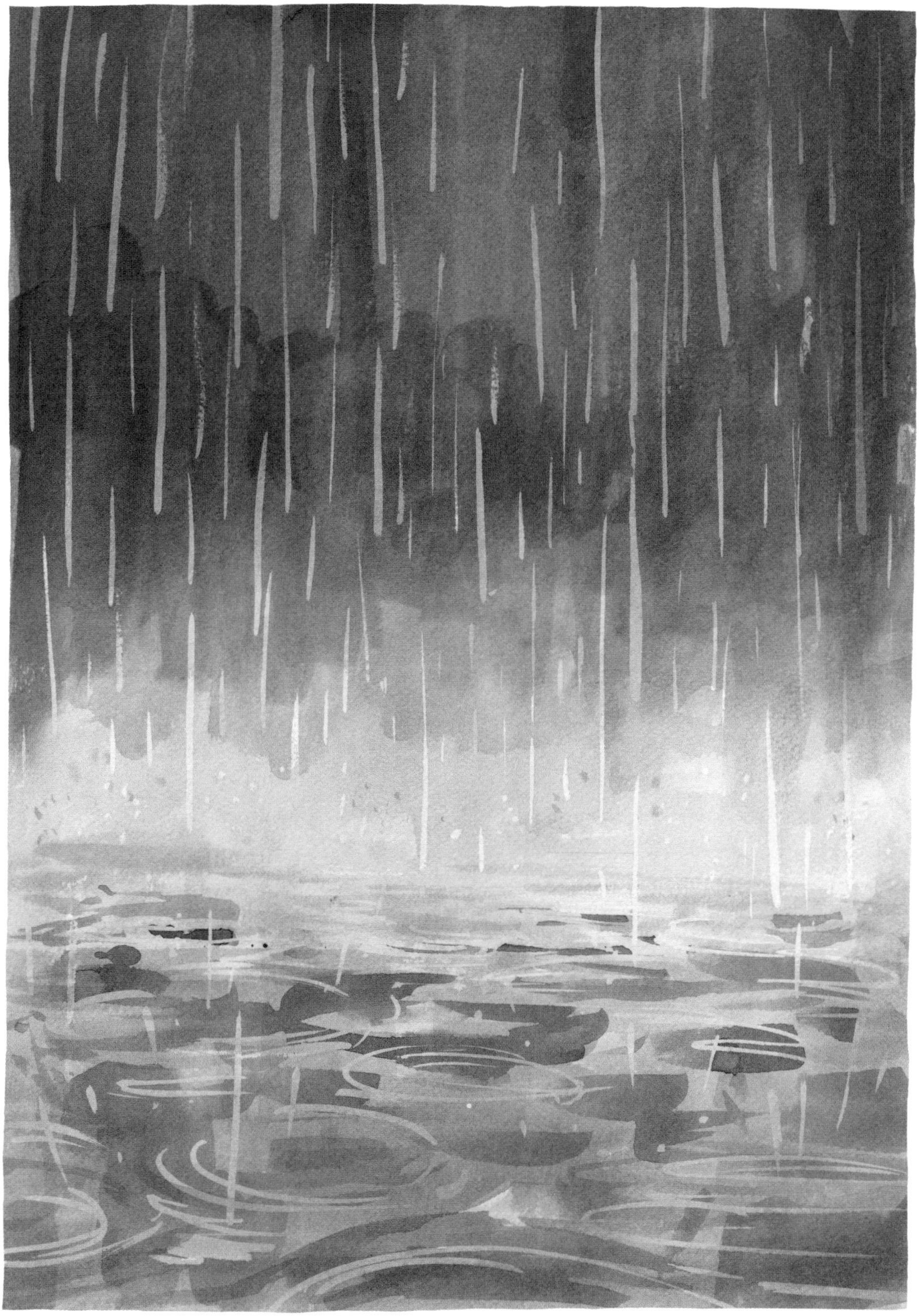

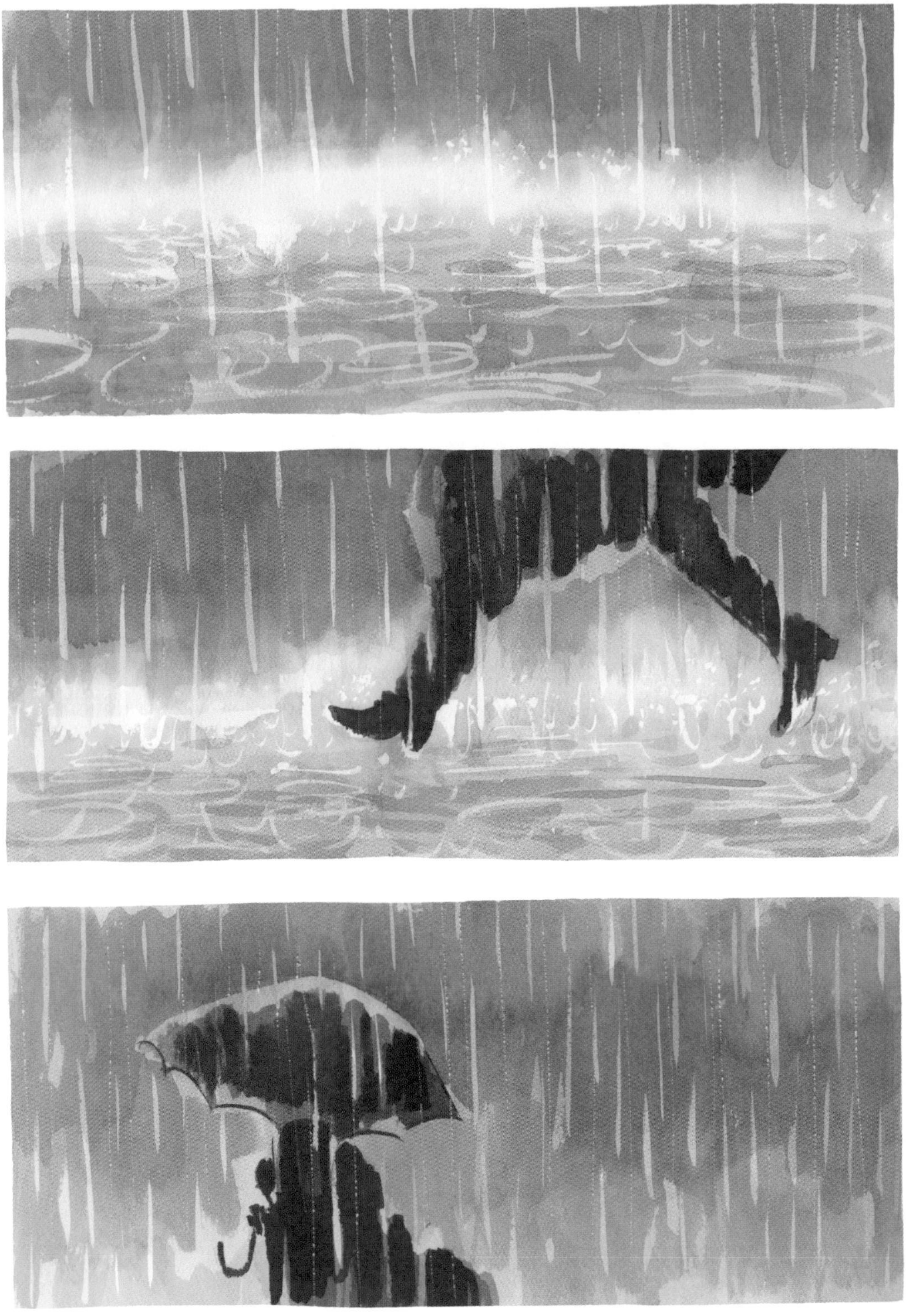

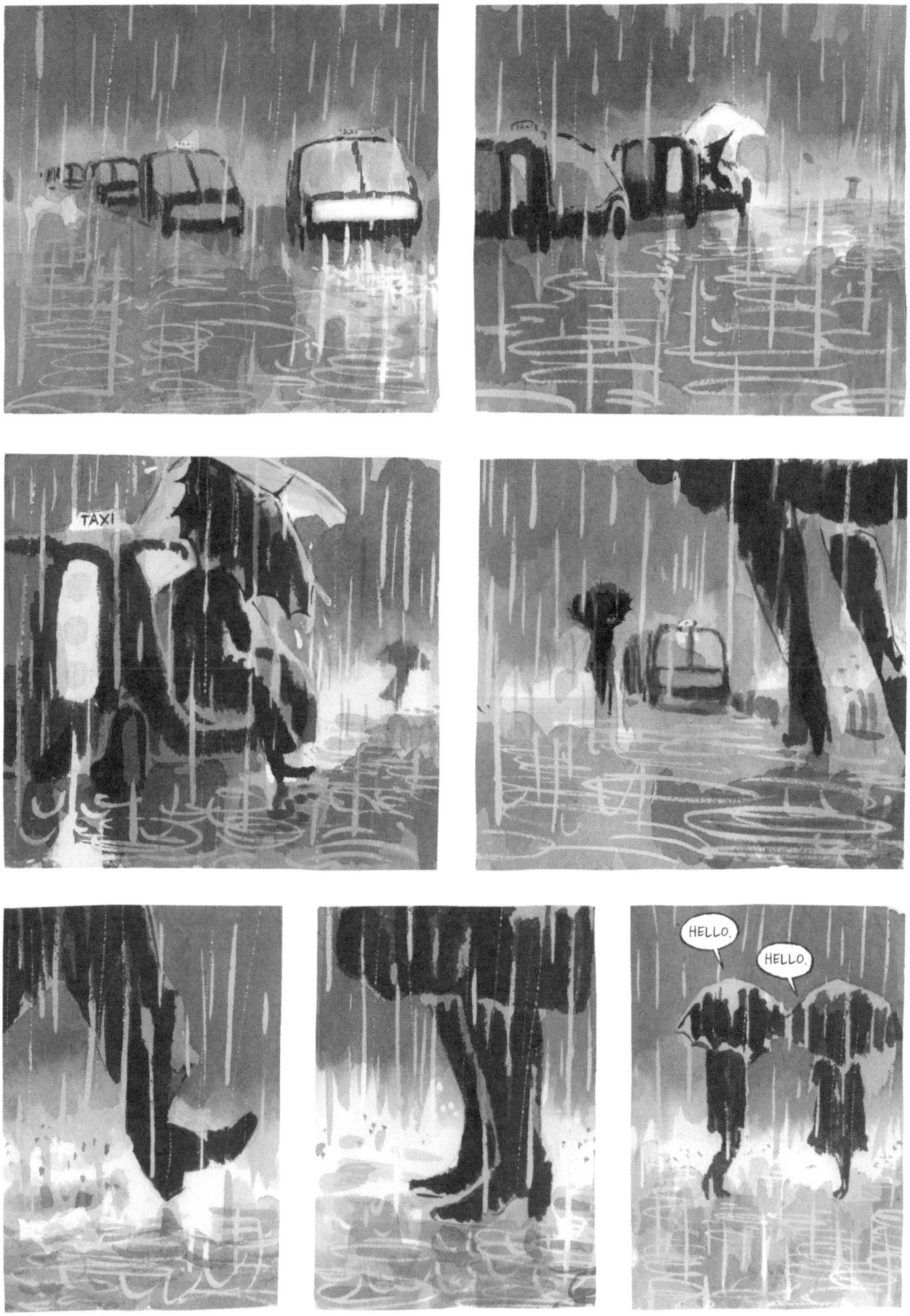
TAXI
TAXI
HELLO.
HELLO.

THE KITCHEN IS CLOSED, I'M SORRY.

THAT'S NO PROBLEM, CAN WE HAVE A DRINK?

THAT BOTTLE THERE'S FINE, THANK YOU.

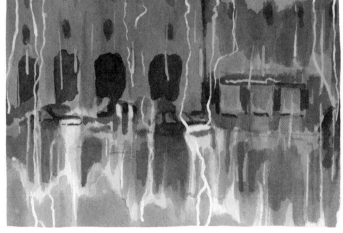

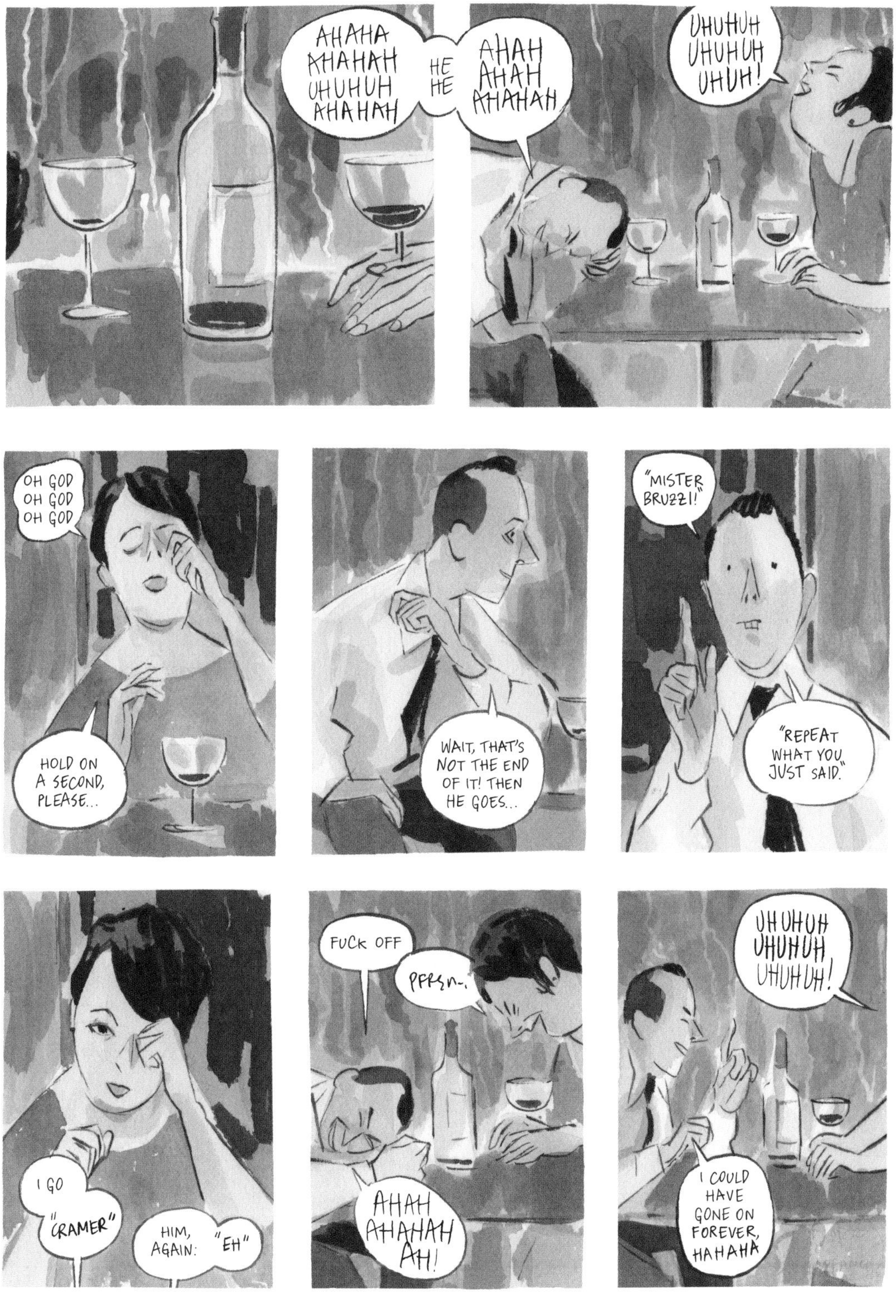
AHAHA AHAHAH UHUHUH AHAHAH
HE HE
AHAH AHAH AHAHAH
UHUHUH UHUHUH UHUH!
OH GOD OH GOD OH GOD
HOLD ON A SECOND, PLEASE...
WAIT, THAT'S NOT THE END OF IT! THEN HE GOES...
"MISTER BRUZZI!"
"REPEAT WHAT YOU JUST SAID."
I GO
"CRAMER"
HIM, AGAIN:
"EH"
FUCK OFF
PFFFN...
AHAH AHAHAH AH!
UHUHUH UHUHUH UHUHUH!
I COULD HAVE GONE ON FOREVER, HAHAHA

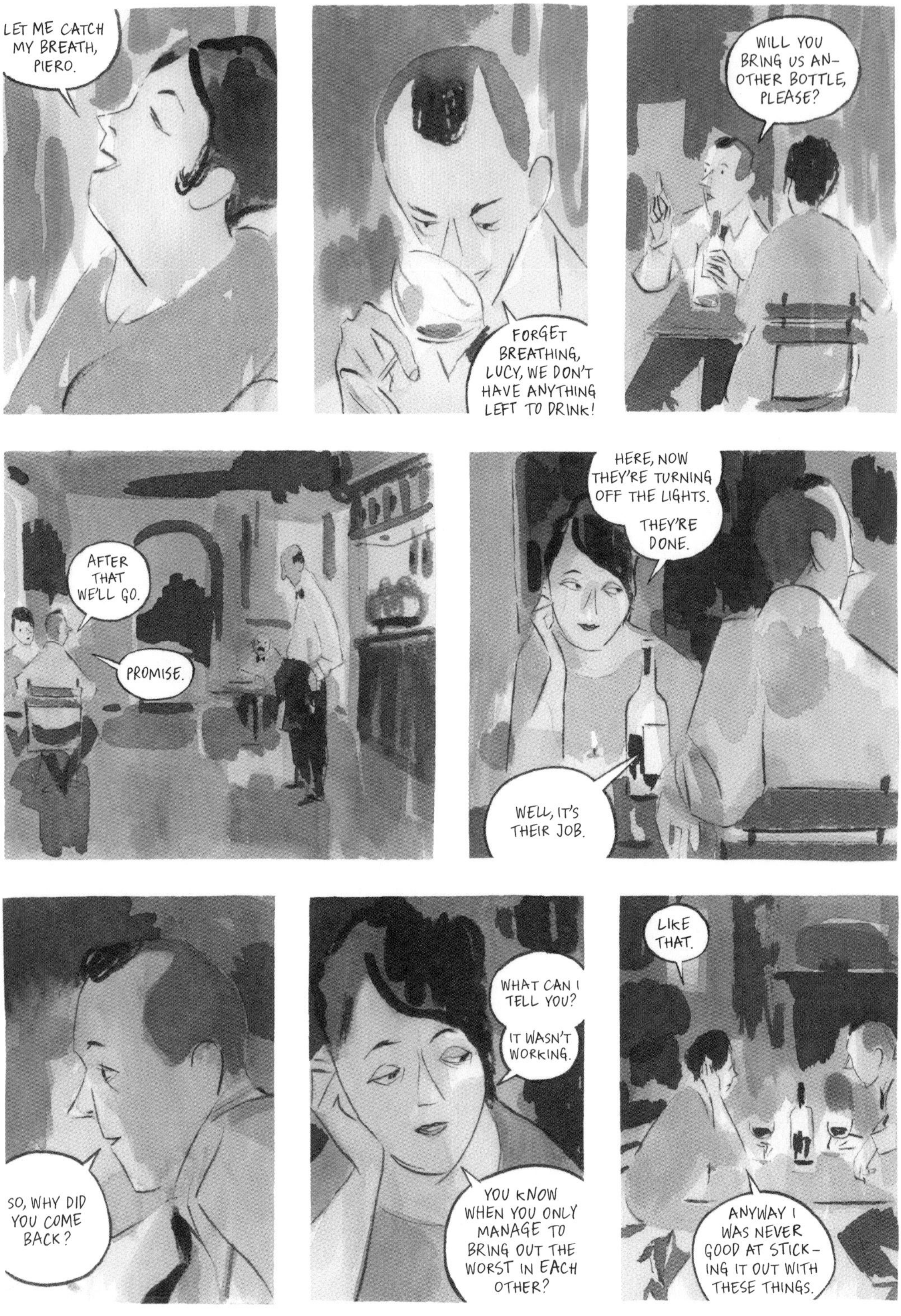
LET ME CATCH MY BREATH, PIERO.
FORGET BREATHING, LUCY, WE DON'T HAVE ANYTHING LEFT TO DRINK!
WILL YOU BRING US AN-OTHER BOTTLE, PLEASE?
AFTER THAT WE'LL GO.
PROMISE.
HERE, NOW THEY'RE TURNING OFF THE LIGHTS.
THEY'RE DONE.
WELL, IT'S THEIR JOB.
SO, WHY DID YOU COME BACK?
WHAT CAN I TELL YOU?
IT WASN'T WORKING.
YOU KNOW WHEN YOU ONLY MANAGE TO BRING OUT THE WORST IN EACH OTHER?
LIKE THAT.
ANYWAY I WAS NEVER GOOD AT STICK-ING IT OUT WITH THESE THINGS.

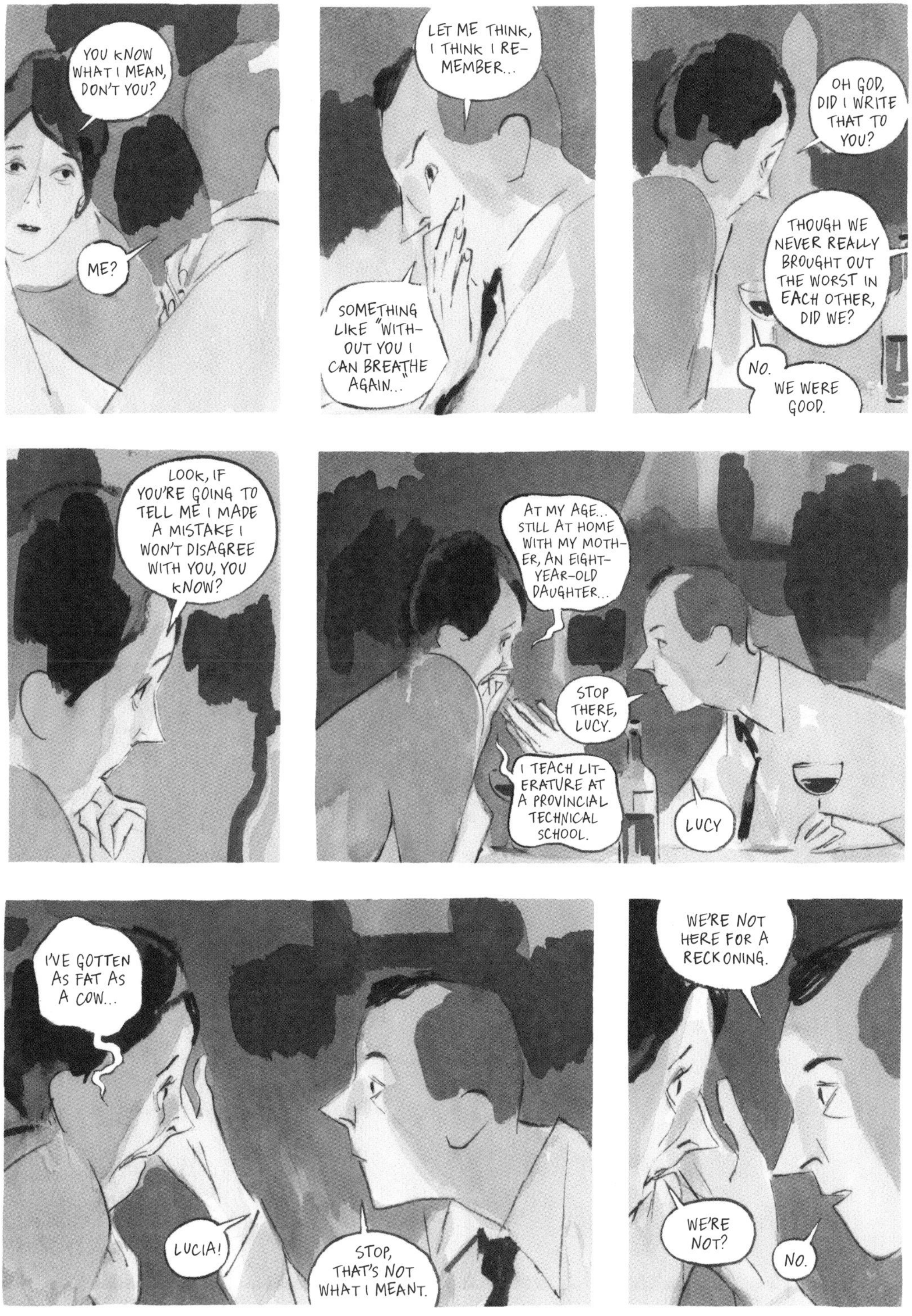
YOU KNOW WHAT I MEAN, DON'T YOU?
ME?
LET ME THINK, I THINK I RE-MEMBER...
SOMETHING LIKE "WITH-OUT YOU I CAN BREATHE AGAIN..."
OH GOD, DID I WRITE THAT TO YOU?
THOUGH WE NEVER REALLY BROUGHT OUT THE WORST IN EACH OTHER, DID WE?
NO.
WE WERE GOOD.
LOOK, IF YOU'RE GOING TO TELL ME I MADE A MISTAKE I WON'T DISAGREE WITH YOU, YOU KNOW?
AT MY AGE... STILL AT HOME WITH MY MOTH-ER, AN EIGHT-YEAR-OLD DAUGHTER...
STOP THERE, LUCY.
I TEACH LIT-ERATURE AT A PROVINCIAL TECHNICAL SCHOOL.
LUCY
I'VE GOTTEN AS FAT AS A COW...
LUCIA!
STOP, THAT'S NOT WHAT I MEANT.
WE'RE NOT HERE FOR A RECKONING.
WE'RE NOT?
NO.

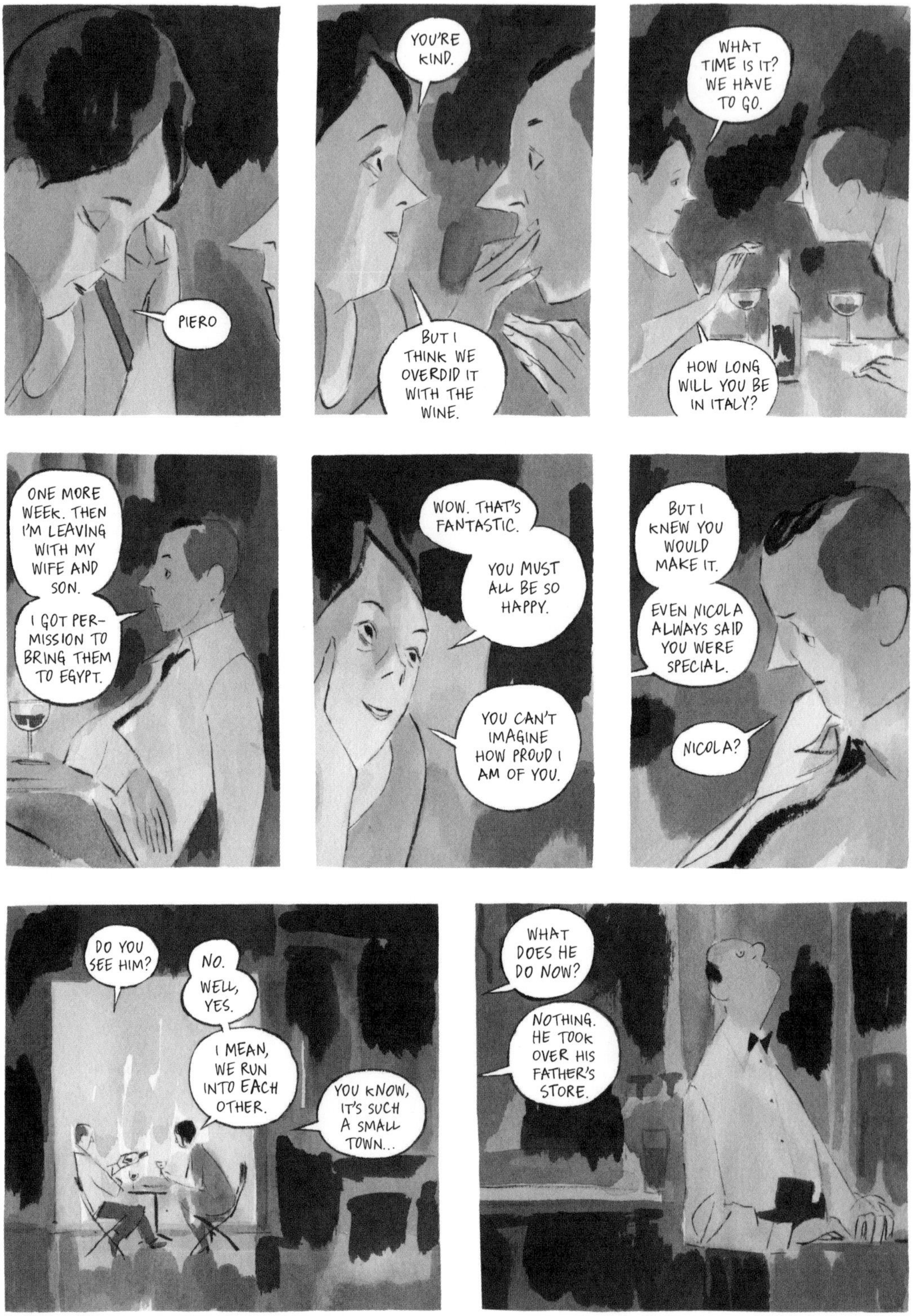
PIERO
YOU'RE KIND.
BUT I THINK WE OVERDID IT WITH THE WINE.
WHAT TIME IS IT? WE HAVE TO GO.
HOW LONG WILL YOU BE IN ITALY?
ONE MORE WEEK. THEN I'M LEAVING WITH MY WIFE AND SON.
I GOT PER-MISSION TO BRING THEM TO EGYPT.
WOW. THAT'S FANTASTIC.
YOU MUST ALL BE SO HAPPY.
YOU CAN'T IMAGINE HOW PROUD I AM OF YOU.
BUT I KNEW YOU WOULD MAKE IT.
EVEN NICOLA ALWAYS SAID YOU WERE SPECIAL.
NICOLA?
DO YOU SEE HIM?
NO.
WELL, YES.
I MEAN, WE RUN INTO EACH OTHER.
YOU KNOW, IT'S SUCH A SMALL TOWN...
WHAT DOES HE DO NOW?
NOTHING. HE TOOK OVER HIS FATHER'S STORE.

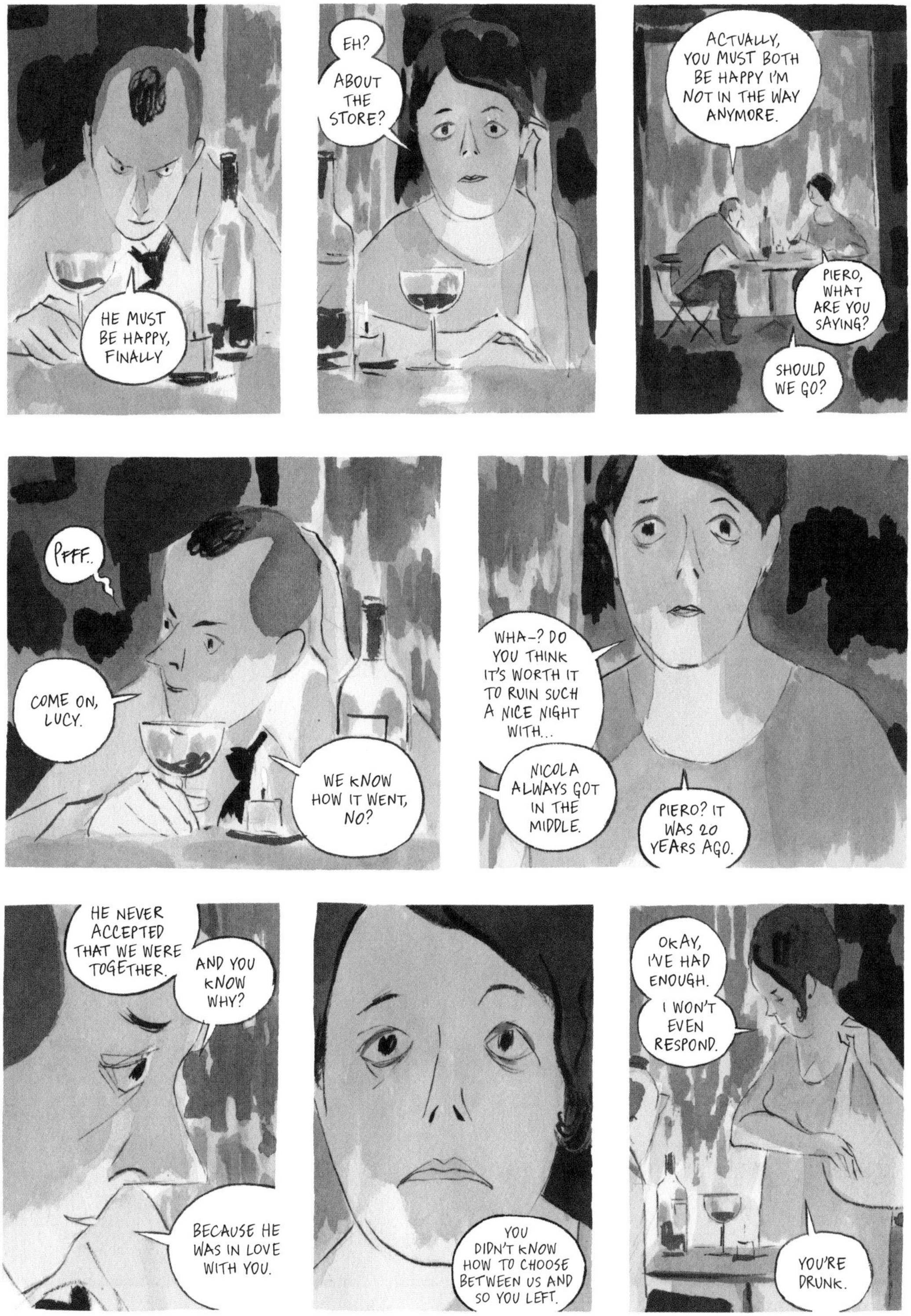

HE MUST BE HAPPY, FINALLY
EH?
ABOUT THE STORE?
ACTUALLY, YOU MUST BOTH BE HAPPY I'M NOT IN THE WAY ANYMORE.
PIERO, WHAT ARE YOU SAYING?
SHOULD WE GO?
PFFF..
COME ON, LUCY.
WE KNOW HOW IT WENT, NO?
WHA-? DO YOU THINK IT'S WORTH IT TO RUIN SUCH A NICE NIGHT WITH...
NICOLA ALWAYS GOT IN THE MIDDLE.
PIERO? IT WAS 20 YEARS AGO.
HE NEVER ACCEPTED THAT WE WERE TOGETHER.
AND YOU KNOW WHY?
BECAUSE HE WAS IN LOVE WITH YOU.
YOU DIDN'T KNOW HOW TO CHOOSE BETWEEN US AND SO YOU LEFT.
OKAY, I'VE HAD ENOUGH.
I WON'T EVEN RESPOND.
YOU'RE DRUNK.

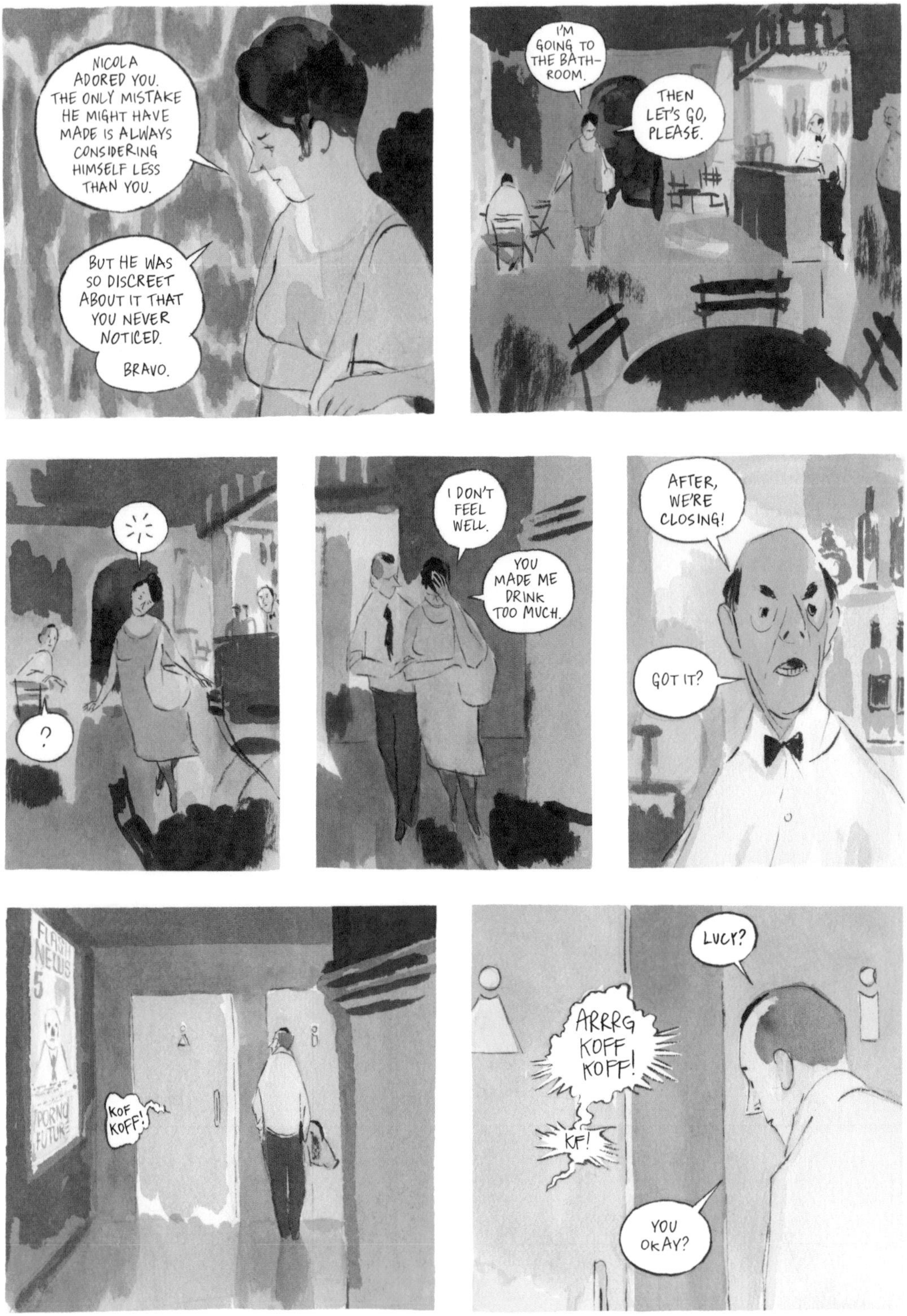
NICOLA ADORED YOU. THE ONLY MISTAKE HE MIGHT HAVE MADE IS ALWAYS CONSIDERING HIMSELF LESS THAN YOU.
BUT HE WAS SO DISCREET ABOUT IT THAT YOU NEVER NOTICED.
BRAVO.
I'M GOING TO THE BATH-ROOM.
THEN LET'S GO, PLEASE.
?
I DON'T FEEL WELL.
YOU MADE ME DRINK TOO MUCH.
AFTER, WE'RE CLOSING!
GOT IT?
FLASH NEWS 5
PORNO FUTURE
KOF KOFF!
LUCY?
ARRRG KOFF KOFF!
KF!
YOU OKAY?

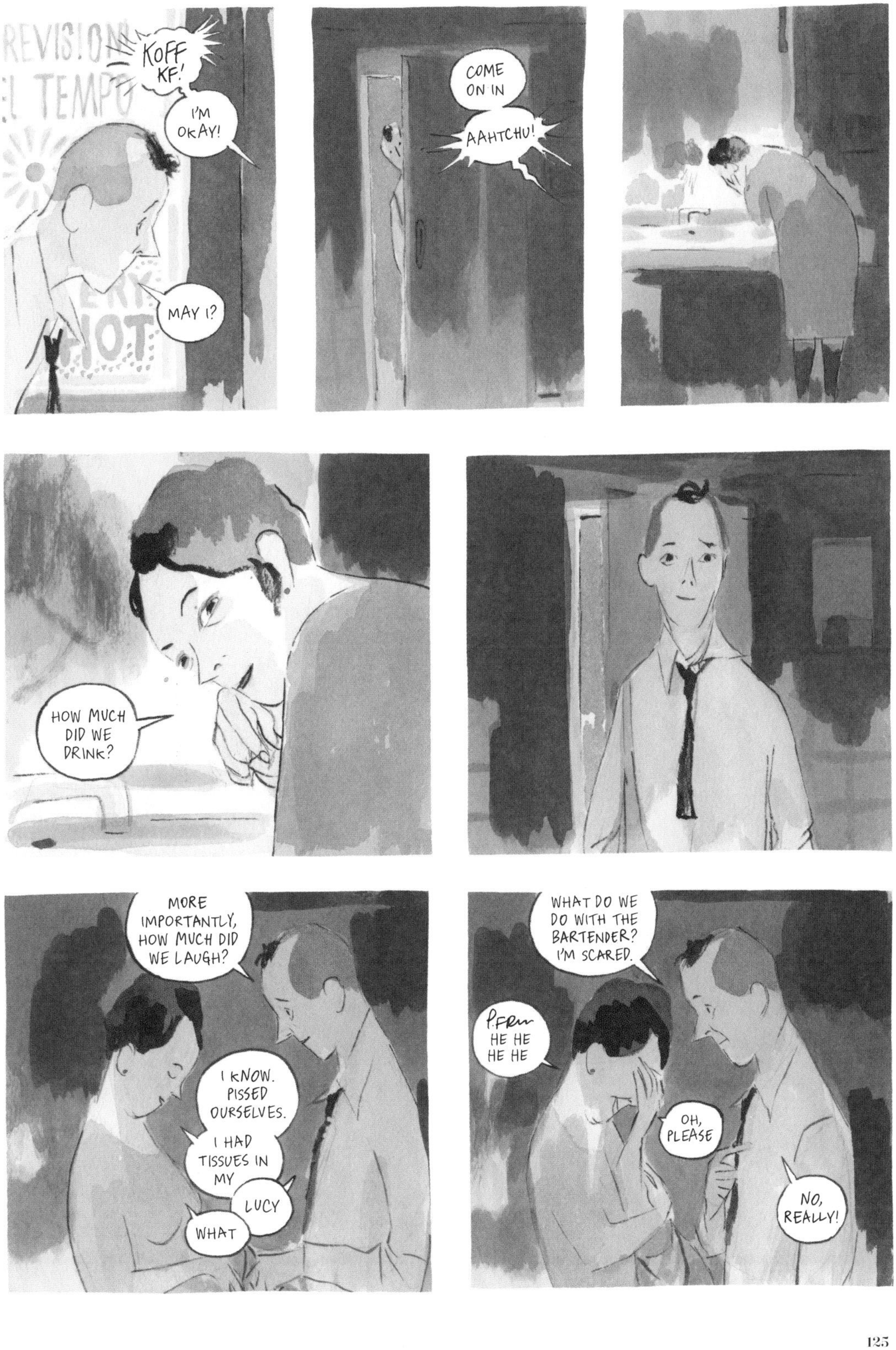
KOFF KF!
I'M OKAY!
MAY I?
COME ON IN
AAHTCHU!
HOW MUCH DID WE DRINK?
MORE IMPORTANTLY, HOW MUCH DID WE LAUGH?
I KNOW. PISSED OURSELVES.
I HAD TISSUES IN MY
LUCY
WHAT
WHAT DO WE DO WITH THE BARTENDER? I'M SCARED.
HE HE HE HE
OH, PLEASE
NO, REALLY!

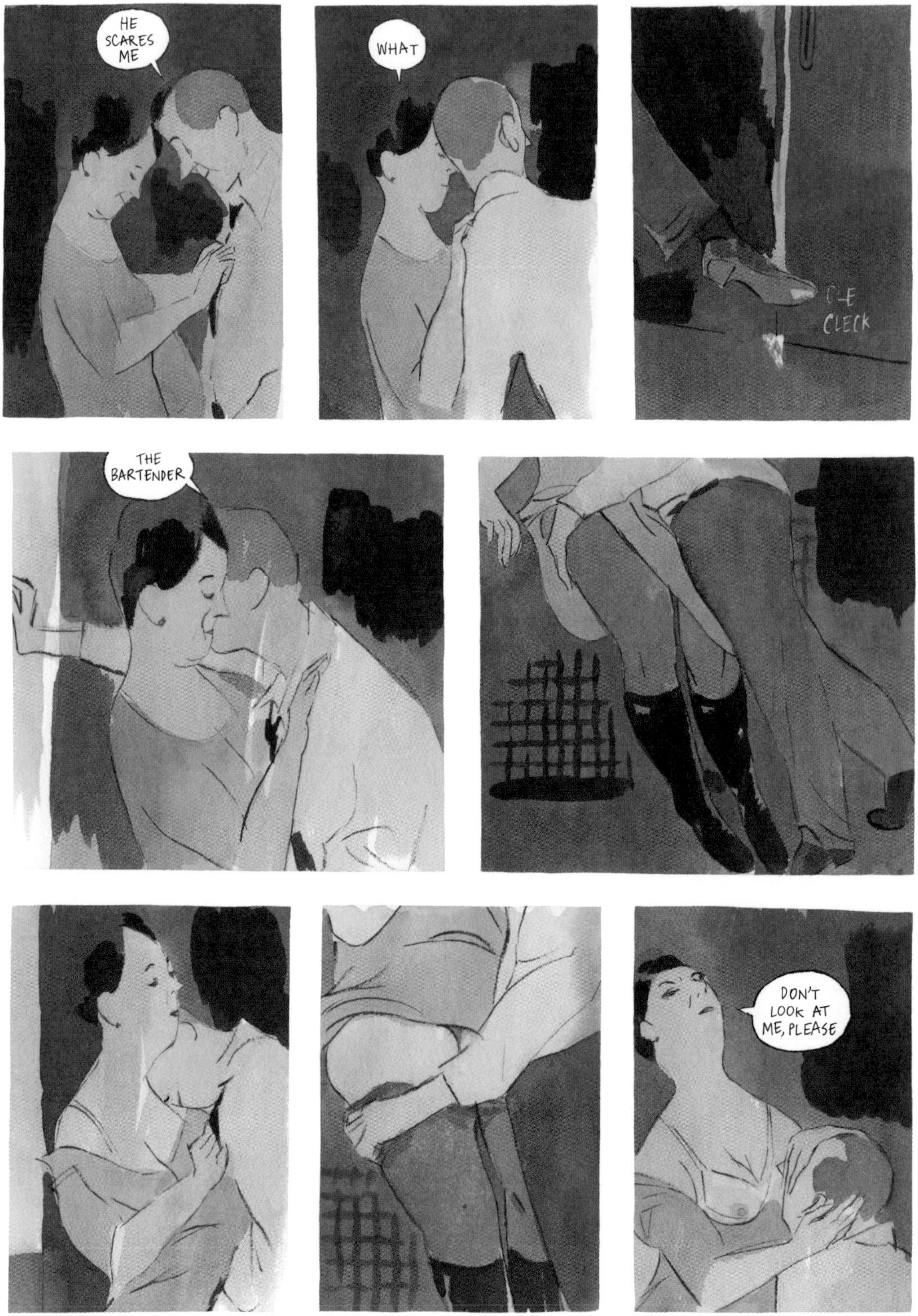
HE SCARES ME
WHAT
CLE
CLECK
THE BARTENDER
DON'T LOOK AT ME, PLEASE

WHY NOT?

DON'T LOOK AT ME. I DON'T WANT YOU TO.

OKAY.

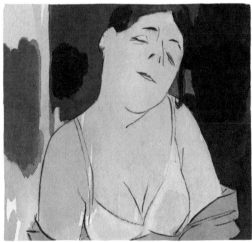

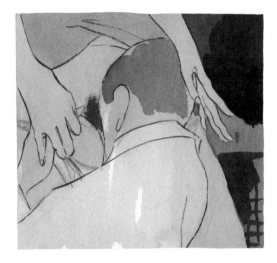

DON'T STOP WHERE ARE YOU GOING

WAIT A SECOND

HURRY UP

KEEP YOUR EYES CLOSED!

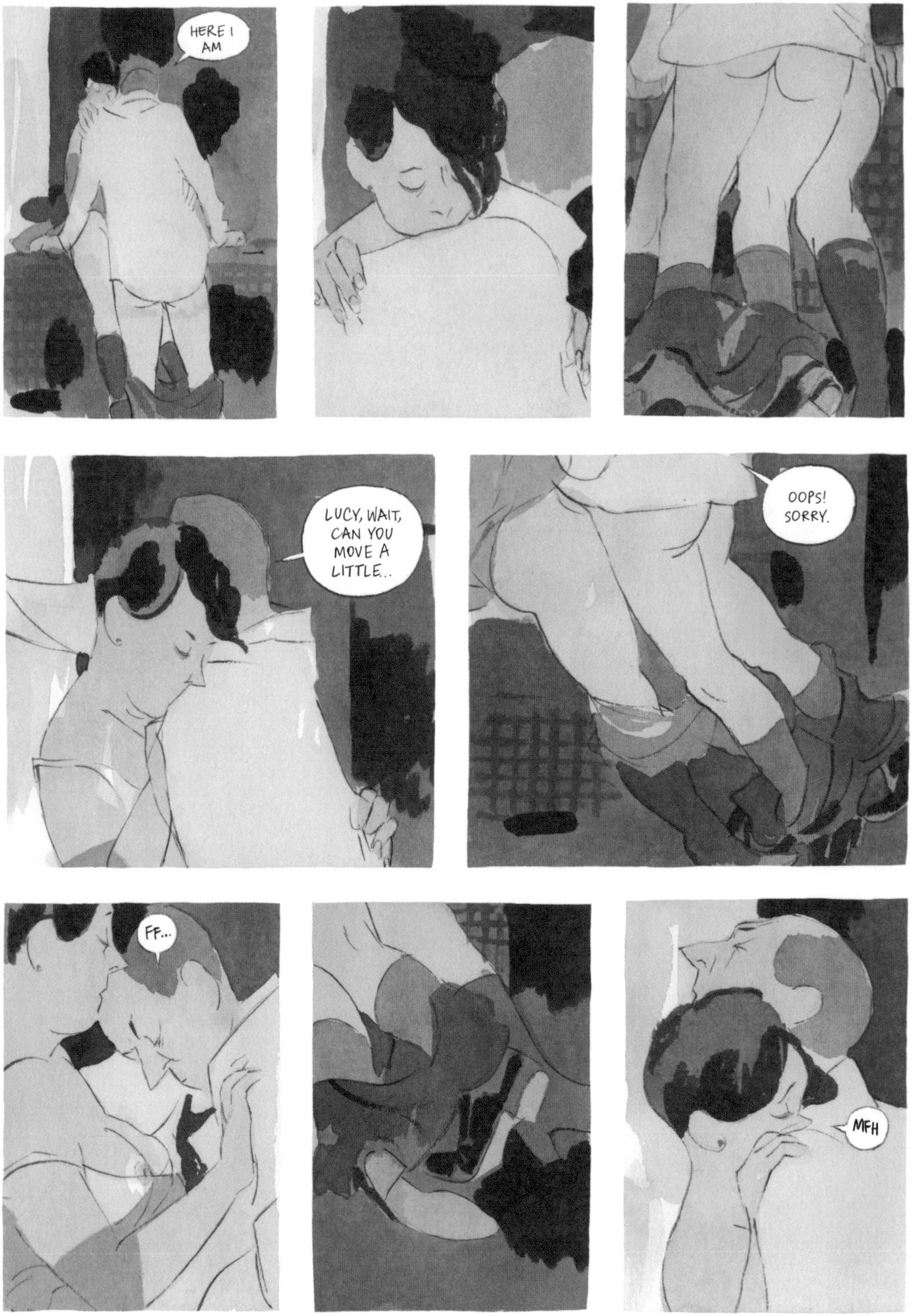
HERE I AM
LUCY, WAIT, CAN YOU MOVE A LITTLE..
OOPS! SORRY.
FF...
MFH

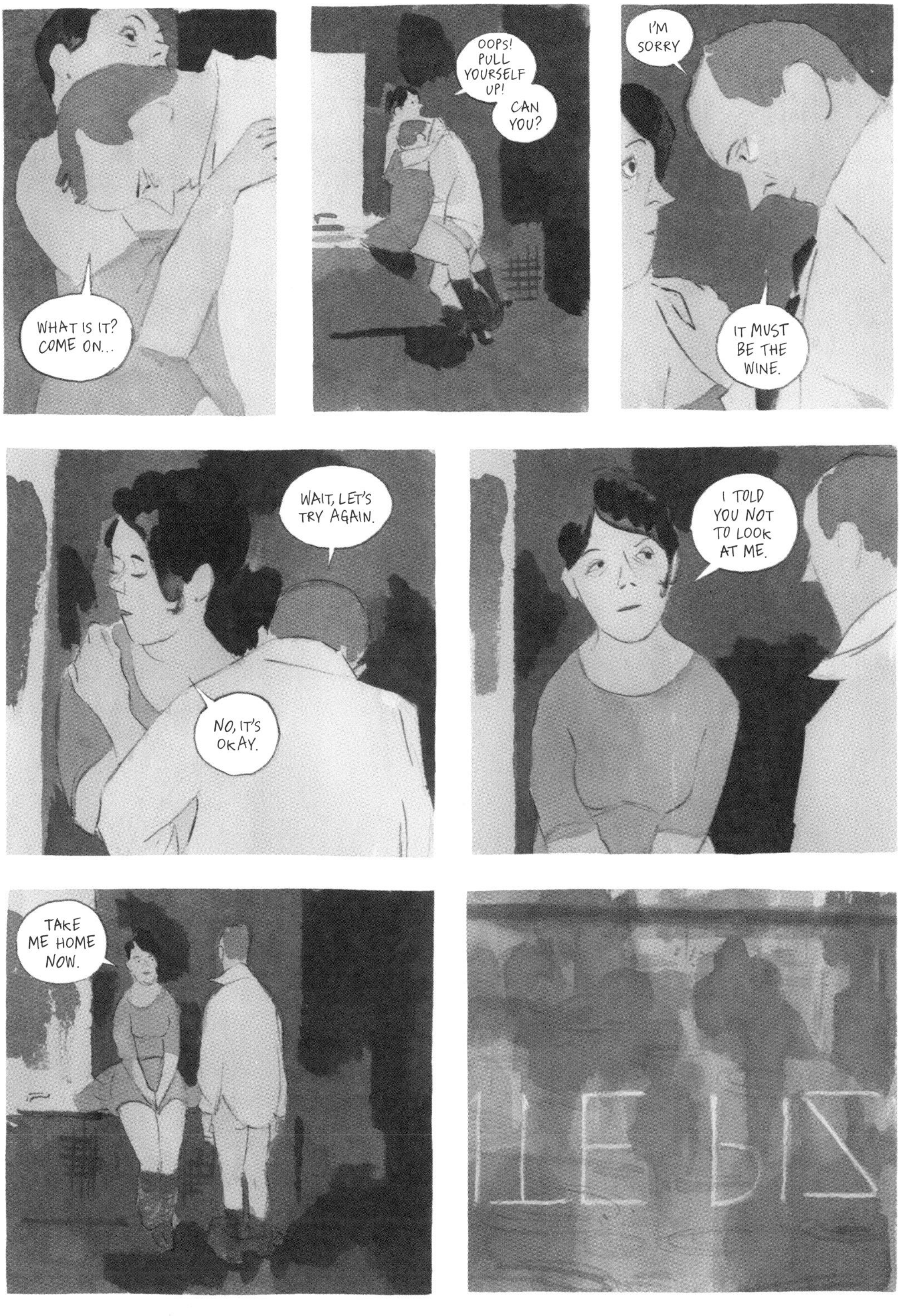
WHAT IS IT? COME ON...
OOPS! PULL YOURSELF UP!
CAN YOU?
I'M SORRY
IT MUST BE THE WINE.
WAIT, LET'S TRY AGAIN.
NO, IT'S OKAY.
I TOLD YOU NOT TO LOOK AT ME.
TAKE ME HOME NOW.

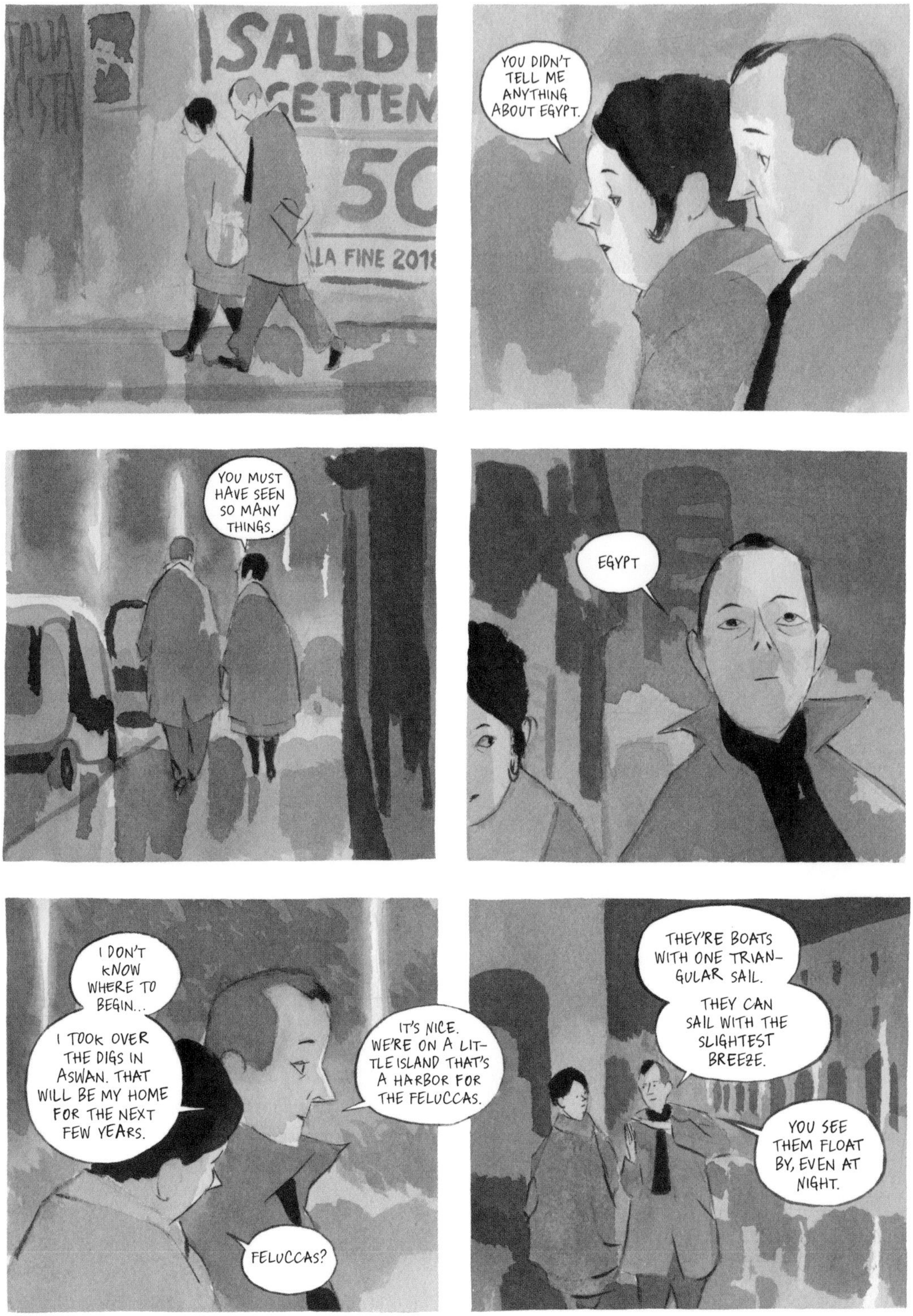
SALDI
SETTEM
50
LA FINE 2018
YOU DIDN'T TELL ME ANYTHING ABOUT EGYPT.
YOU MUST HAVE SEEN SO MANY THINGS.
EGYPT
I DON'T KNOW WHERE TO BEGIN...
I TOOK OVER THE DIGS IN ASWAN. THAT WILL BE MY HOME FOR THE NEXT FEW YEARS.
IT'S NICE. WE'RE ON A LITTLE ISLAND THAT'S A HARBOR FOR THE FELUCCAS.
FELUCCAS?
THEY'RE BOATS WITH ONE TRIANGULAR SAIL.
THEY CAN SAIL WITH THE SLIGHTEST BREEZE.
YOU SEE THEM FLOAT BY, EVEN AT NIGHT.

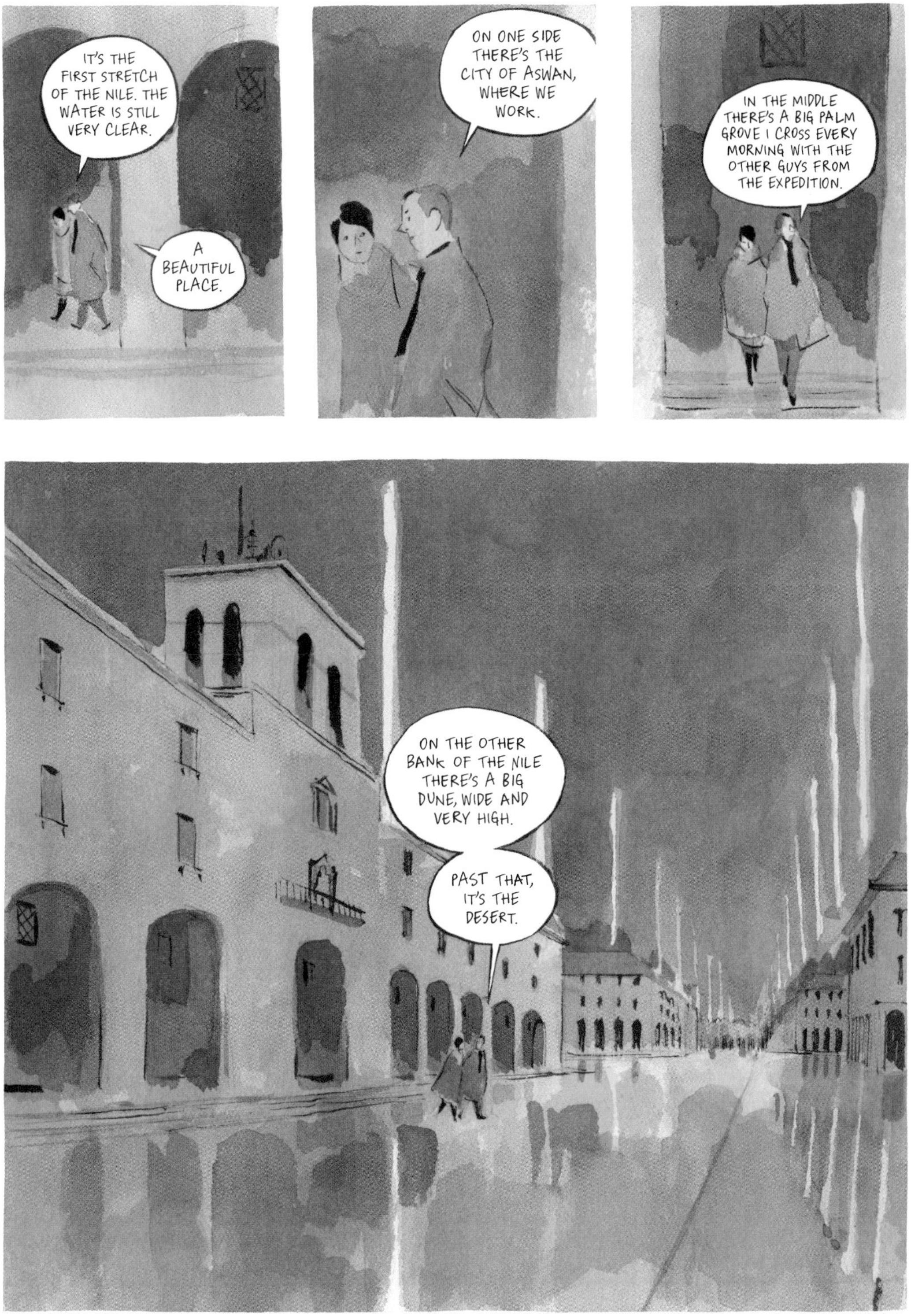
IT'S THE FIRST STRETCH OF THE NILE. THE WATER IS STILL VERY CLEAR.
A BEAUTIFUL PLACE.
ON ONE SIDE THERE'S THE CITY OF ASWAN, WHERE WE WORK.
IN THE MIDDLE THERE'S A BIG PALM GROVE I CROSS EVERY MORNING WITH THE OTHER GUYS FROM THE EXPEDITION.
ON THE OTHER BANK OF THE NILE THERE'S A BIG DUNE, WIDE AND VERY HIGH.
PAST THAT, IT'S THE DESERT.

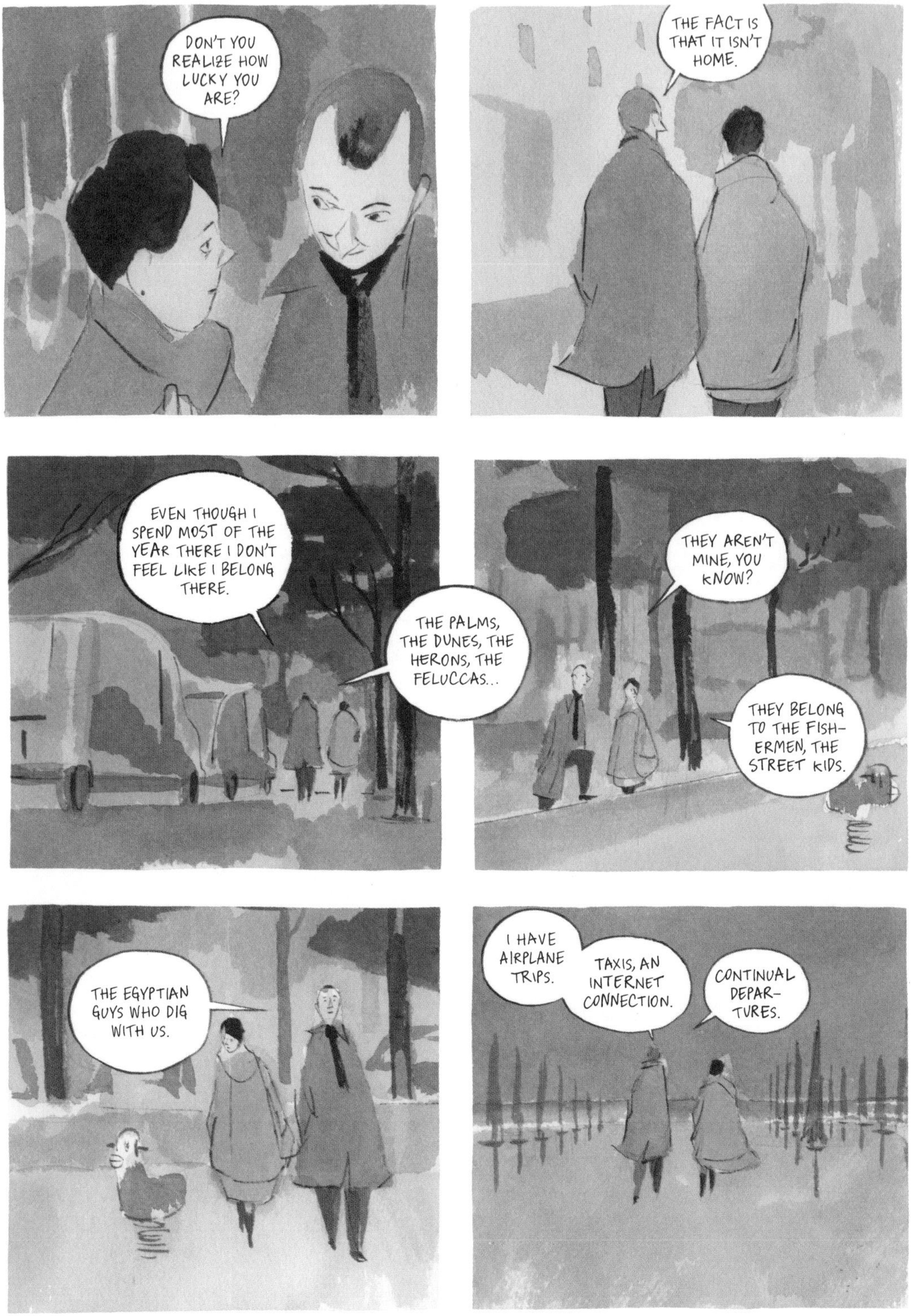
DON'T YOU REALIZE HOW LUCKY YOU ARE?
THE FACT IS THAT IT ISN'T HOME.
EVEN THOUGH I SPEND MOST OF THE YEAR THERE I DON'T FEEL LIKE I BELONG THERE.
THE PALMS, THE DUNES, THE HERONS, THE FELUCCAS...
THEY AREN'T MINE, YOU KNOW?
THEY BELONG TO THE FISH-ERMEN, THE STREET KIDS.
THE EGYPTIAN GUYS WHO DIG WITH US.
I HAVE AIRPLANE TRIPS.
TAXIS, AN INTERNET CONNECTION.
CONTINUAL DEPAR-TURES.

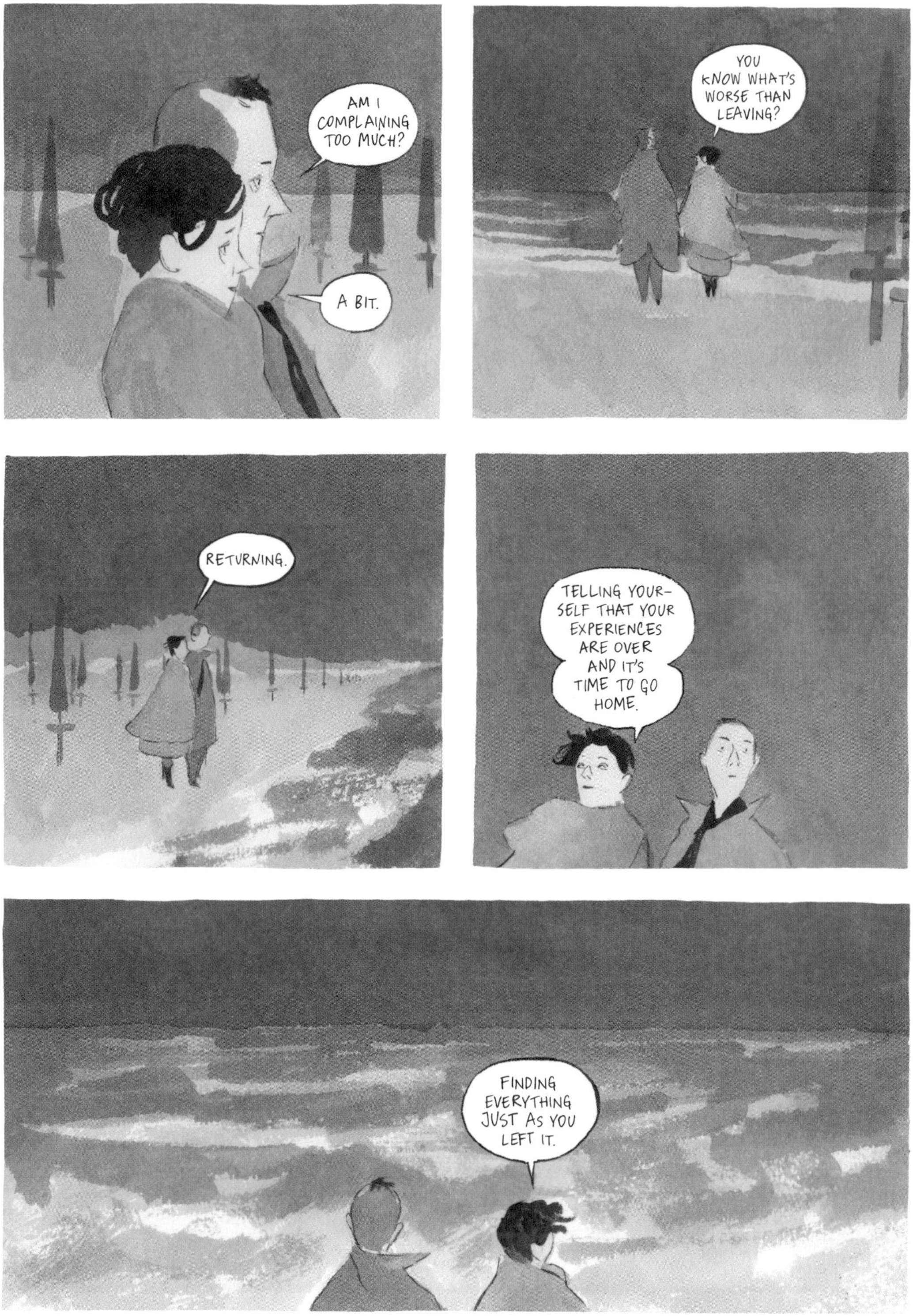
AM I COMPLAINING TOO MUCH?
A BIT.
YOU KNOW WHAT'S WORSE THAN LEAVING?
RETURNING.
TELLING YOURSELF THAT YOUR EXPERIENCES ARE OVER AND IT'S TIME TO GO HOME.
FINDING EVERYTHING JUST AS YOU LEFT IT.

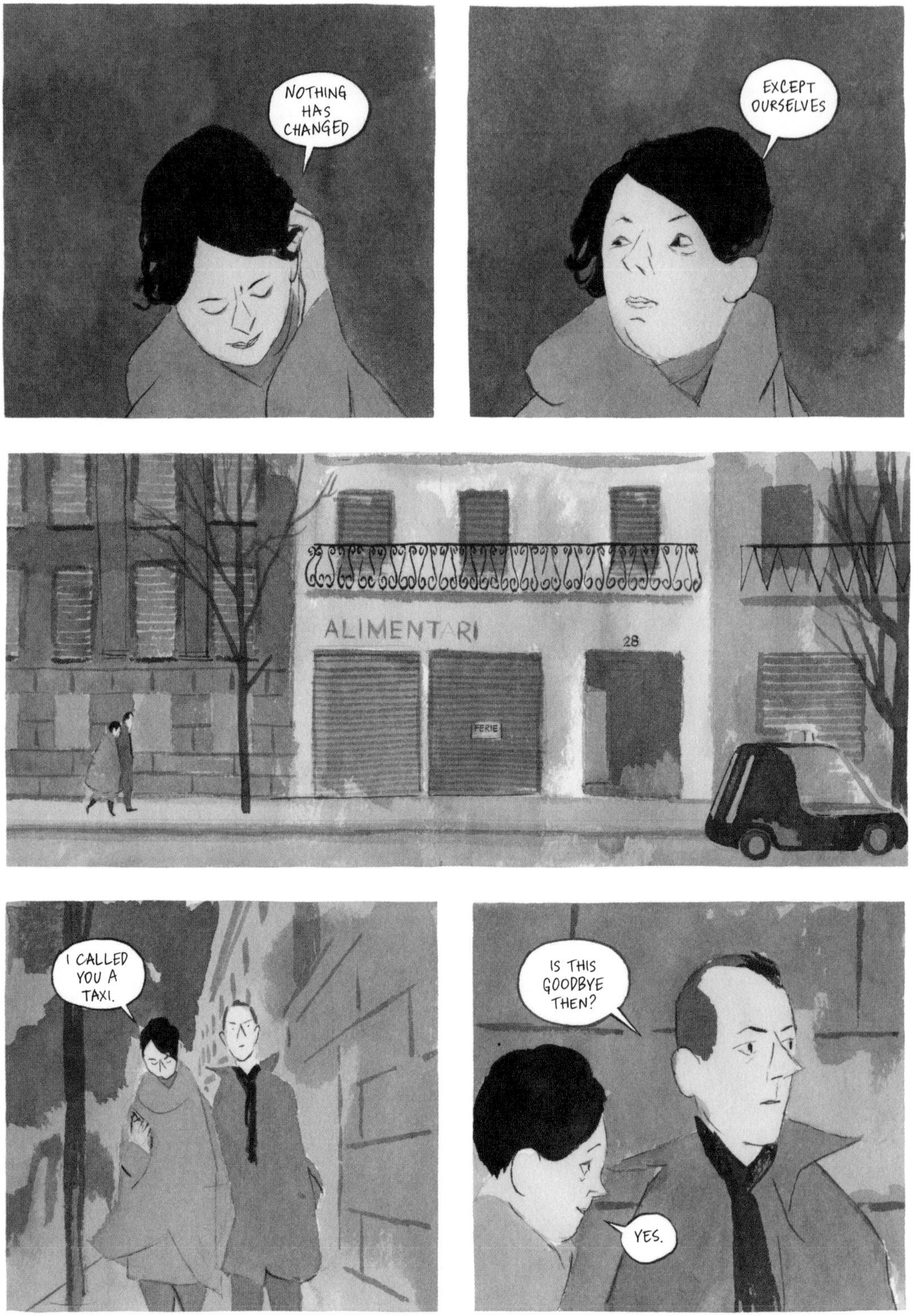
NOTHING HAS CHANGED
EXCEPT OURSELVES
ALIMENTARI
28
FERIE
I CALLED YOU A TAXI.
IS THIS GOODBYE THEN?
YES.

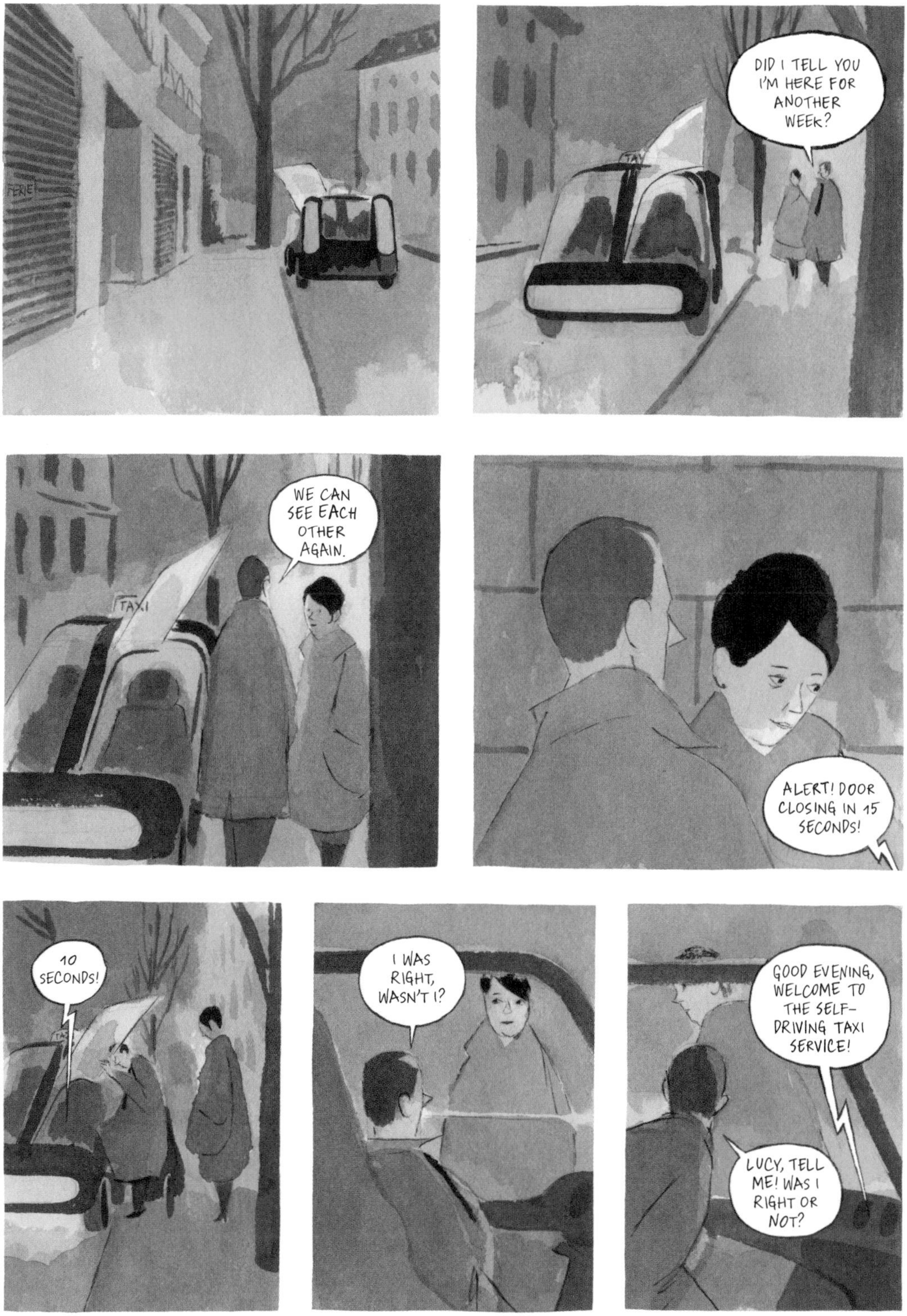
FERIE
DID I TELL YOU I'M HERE FOR ANOTHER WEEK?
TAXI
WE CAN SEE EACH OTHER AGAIN.
ALERT! DOOR CLOSING IN 15 SECONDS!
10 SECONDS!
I WAS RIGHT, WASN'T I?
GOOD EVENING, WELCOME TO THE SELF-DRIVING TAXI SERVICE!
LUCY, TELL ME! WAS I RIGHT OR NOT?

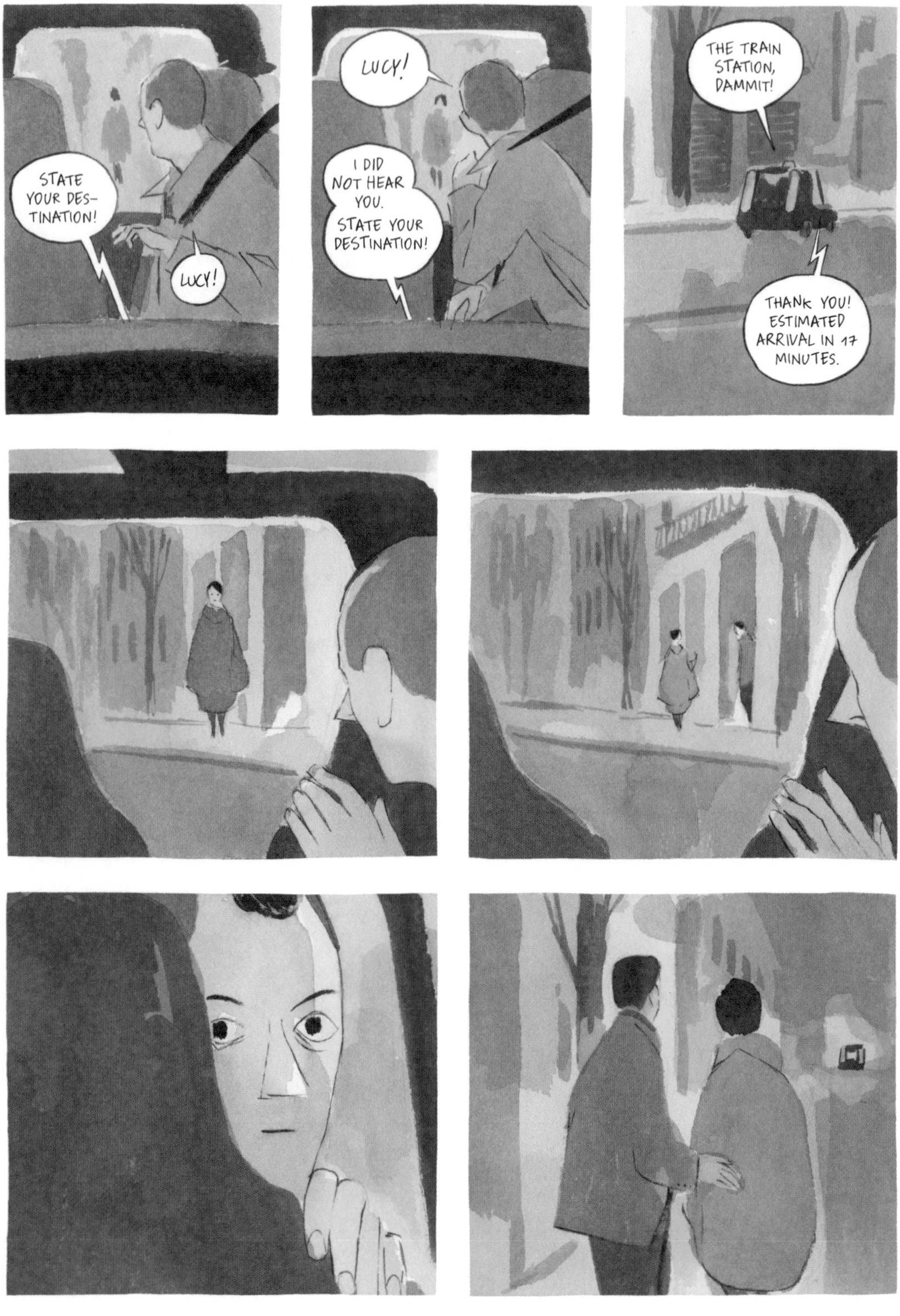
STATE YOUR DES-TINATION!
LUCY!
LUCY!
I DID NOT HEAR YOU. STATE YOUR DESTINATION!
THE TRAIN STATION, DAMMIT!
THANK YOU! ESTIMATED ARRIVAL IN 17 MINUTES.

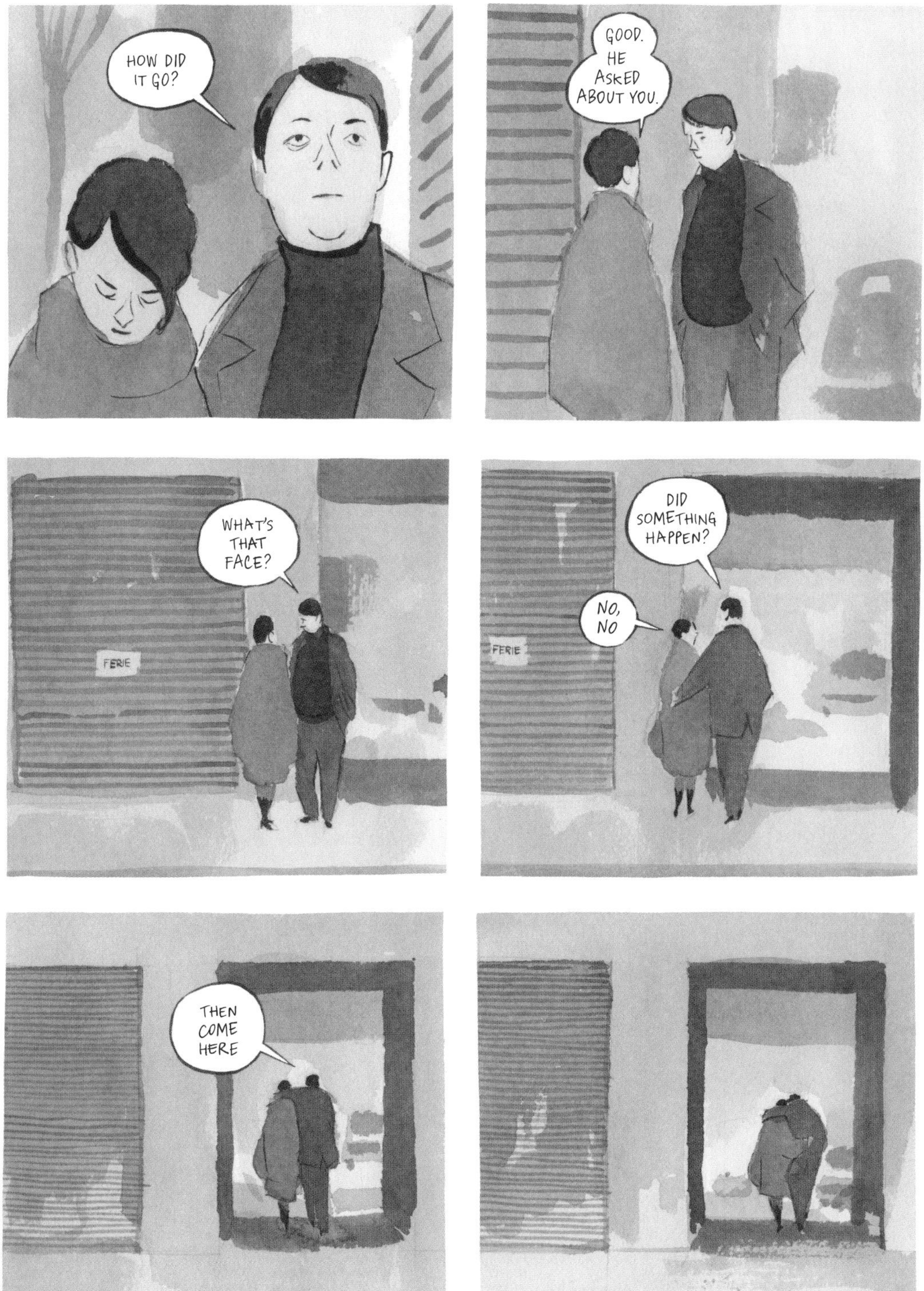
HOW DID IT GO?
GOOD. HE ASKED ABOUT YOU.
FERIE
WHAT'S THAT FACE?
FERIE
DID SOMETHING HAPPEN?
NO, NO
THEN COME HERE

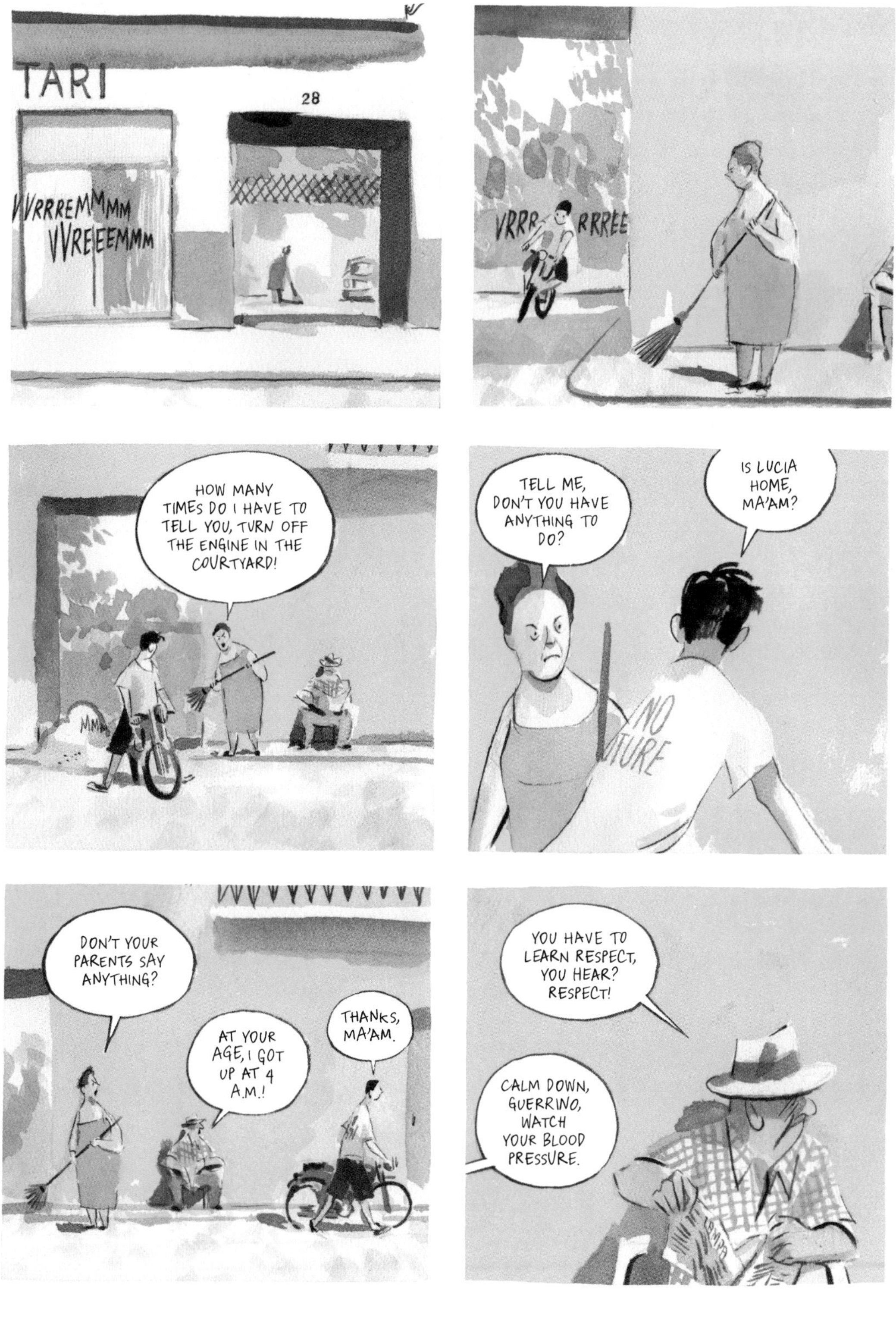
TARI
28
VRRREMMMM
VVREEEMMM
VRRR
RRREE
HOW MANY TIMES DO I HAVE TO TELL YOU, TURN OFF THE ENGINE IN THE COURTYARD!
MMM
TELL ME, DON'T YOU HAVE ANYTHING TO DO?
IS LUCIA HOME, MA'AM?
DON'T YOUR PARENTS SAY ANYTHING?
AT YOUR AGE, I GOT UP AT 4 A.M.!
THANKS, MA'AM.
YOU HAVE TO LEARN RESPECT, YOU HEAR? RESPECT!
CALM DOWN, GUERRINO, WATCH YOUR BLOOD PRESSURE.

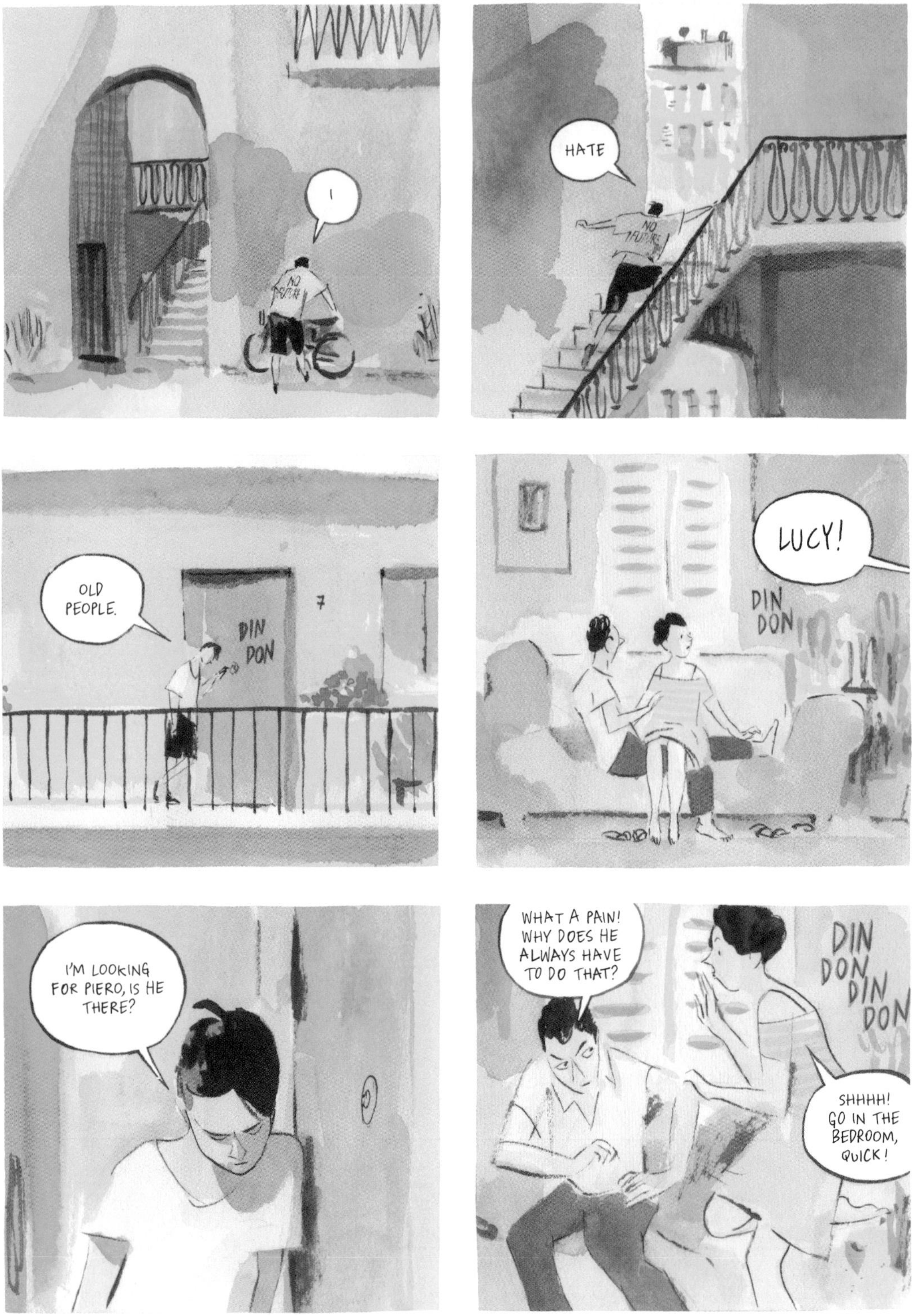
I
HATE
OLD PEOPLE.
DIN DON
LUCY!
DIN DON
I'M LOOKING FOR PIERO, IS HE THERE?
WHAT A PAIN! WHY DOES HE ALWAYS HAVE TO DO THAT?
DIN DON DIN DON
SHHHH! GO IN THE BEDROOM, QUICK!

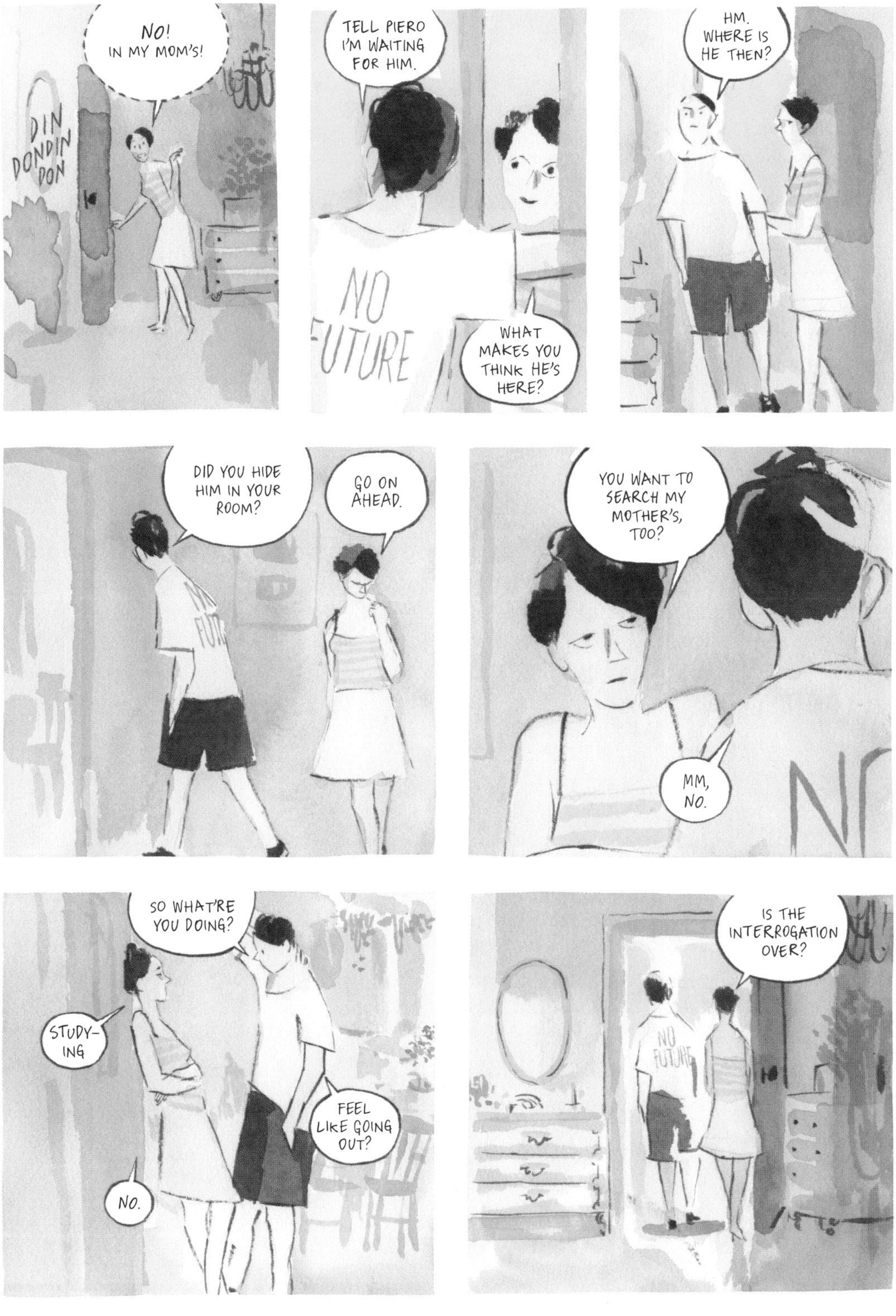

NO! IN MY MOM'S!
DIN DONDIN DON
TELL PIERO I'M WAITING FOR HIM.
NO FUTURE
WHAT MAKES YOU THINK HE'S HERE?
HM. WHERE IS HE THEN?
DID YOU HIDE HIM IN YOUR ROOM?
GO ON AHEAD.
YOU WANT TO SEARCH MY MOTHER'S, TOO?
MM, NO.
SO WHAT'RE YOU DOING?
STUDY-ING
FEEL LIKE GOING OUT?
NO.
IS THE INTERROGATION OVER?
NO FUTURE

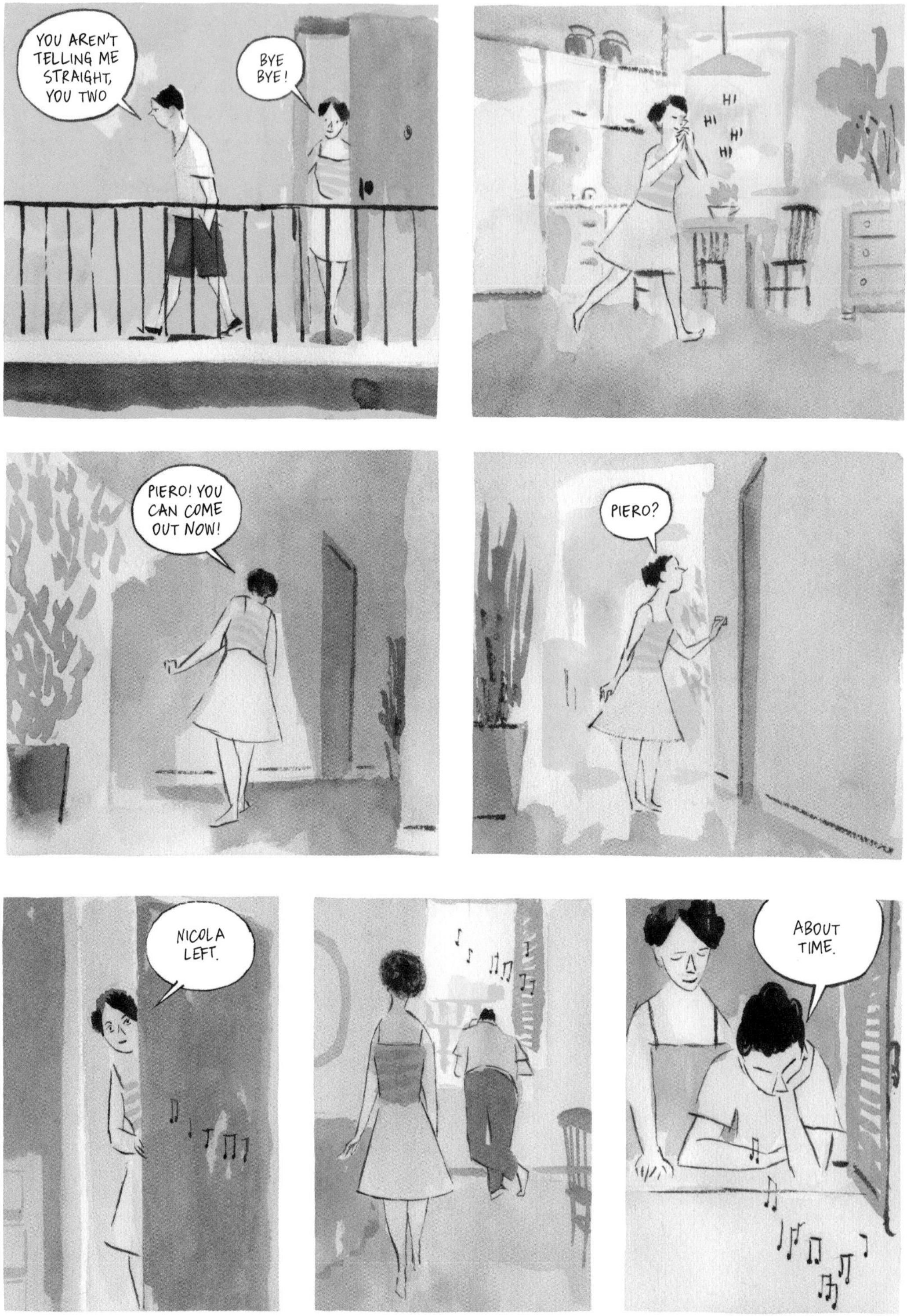
YOU AREN'T TELLING ME STRAIGHT, YOU TWO
BYE BYE!
HI
HI
HI
HI
PIERO! YOU CAN COME OUT NOW!
PIERO?
NICOLA LEFT.
ABOUT TIME.

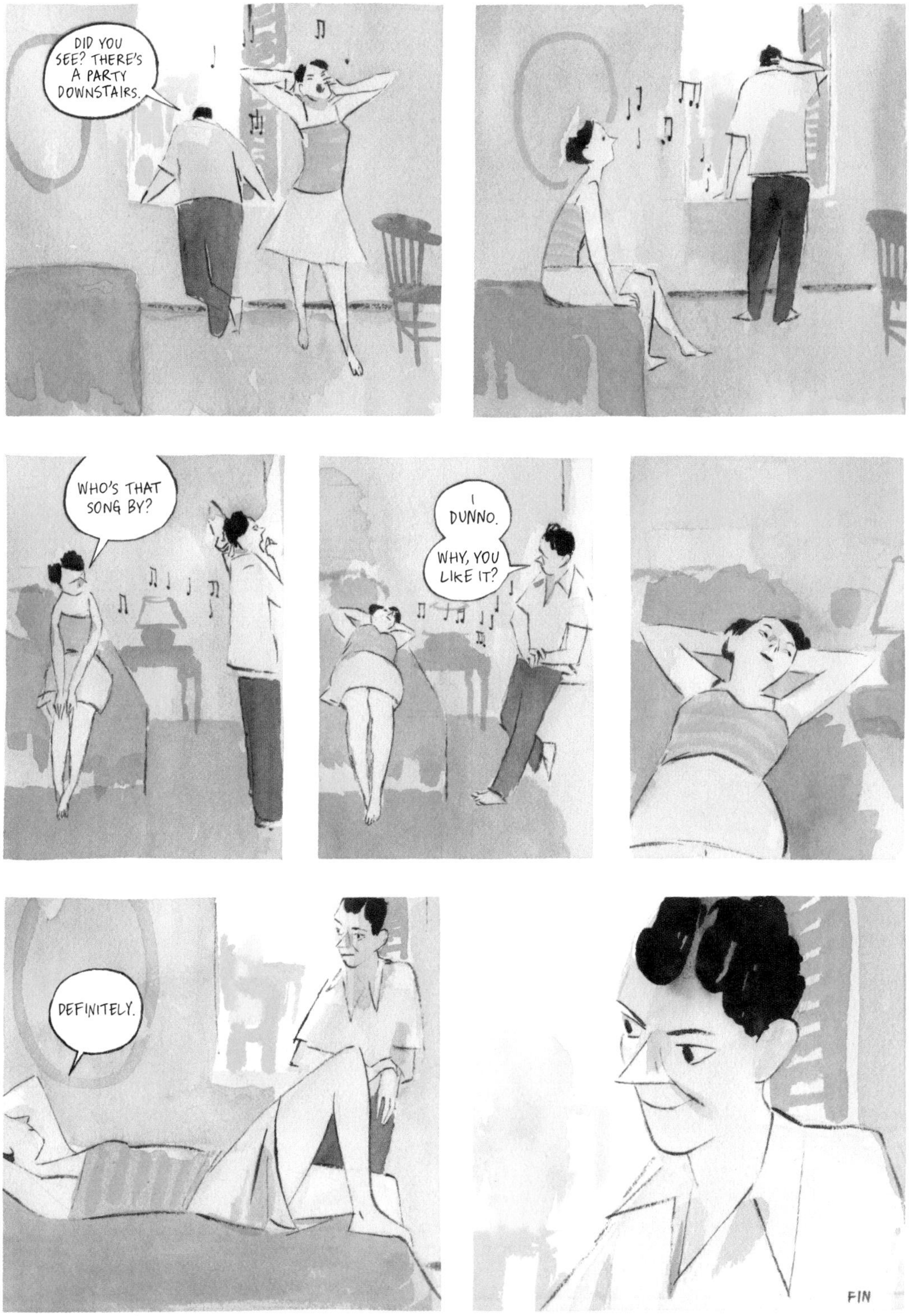
DID YOU SEE? THERE'S A PARTY DOWNSTAIRS.
WHO'S THAT SONG BY?
I DUNNO.
WHY, YOU LIKE IT?
DEFINITELY.
FIN

Fantagraphics Books

7563 Lake City Way NE
Seattle, Washington, 98115
www.fantagraphics.com

Translated from Italian by Jamie Richards
Editor and associate publisher: Eric Reynolds
Book design: Michael Heck
Production: Paul Baresh
Publisher: Gary Groth

ISBN 978-1-60699-666-9
Library of Congress Control Number: 2015957943

First printing: April 2016
Printed in Singapore